Math in Focus

Singapore Math®
by Marshall Cavendish

Student Edition

Program Consultant and Author
Dr. Fong Ho Kheong

Authors
Gan Kee Soon
Chelvi Ramakrishnan

Marshall Cavendish
Education

U.S. Distributor

Houghton Mifflin Harcourt.
The Learning Company™

Grade
5A

Contents

Chapter 1 — Whole Numbers and the Four Operations

▶ Hands-on Activity

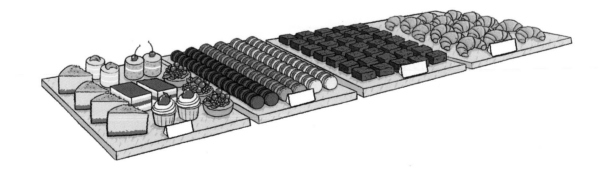

© 2020 Marshall Cavendish Education Pte Ltd

Chapter

2 Fractions and Mixed Numbers

Chapter Opener — 107

How are fractions and division related? How is adding and subtracting unlike fractions and mixed numbers similar to adding and subtracting like fractions?

RECALL PRIOR KNOWLEDGE — 108

Like and unlike fractions • Finding equivalent fractions • Expressing fractions in simplest form • Representing fractions on a number line • Understanding mixed numbers • Expressing improper fractions as mixed numbers • Expressing mixed numbers as improper fractions • Adding and subtracting like fractions

Hands-on Activity

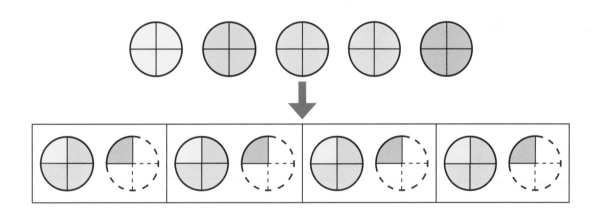

Chapter

3 Multiplying and Dividing Fractions and Mixed Numbers

Chapter Opener   **181**

 How do we multiply and divide fractions, mixed numbers, and whole numbers? How do the factors affect the product if one of the factors is a fraction?

RECALL PRIOR KNOWLEDGE   **182**

Finding equivalent fractions • Simplifying fractions • Expressing improper fractions as mixed numbers and mixed numbers as improper fractions in simplest form • Expressing fractions as decimals • Finding the number of units to solve a problem • Drawing a bar model to represent the problem • Using order of operations to simplify expressions

Hands-on Activity

© 2020 Marshall Cavendish Education Pte Ltd

4 Decimals

Chapter Opener

❓ What is the value of the second decimal place? What will be the value of the third decimal place?

RECALL PRIOR KNOWLEDGE

Understanding tenths • Understanding hundredths • Understanding tenths and hundredths • Comparing decimals • Expressing fractions as decimals • Expressing mixed numbers as decimals • Rounding decimals to the nearest whole number • Rounding decimals to the nearest tenth

▶ Hands-on Activity

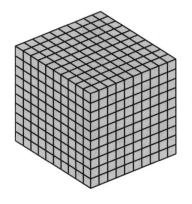
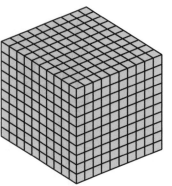
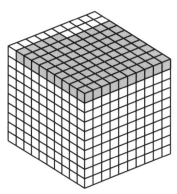

Four Operations of Decimals

Chapter Opener 331

 How can decimals be added, subtracted, multiplied and divided?

RECALL PRIOR KNOWLEDGE 332

Regrouping ones • Regrouping tenths • Regrouping hundredths • Multiplying tens, hundreds, and thousands by a 1-digit number • Dividing a 1-digit number with and without remainder • Rounding Decimals

Hands-on Activity

© 2020 Marshall Cavendish Education Pte Ltd

Manipulative List

 Connecting cubes

 Counters

 Fraction circle

 Place-value chips

 Place-value chip–0.001

 Place-value chip–0.01

 Place-value chip–0.1

 Place-value chip–1

 Place-value chip–10

 Place-value chip–100

 Place-value chip–1,000

 Place-value chip–10,000

 Place-value chip–100,000

 Place-value chip–1,000,000

 Place-value strips

Preface

Welcome!

Math in Focus® is a program that puts **you** at the center of an exciting learning experience! This experience is all about helping you to build skills and math ideas that make sense, sharing your thinking to deepen your understanding, and learning to become a strong and confident problem solver!

What's in your book?

Each chapter in this book begins with a real-world example of the math topic you are about to learn.

In each chapter, you will see the following features:

THINK introduces a problem for the whole section, to get you thinking creatively and critically. You may not be able to answer the problem right away but you can come back to it a few times as you work through the section.

ENGAGE introduces tasks that link what you already know with what you will be learning next. The tasks will have you exploring and discussing math concepts with your classmates.

LEARN introduces you to new math concepts through a Concrete-Pictorial-Abstract (C-P-A) approach, using examples and activities.

Hands-on Activity provides you with the experience of working very closely with your classmates. These Hands-On Activities allow you to become more confident in what you have learned and help you to uncover new concepts.

TRY provides you with the opportunity to practice what you are learning, with support and guidance.

INDEPENDENT PRACTICE allows you to work on different kinds of problems and apply the concepts and skills you have learned to solve these problems on your own.

Additional features include:

RECALL PRIOR KNOWLEDGE	Math Talk	MATH SHARING	GAME
Helps you recall related concepts you learned before, accompanied by practice questions	Invites you to explain your reasoning and communicate your ideas to your classmates and teachers	Encourages you to create strategies, discover methods, and share them with your classmates and teachers using mathematical language	Helps you to really master the concepts you learned, through fun partner games
LET'S EXPLORE	**MATH JOURNAL**	**PUT ON YOUR THINKING CAP!**	**CHAPTER WRAP-UP**
Extends your learning through investigation	Allows you to reflect on your learning when you write down your thoughts about the concepts learned	Challenges you to apply the concepts to solve problems in different ways	Summarizes your learning in a flow chart and helps you to make connections within the chapter
CHAPTER REVIEW	Assessment Prep	PERFORMANCE TASK	STEAM
Provides you with a lot of practice in the concepts learned	Prepares you for state tests with assessment-type problems	Assesses your learning through problems that allow you to demonstrate your understanding and knowledge	Promotes collaboration with your classmates through interesting projects that allow you to use math in creative ways

Let's begin your exciting learning journey with us! Are you ready?

When do we use 7-digit numbers in real-world situations? Why are the four operations of whole numbers important in everyday life?

Name: _____   Date: _____

Reading and writing numbers

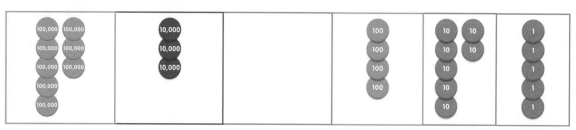

Hundred Thousands	Ten Thousands	Thousands	Hundreds	Tens	Ones
8	3	0	4	7	5

stands for **8 hundred thousands** 800,000 | stands for **3 ten thousands** 30,000 | stands for **0 thousands** 0 | stands for **4 hundreds** 400 | stands for **7 tens** 70 | stands for **5 ones** 5

830,475

Expanded form: 800,000 + 30,000 + 0 + 400 + 70 + 5

Standard form: 830,475

Word form: eight hundred thirty thousand, four hundred seventy-five

▶ Quick Check

Write in expanded form, standard form, and word form.

1
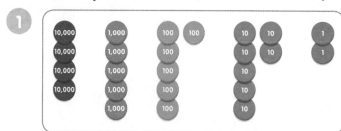

Expanded form: _____

Standard form: _____

Word form: _____

Write the number in standard form.

2 fifty thousand twelve _____

Write the number in word form.

3 388,502 _____

_____

Complete each expanded form.

4 _____ + 3,000 + 20 = 33,020

5 159,643 = 100,000 + 50,000 + 9,000 + _____ + 40 + 3

6 280,954 = 280,000 + 900 + _____ + 4

Write the value of each digit.

7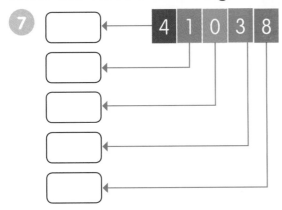

8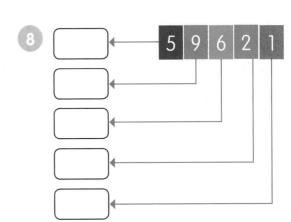

Fill in each blank.

9   In 33,020, the value of the digit 2 is _____.

10 In 759,643, the value of the digit 6 is _____.

11 In 80,215, the digit _____ stands for 80,000.

12 In 240,138, the digit _____ is in the ones place.

13 In 729,650, the digit with the value of 9,000 is in the _____ place.

Multiplying by a 1-digit number without regrouping

Find 3,403 × 2.

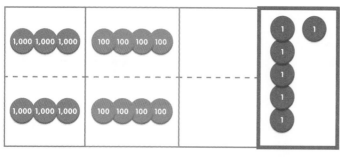

Step 1 Multiply the ones by 2.
3 ones × 2 = 6 ones

	3,	4	0	3
×				2
				6

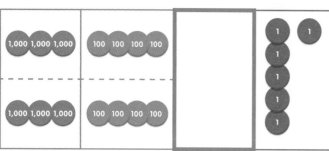

Step 2 Multiply the tens by 2.
0 tens × 2 = 0 tens

	3,	4	0	3
×				2
			0	6

© 2020 Marshall Cavendish Education Pte Ltd

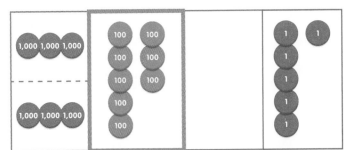

Step 3
Multiply the hundreds by 2.
4 hundreds × 2 = 8 hundreds

	3,	4	0	3
×				2
		8	0	6

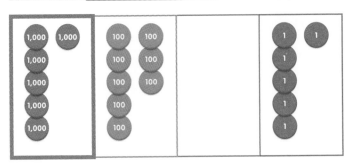

Step 4
Multiply the thousands by 2.
3 thousands × 2 = 6 thousands

	3,	4	0	3
×				2
6,	8	0	6

▶ **Quick Check**

Multiply.

(14) 200 × 3 = _____

(15) 1,023 × 3 = _____

Multiplying by a 1-digit number with regrouping
Multiply 1,946 by 8.

	7	3	4	
	1,	9	4	6
×				8
1	5,	5	6	8

1,946 × 8 = 15,568

▶ **Quick Check**

Multiply.

(16) $7,921 \times 4 = $ _____

(17) $3,618 \times 8 = $ _____

Dividing by a 1-digit number without remainder

Find $2,247 \div 7$.

Step 1	Step 2	Step 3

Step 1:
```
      3
7)2,2 4 7
  2 1
      1
```

Step 2:
```
      3 2
7)2,2 4 7
  2 1
    1 4
    1 4
```

Step 3:
```
      3 2 1
7)2,2 4 7
  2 1
    1 4
    1 4
        7
        7
        0
```

$2,247 \div 7 = 321$

▶ **Quick Check**

Divide.

18 2,055 ÷ 5 = _____

19 8,324 ÷ 4 = _____

Dividing by a 1-digit number with remainder

Find 2,414 ÷ 6.

Step 1	Step 2	Step 3
4 6)2,4 1 4 **2 4**	4 **0** 6)2,4 1 4 2 4 1 **0** 1	4 0 **2** 6)2,4 1 4 2 4 1 0 1 **4** **1 2** **2**

2,414 ÷ 6 = 402 R 2

▶ **Quick Check**

Divide.

20 5,320 ÷ 6 = _____

21 4,581 ÷ 8 = _____

Using bar models to solve real-world problems

Stores A, B, and C had 4,265 keychains in all.
Store A had 750 more keychains than Store B.
Store C had 3 times as many keychains as Store B.

a How many keychains did Store B have?

b How many keychains did Store C have?

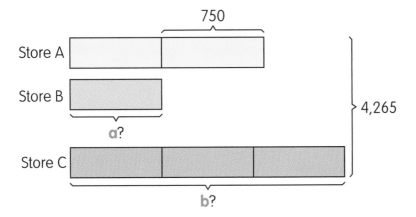

a 4,265 − 750 = 3,515

5 units = 3,515
1 unit = 3,515 ÷ 5
= 703

Store B had 703 keychains.

b 1 unit = 703
3 units = 703 × 3
= 2,109

Store C had 2,109 keychains.

▶ **Quick Check**

Solve. Draw a bar model to help you.

22 A baker baked some cookies. He packed 5 bags of 35 cookies each and had 205 cookies left. How many cookies did the baker bake?

23 Samuel and Riley had 104 stickers in all. After Samuel gave away 20 stickers, Riley had three times as many stickers as Samuel. How many stickers did Riley have?

2 Multiplying by Tens, Hundreds, Thousands, and Powers of Tens

Learning Objectives:
- Use patterns to multiply numbers by 10, 100, and 1,000.
- Use multiples or powers of 10 to multiply.

New Vocabulary
base   exponent
power   square
cube

THINK

1   Find two possible sets of digits in each blank that will make the equation true: 13,000 = 1_____ × _____00.

2   Find all possible sets of digits in each blank that will make the equation true: _____0 × _____00 = 24,000.

ENGAGE

a   How do you multiply 1 ten and 2 ones by 10?
b   How do you multiply 1 ten and 2 ones by 100?
c   How do you multiply 1 ten and 2 ones by 1,000?
Use  to explain how you get the answer in each case.
What pattern do you notice? Use the pattern to find 140 × 1,000.

LEARN Multiply whole numbers by 10

1   ① ① ① ① ① ① ① ① ① ① ⟶ ⑩

$$1 \times 10 = 10$$

⑩ ⑩ ⑩ ⑩ ⑩ ⑩ ⑩ ⑩ ⑩ ⑩ ⟶ ⑩⓪

$$10 \times 10 = 100$$

⑩⓪ ⑩⓪ ⑩⓪ ⑩⓪ ⑩⓪ ⑩⓪ ⑩⓪ ⑩⓪ ⑩⓪ ⑩⓪ ⟶ ①,⓪⓪⓪

$$100 \times 10 = 1,000$$

①,⓪⓪⓪ ①,⓪⓪⓪ ①,⓪⓪⓪ ①,⓪⓪⓪ ①,⓪⓪⓪ ①,⓪⓪⓪ ①,⓪⓪⓪ ①,⓪⓪⓪ ①,⓪⓪⓪ ①,⓪⓪⓪ ⟶ ⑩,⓪⓪⓪

$$1,000 \times 10 = 10,000$$

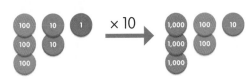

2 **a** What is 321 × 10?

$$321 \times 10 = 3{,}210$$

b What is 4,538 × 10?

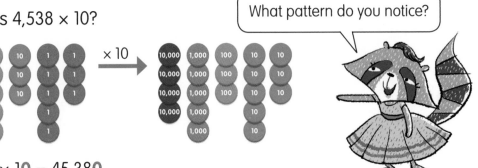

What pattern do you notice?

$$4{,}538 \times 10 = 45{,}380$$

Hands-on Activity Multiplying by 10

1 Use ⬤⬤⬤⬤⬤⬤⬤ to show 73. Then, use ⬤⬤⬤⬤⬤⬤⬤ to show the result of 73 × 10. Fill in the table. Draw arrows to show how each digit moves in the table.

	Ten Thousands	Thousands	Hundreds	Tens	Ones
73					
73 × 10					
240					
240 × 10					
1,206					
1,206 × 10					

2 **Mathematical Habits 8** **Look for patterns**
What pattern do you notice?

TRY Practice multiplying whole numbers by 10

Multiply.

1 $6 \times 10 =$ _____

2 $45 \times 10 =$ _____

3 $432 \times 10 =$ _____

4 $2,584 \times 10 =$ _____

Find each product.

5 5 and 10

_____

6 10 and 29

_____

7 124 and 10

_____

8 10 and 800

_____

Fill in each blank.

9 _____ $\times 8 = 80$

10 $10 \times$ _____ $= 90$

11 $23 \times$ _____ $= 230$

12 _____ $\times 10 = 340$

13 _____ $\times 452 = 4,520$

14 $10 \times$ _____ $= 5,600$

15 $3,650 \times$ _____ $= 36,500$

16 _____ $\times 10 = 42,810$

Math Talk

Liam says that when a number is multiplied by 10, each digit in the number moves one place to the left. Explain why.

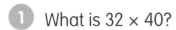 **ENGAGE**

Find each of the following.

a 3 × 20   **b** 5 × 30   **c** 6 × 40

Look at the results. What pattern can you observe? Explain the pattern.

Use the pattern to find 13 × 40.

LEARN Multiply whole numbers by tens

1 What is 32 × 40?

32 × 4**0**
= (32 × 4) × 1**0**
= 128 × 1**0**
= 1,28**0**

$$\begin{array}{r} 3\ 2 \\ \times\ \ \ 4 \\ \hline 1\ 2\ 8 \end{array}$$

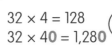

32 × 4 = 128
32 × 4**0** = 1,28**0**

2 What is 301 × 20?

301 × 2**0**
= (301 × 2) × 1**0**
= 602 × 1**0**
= 6,02**0**

$$\begin{array}{r} 3\ 0\ 1 \\ \times\ \ \ \ \ 2 \\ \hline 6\ 0\ 2 \end{array}$$

301 × 2 = 602
301 × 2**0** = 6,02**0**

TRY Practice multiplying whole numbers by tens

Multiply.

1 24 × 30

= (24 × _____) × 10

= _____ × 10

= _____

2 439 × 20

= (439 × _____) × 10

= _____ × 10

= _____

Multiply. Show your work.

3 15 × 80

4 217 × 50

ENGAGE

1 A box contains 144 paper clips. How many paper clips are there in

    a 10 boxes?   **b** 100 boxes?   **c** 1,000 boxes?

Use ⚫🔘⚫🔘🔘🔘⚪ and 🃏 to show your answers.

2 How can you find the number of paper clips in 20 boxes and 200 boxes? What is a quick way to find your answers?

LEARN Multiply whole numbers by 100 and 1,000

1 **a** What is 5 × 100?

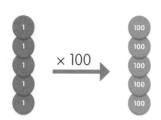

$$5 \times 100 = 500$$

b What is 50 × 100?

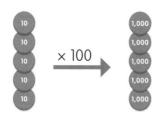

$$50 \times 100 = 5,000$$

c What is 500 × 100?

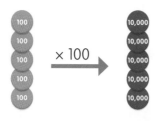

$$500 \times 100 = 50,000$$

$$1 \times 100 = 100$$

$$10 \times 100 = 1,000$$

$$100 \times 100 = 10,000$$

2 **a** What is 6 × 1,000?

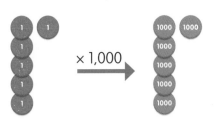

6 × 1,**000** = 6,**000**

b What is 60 × 1,000?

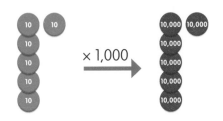

60 × 1,**000** = 60,**000**

c What is 600 × 1,000?

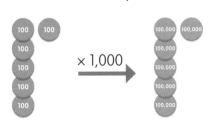

600 × 1,**000** = 600,**000**

d What is 6,000 × 1,000?

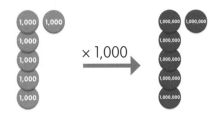

6,000 × 1,**000** = 6,000,**000**

What pattern do you notice?

Multiplying whole numbers by 100 and 1,000

① Use ⬤⬤⬤⬤⬤⬤⬤ to show 8. Then, use ⬤⬤⬤⬤⬤⬤⬤ to show the result of 8 × 100 and 8 × 1,000. Fill in the table and draw arrows to show how each digit moves in the table.

	Hundred Thousands	Ten Thousands	Thousands	Hundreds	Tens	Ones
8						
8 × 100						
8						
8 × 1,000						
65						
65 × 100						
65						
65 × 1,000						
409						
409 × 100						
409						
409 × 1,000						

② **Mathematical Habits 8** **Look for patterns**
What pattern do you notice?

TRY Practice multiplying whole numbers by 100 and 1,000

Multiply.

1. $4 \times 100 =$ _____

2. $39 \times 100 =$ _____

3. $561 \times 100 =$ _____

4. $7 \times 1,000 =$ _____

5. $53 \times 1,000 =$ _____

6. $687 \times 1,000 =$ _____

Find each product.

7. 9 and 100

_____

8. 100 and 65

_____

9. 2 and 1,000

_____

10. 1,000 and 128

_____

Fill in each blank.

11. _____ $\times 26 = 2,600$

12. $10 \times$ _____ $= 90$

13. $218 \times$ _____ $= 218,000$

14. _____ $\times 100 = 725,000$

15. _____ $\times 95 = 95,000$

16. $1,000 \times$ _____ $= 68,000$

17. $287 \times$ _____ $= 287,000$

18. _____ $\times 1,000 = 3,085,000$

Math Talk

Jason says that when you multiply a number by 100, each digit moves 2 places to the left and when you multiply a number by 1,000, each digit moves 3 places to the left. Explain why.

1 Use  to find a pattern.

What is 12 × 100? What is 12 × 300? What is 12 × 1,000? What is 12 × 3,000? What do you predict 12 × 50,000 equals? Explain your thinking to your partner.

2 Find the missing number in the equation: _____ × 8000 = 120,000.

LEARN Multiply whole numbers by hundreds and thousands

1 What is 23 × 300?

23 × 3**00**
= (23 × 3) × 1**00**
= 69 × 1**00**
= 6,9**00**

```
   2 3
 ×   3
   6 9
```

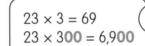

23 × 3 = 69
23 × 3**00** = 6,9**00**

2 What is 120 × 400?

120 × 4**00**
= (120 × 4) × 1**00**
= 480 × 1**00**
= 48,0**00**

```
   1 2 0
 ×     4
   4 8 0
```

120 × 4 = 480
120 × 4**00** = 48,0**00**

3 What is 41 × 2,000?

41 × 2,**000**
= (41 × 2) × 1,**000**
= 82 × 1,**000**
= 82,**000**

```
   4 1
 ×   2
   8 2
```

41 × 2 = 82
41 × 2,**000** = 82,000

4 What is 304 × 2,000?

304 × 2,**000**
= (304 × 2) × 1,**000**
= 608 × 1,**000**
= 608,**000**

```
   3 0 4
 ×     2
   6 0 8
```

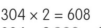

304 × 2 = 608
304 × 2,**000** = 608,000

TRY Practice multiplying whole numbers by hundreds and thousands

Multiply.

1 42 × 600

= (42 × _____) × 100

= _____ × 100

= _____

2 42 × 6,000

= (42 × _____) × 1,000

= _____ × 1,000

= _____

3 6 × 400

4 81 × 600

5 7,510 × 200

6 20 × 900

7 12 × 7,000

8 549 × 3,000

Find each product.

9 9 and 200

10 500 and 348

11 45 and 3,000

12 720 and 800

Fill in the table.

		× 5	× 50	× 500	× 5,000
13	71				
14	395				
15	1,046				

ENGAGE

1 Chris wrote 10 as 10^1 and 100 as 10^2. Explain the pattern you see to your partner. Then, using the pattern to find the missing number in the equation.

$10^{\square} = 10,000$

2 Find each missing number in the equation. $700,000 = \underline{\hspace{3cm}} \times 10^{\square}$

LEARN Multiply whole numbers by powers of 10

1 You can use exponents to multiply a number by itself.

exponent

$1 \times 1 = 1^2$

base

The **base** is the factor, or the number being multiplied.

The **exponent** or power, tells you how many times to use the base as a factor.

a 10 × 10 is 10 multiplied by itself once.

10 × 10 is the **square** of 10.

10 × 10 is written as 10^2. ——— 10^2 is read as "10 squared."

b 10 × 10 × 10 is 10 multiplied by itself twice.

10 × 10 × 10 is the **cube** of 10.

10 × 10 × 10 is written as 10^3. ——— 10^3 is read as "10 cubed."

2 Find 23×10^2.

$$23 \times \mathbf{10^2} = 23 \times (10 \times 10)$$
$$= 23 \times 100$$
$$= 2,3\mathbf{00}$$

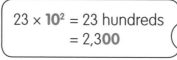

$23 \times \mathbf{10^2} = 23$ hundreds
$= 2,3\mathbf{00}$

3 Find 605×10^3.

$$605 \times \mathbf{10^3} = 605 \times (10 \times 10 \times 10)$$
$$= 605 \times 1,000$$
$$= 605,\mathbf{000}$$

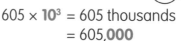

$605 \times \mathbf{10^3} = 605$ thousands
$= 605,\mathbf{000}$

TRY Practice multiplying whole numbers by powers of 10

Multiply.

1 35×10^2

2 140×10^2

3 $9,465 \times 10^2$

4 88×10^3

5 315×10^3

6 $7,008 \times 10^3$

INDEPENDENT PRACTICE

Multiply.

1. 412×10

2. $7,921 \times 100$

3. $744 \times 1,000$

4. $7,035 \times 60$

5. 81×700

6. $169 \times 3,000$

Fill in each blank.

7. $152 \times \rule{2cm}{0.4pt} = 1,520$

8. $303 \times 300 = \rule{2cm}{0.4pt}$

9. $864 \times \rule{2cm}{0.4pt} = 864,000$

10. $25 \times 30 = \rule{2cm}{0.4pt}$

11. $\rule{2cm}{0.4pt} \times 45 = 4,500$

12. $\rule{2cm}{0.4pt} \times 1,000 = 4,000,000$

Multiply.

13 27×10^2

14 80×10^2

15 306×10^2

16 $1,405 \times 10^2$

17 $5,200 \times 10^2$

18 60×10^3

19 48×10^3

20 143×10^3

21 630×10^3

22 $3,146 \times 10^3$

3 Dividing by Tens, Hundreds, and Thousands

Learning Objectives:
- Use patterns to divide numbers by 10, 100, and 1,000.
- Use multiples of 10, 100, and 1,000 to divide.

 THINK

Find two possible pairs of numbers to make the equation true.

$9,000 ÷$ _____ $÷ 3 = 1,200 ÷ 4 ÷$ _____

ENGAGE

Find the answer by representing the problem using **a** multiplication equations and **b** division equations.

Noah puts 40 buttons into bags of 10. How many bags does he use?

Savannah puts 600 pennies into bags of 100. How many bags does she use?

Ian puts 12,000 building blocks into bags of 1,000. How many bags does he use?

What pattern do you see? Explain your thinking to your partner.

Find the missing digits. _____ × 1_____ = 22,000

LEARN Divide whole numbers by 10

1. ⬤ 10 = ⬤⬤⬤⬤⬤⬤⬤⬤⬤⬤ $\xrightarrow{÷ 10}$ ⬤

$10 ÷ 10 = 1$

100 = 10 10 10 10 10 10 10 10 10 10 $\xrightarrow{÷ 10}$ 10

$100 ÷ 10 = 10$

$1,000$ = 100 100 100 100 100 100 100 100 100 100 $\xrightarrow{÷ 10}$ 100

$1,000 ÷ 10 = 100$

$10,000$ = $1,000$ $1,000$ $1,000$ $1,000$ $1,000$ $1,000$ $1,000$ $1,000$ $1,000$ $1,000$ $\xrightarrow{÷ 10}$ $1,000$

$10,000 ÷ 10 = 1,000$

2 **a** What is 30 ÷ 10?

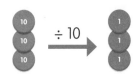

30 ÷ 10 = 3

b What is 300 ÷ 10?

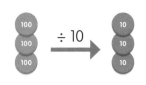

300 ÷ 10 = 30

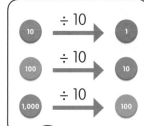

c What is 3,000 ÷ 10?

3,000 ÷ 10 = 300

What pattern do you notice?

Hands-on Activity Dividing whole numbers by 10

1 Use 🔵🔵🔵🔵🔵🔵🔵🔵 to show 90. Then, use 🔵🔵🔵🔵🔵🔵🔵🔵 to show the result of 90 ÷ 10. Fill in the table. Draw arrows to show how each digit moves in the table.

	Thousands	Hundreds	Tens	Ones	Tenths
90					
90 ÷ 10					
140					
140 ÷ 10					
3,500					
3,500 ÷ 10					

2 **Mathematical Habits 8** **Look for patterns**
What pattern do you notice?

TRY Practice dividing whole numbers by 10

Divide.

1 360 ÷ 10 = _____

2 790 ÷ 10 = _____

3 1,580 ÷ 10 = _____

4 2,160 ÷ 10 = _____

Fill in each blank.

5 _____ ÷ 10 = 70

6 560 ÷ _____ = 56

7 _____ ÷ 10 = 345

8 5,090 ÷ _____ = 509

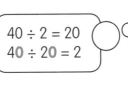 **Math Talk**

What pattern do you observe when a number is divided by 10?

ENGAGE

1 Use ⬤ to divide 60 by 20. Describe the steps you followed to your partner.

2 Use the same way in **1** to solve each equation.
a 80 ÷ 20 **b** 120 ÷ 20
What pattern can you observe? Explain the pattern.
Use the pattern to find 180 ÷ 30.

LEARN Divide whole numbers by tens

1 What is 40 ÷ 20?

$40 ÷ 20$
$= (40 ÷ 10) ÷ 2$
$= 4 ÷ 2$
$= 2$

$40 ÷ 2 = 20$
$40 ÷ 20 = 2$

2 What is 330 ÷ 30?

330 ÷ 30
= (330 ÷ 10) ÷ 3
= 33 ÷ 3
= 11

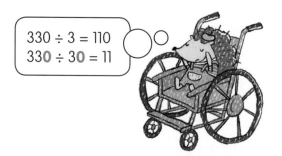

330 ÷ 3 = 110
330 ÷ 30 = 11

3 What is 2,400 ÷ 20?

2,400 ÷ 20
= (2,400 ÷ 10) ÷ 2
= 240 ÷ 2
= 120

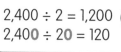

2,400 ÷ 2 = 1,200
2,400 ÷ 20 = 120

TRY Practice dividing by tens

Divide.

1 60 ÷ 30 = (60 ÷ _____) ÷ 3

= _____ ÷ 3

= _____

2 270 ÷ 90 = (270 ÷ _____) ÷ 9

= _____ ÷ 9

= _____

3 7,200 ÷ 80

4 6,320 ÷ 20

ENGAGE

1 Sari packed 300 apples into packs of 10. How many apples are there in each pack?
Find the answer using **a** multiplication and **b** division.
What pattern can you observe?

2 Use the pattern in **1** to find

  a $5 \times \underline{\hspace{2cm}} = 400$ **b** $5 \times \underline{\hspace{2cm}} = 4{,}000$ **c** $5 \times \underline{\hspace{2cm}} = 4{,}400$

LEARN Divide whole numbers by 100 and 1,000

1 **a** What is $500 \div 100$?

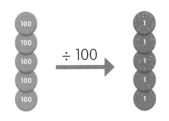

$500 \div 100 = 5$

  b What is $5{,}000 \div 100$?

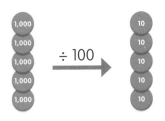

$5{,}000 \div 100 = 50$

  c What is $50{,}000 \div 100$?

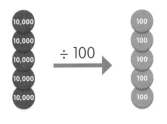

$50{,}000 \div 100 = 500$

2 a What is 6,000 ÷ 1,000?

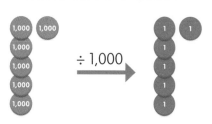

6,000 ÷ 1,000 = 6

b What is 60,000 ÷ 1,000?

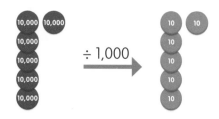

60,000 ÷ 1,000 = 60

c What is 600,000 ÷ 1,000?

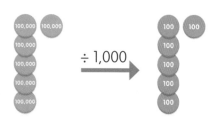

600,000 ÷ 1,000 = 600

What pattern do you notice?

Dividing whole numbers by 100 and 1,000

1 Use ⬤⬤⬤⬤⬤⬤⬤⬤⬤ to show 9,000. Then, use

⬤⬤⬤⬤⬤⬤⬤⬤⬤ to show the result of 9,000 ÷ 100 and

9,000 ÷ 1,000. Do the same for the numbers and divisions in the table and fill in the table. Draw arrows to show how each digit moves in the table.

	Ten Thousands	Thousands	Hundreds	Tens	Ones	Tenths	Hundredths	Thousandths
9,000								
9,000 ÷ 100								
9,000								
9,000 ÷ 1,000								
30,000								
30,000 ÷ 100								
30,000								
30,000 ÷ 1,000								
54,000								
54,000 ÷ 100								
54,000								
54,000 ÷ 1,000								

2 **Mathematical Habits** 8 Look for patterns
What pattern do you notice?

TRY Practice dividing whole numbers by 100 and 1,000

Divide.

1. $5,200 \div 100 = \underline{\hspace{3cm}}$

2. $84,000 \div 100 = \underline{\hspace{3cm}}$

3. $62,000 \div 1,000 = \underline{\hspace{3cm}}$

4. $90,000 \div 1,000 = \underline{\hspace{3cm}}$

ENGAGE

1. Use **1,000,000** **100,000** **10,000** **1,000** **100** **10** **1** to model the problems.
   Farmer Brown packed 400 apples equally into cartons of 200.
   Farmer Hill packed 4,000 apples equally into cartons of 200.
   Farmer Young packed 40,000 apples equally into cartons of 200.
   What pattern do you notice? Explain your thinking to your partner.

2. Write two multiplication equations to find $69,000 \div 3$.

LEARN Divide whole numbers by hundreds and thousands

1. What is $2,200 \div 200$?

   $2,200 \div 200$
   $= (2,200 \div 100) \div 2$
   $= 22 \div 2$
   $= 11$

   $2,200 \div 2 = 1,100$
   $2,200 \div 200 = 11$

2 What is 4,000 ÷ 200?

4,000 ÷ 200
= (4,000 ÷ 100) ÷ 2
= 40 ÷ 2
= 20

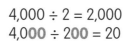

4,000 ÷ 2 = 2,000
4,000 ÷ 200 = 20

3 What is 6,000 ÷ 3,000?

6,000 ÷ 3,000
= (6,000 ÷ 1,000) ÷ 3
= 6 ÷ 3
= 2

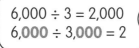

6,000 ÷ 3 = 2,000
6,000 ÷ 3,000 = 2

4 What is 8,000 ÷ 2,000?

8,000 ÷ 2,000
= (8,000 ÷ 1,000) ÷ 2
= 8 ÷ 2
= 4

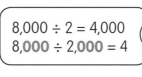

8,000 ÷ 2 = 4,000
8,000 ÷ 2,000 = 4

TRY Practice dividing whole numbers by hundreds and thousands

Divide.

1 6,000 ÷ 300

= (6,000 ÷ _____) ÷ 3

= _____ ÷ 3

= _____

2 6,000 ÷ 3,000

= (6,000 ÷ _____) ÷ 3

= _____ ÷ 3

= _____

3 3,000 ÷ 500

4 3,600 ÷ 400

5. 9,000 ÷ 200

6. 29,400 ÷ 600

7. 8,000 ÷ 2,000

8. 10,000 ÷ 5,000

9. 48,000 ÷ 8,000

10. 70,000 ÷ 2,000

Fill in the table.

		÷ 80	÷ 800	÷ 8000
11	40,000			
12	72,000			
13	128,000			

INDEPENDENT PRACTICE

Divide.

1 870 ÷ 10 = _____

2 9,000 ÷ 10 = _____

3 7,100 ÷ 100 = _____

4 82,000 ÷ 100 = _____

5 3,000 ÷ 1,000 = _____

6 97,000 ÷ 1,000 = _____

Find each quotient.

7 500 ÷ 20

8 7,070 ÷ 70

9 8,100 ÷ 300

10 65,600 ÷ 800

11 6,000 ÷ 3,000

12 54,000 ÷ 9,000

Multiplying and Dividing by 2-Digit Numbers Fluently

Learning Objectives:
- Multiply by a 2-digit number fluently.
- Divide by a 2-digit number fluently.

THINK

Sydney multiplied a 3-digit number by 12. She then multiplied 288 by the quotient of the 3-digit number and 24. She observed that the answers are the same. What is the 3-digit number?

ENGAGE

Use .

What is 56×3? What is 56×20?

How do you use your answers to find 56×23? Explain your reasoning.

Can you use the same method to find 549×28? What is another way to find the answer? Explain your thinking to your partner.

LEARN Multiply by a 2-digit number fluently

① Multiply 63 by 28.

```
      2
      6 3
  ×   2 8
      5 0 4   ← multiply 63 by 8 ones
  1, 2 6 0    ← multiply 63 by 2 tens
  1, 7 6 4    ← add
```

Check
Estimate the value of 63×28.
63 rounds to 60.
28 rounds to 30.
$60 \times 30 = 1,800$
The estimate shows that the answer 1,764 is reasonable.

2 Multiply 623 by 32.

```
        6 2 3
    ×     3 2
      1, 2 4 6  ← multiply 623 by 2 ones
    1 8, 6 9 0  ← multiply 623 by 3 tens
    1 9, 9 3 6  ← add
```

Check

Estimate the value of
623 × 32.
623 rounds to 600.
32 rounds to 30.
600 × 30 = 18,000
The estimate shows
that the answer 19,936
is reasonable.

When both factors are **rounded down**, the estimate will be **less** than the actual product.

When both factors are **rounded up**, the estimate will be **greater** than the actual product.

What happens when one factor is rounded up and the other is rounded down?

3 Multiply 5,362 by 76.

```
      2  4  1
      2  3  1
      5, 3 6 2
    ×      7 6
      3 2, 1 7 2  ← multiply 5,362 by 6 ones
    3 7 5, 3 4 0  ← multiply 5,362 by 7 tens
    4 0 7, 5 1 2  ← add
```

Check

Estimate the value of
5,362 × 76.
5,362 rounds to 5,000.
76 rounds to 80.
5,000 × 80 = 400,000
The estimate shows
that the answer
407,512 is reasonable.

TRY Practice multiplying by a 2-digit number fluently

Multiply.

1)

```
      9 7
  ×   5 3
```
[_____] ← multiply 97 by ____ ones
[_____] ← multiply 97 by ____ tens
[_____] ← add

Check

Estimate the value of 97 × 53.

97 rounds to _____.

53 rounds to _____.

____ × ____ = _____

The estimate shows that the

answer _____

is _____.

Multiply. Estimate to check that each answer is reasonable.

2) $19 \times 12 =$ _____

3) $65 \times 44 =$ _____

4) $38 \times 72 =$ _____

5) $99 \times 95 =$ _____

Multiply.

6
```
    5 1 4
×     7 2
```

[⬚] ← multiply 514 by ____ ones

[⬚] ← multiply 514 by ____ tens

[⬚] ← add

Check

Estimate the value of 514 × 72.

514 rounds to _____.

72 rounds to _____.

_____ × _____ = _____

The estimate shows that the

answer _____ is

_____.

Multiply. Estimate to check that each answer is reasonable.

7 413 × 12 = _____

8 294 × 48 = _____

9 519 × 36 = _____

10 608 × 94 = _____

Multiply.

11
$$
\begin{array}{r}
9{,}2\ 0\ 5 \\
\times\qquad 2\ 4 \\
\end{array}
$$

⬚ ← multiply 9,205 by ____ ones

⬚ ← multiply 9,205 by ____ tens

⬚ ← add

Check

Estimate the value of

9,205 × 24.

9,205 rounds to ____.

24 rounds to ____.

____ × ____ = ____

The estimate shows that the

answer _____ is

_____.

Multiply. Estimate to check that each answer is reasonable.

12 3,352 × 14 = _____

13 9,540 × 36 = _____

14 1,598 × 72 = _____

15 2,535 × 47 = _____

ENGAGE

1 Xavier needs 36 eggs. How many cartons of 12 eggs does he need to buy? Use  to prove your answer.

2 Find the factor that makes the equation true. 78 ÷ _____ = 6

Explain how you find your answer and prove that it is correct.

LEARN Divide by a 2-digit number fluently

1 Divide 180 by 20.

▶ **Method 1**

$18\cancel{0} \div 2\cancel{0} = 9$

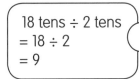

18 tens ÷ 2 tens
= 18 ÷ 2
= 9

▶ **Method 2**

```
              9  ── quotient
divisor ── 20) 1 8 0 ────── dividend
              1 8 0 ◀── 9 × 20
              ─────
                  0 ────── remainder
```

Use Method 2 when the dividend cannot be exactly divided by the divisor. For 180 ÷ 40, dropping the zeros gives an incorrect remainder.

Incorrect

2 is the remainder.
$18\cancel{0} \div 4\cancel{0} = 4 \text{ R } 2$

```
         4
      4) 1 8
         1 6
         ───
           2
```

Correct

20 is the remainder.
180 ÷ 40 = 4 R 20

```
          4
     40) 1 8 0
         1 6 0
         ─────
           2 0
```

2 Divide 63 by 17.

17 rounds to 20.

Estimate the quotient.
$3 \times 20 = 60$

$$20 \overline{)\begin{array}{c} 3 \\ 6 \ 3 \end{array}}$$

$$17 \overline{)\begin{array}{r} 3 \\ 6 \ 3 \\ 5 \ 1 \\ \hline 1 \ 2 \end{array}}$$

$63 \div 17 = 3$ R 12

The quotient is 3 and the remainder is 12.

3 Divide 83 by 15.

15 rounds to 20.

Estimate the quotient.
$4 \times 20 = 80$

$$20 \overline{)\begin{array}{c} 4 \\ 8 \ 3 \end{array}}$$

$$15 \overline{)\begin{array}{r} 4 \\ 8 \ 3 \\ 6 \ 0 \\ \hline 2 \ 3 \end{array}} \longleftarrow \text{This should be less than 15.}$$

The estimated quotient is too small. Try 5.

$$15 \overline{)\begin{array}{r} 5 \ \text{R} \ 8 \\ 8 \ 3 \\ 7 \ 5 \\ \hline 8 \end{array}}$$

The quotient is 5 and the remainder is 8.

 **Math Talk**

Diego divided 88 by 23.
He estimated the quotient as 4. Do you agree with him? Explain.

4 You can use different methods to divide 3-digit numbers by 2-digit numbers.

a Estimate the quotient.

Divide 235 by 32.

```
        7 R 11
32) 2 3 5
    2 2 4  ←— 7 × 32
      1 1
```

32 rounds to 30.

Estimate the quotient.
7 × 30 = 210
8 × 30 = 240

The quotient is about 7.

The quotient is 7 and the remainder is 11.

b Divide the tens before dividing the ones.

Divide 765 by 23.

```
       3 3 R 6
23) 7 6 5
    6 9      ←— 23 × 3 tens
    7 5
    6 9   ←— 23 × 3
      6
```

7 hundreds 6 tens = 76 tens
76 tens ÷ 23 = 3 tens R 7 tens

7 tens 5 ones = 75 ones
75 ÷ 23 = 3 R 6

The quotient is 33 and the remainder is 6.

c Use an area model to decompose the dividend.

Divide 368 by 15.

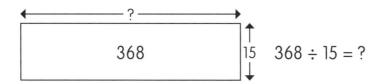

368 ÷ 15 = ?

368 = 300 + 60 + 8

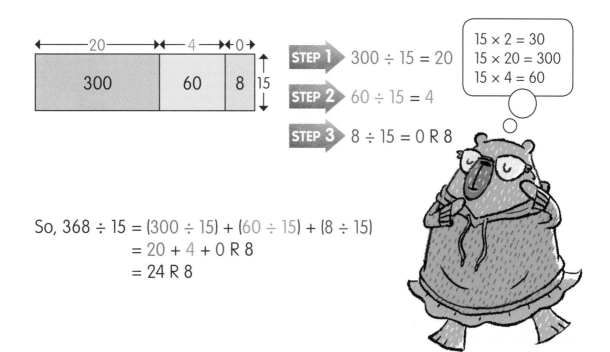

STEP 1 300 ÷ 15 = 20

STEP 2 60 ÷ 15 = 4

STEP 3 8 ÷ 15 = 0 R 8

15 × 2 = 30
15 × 20 = 300
15 × 4 = 60

So, 368 ÷ 15 = (300 ÷ 15) + (60 ÷ 15) + (8 ÷ 15)
= 20 + 4 + 0 R 8
= 24 R 8

 **Math Talk**

Discuss other ways to decompose 368 and other ways to divide 368 by 15 with your classmates.

5 You can divide 4-digit numbers by a 2-digit number in different ways.

a Divide the tens before dividing the ones.

Divide 6,118 by 75.

```
            8 1  R 43
    75)6, 1 1 8
        6 0 0   ← 75 × 8 tens
        1 1 8
          7 5   ← 75 × 1
          4 3
```

> 6 thousands 1 hundred 1 ten = 611 tens
> 611 tens ÷ 75 = 8 tens R 11 tens
>
> 11 tens 8 ones = 118 ones
> 118 ÷ 75 = 1 R 43

The quotient is 81 and the remainder is 43.

b Divide the hundreds, then the tens, and then divide the ones.

Divide 5,213 by 15.

```
        3 4 7  R 8
  15)5, 2 1 3
      4 5        ← 15 × 3 hundreds
      7 1
      6 0        ← 15 × 4 tens
      1 1 3
      1 0 5      ← 15 × 7
          8
```

> 5 thousands 2 hundreds
> = 52 hundreds
>
> 52 hundreds ÷ 15
> = 3 hundreds R 7 hundreds
>
> 7 hundreds 1 ten = 71 tens
> 71 tens ÷ 15 = 4 tens R 11 tens
>
> 11 tens 3 ones = 113 ones
> 113 ÷ 15 = 7 R 8

The quotient is 347 and the remainder is 8.

c Use an area model to decompose the dividend.

Divide 2,766 by 24.

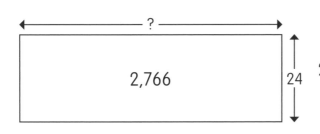

To divide by 24 easily, decompose the number into multiples of 24.

$2,766 \div 24 = ?$

$2,766 = 2,400 + 240 + 120 + 6$

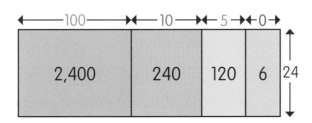

STEP 1 $2,400 \div 24 = 100$

STEP 2 $240 \div 24 = 10$

STEP 3 $120 \div 24 = 5$

STEP 4 $6 \div 24 = 0 \text{ R } 6$

So, $2,766 \div 24 = (2,400 \div 24) + (240 \div 24) + (120 \div 24) + (6 \div 24)$
$= 100 + 10 + 5 + 0 \text{ R } 6$
$= 115 \text{ R } 6$

TRY Practice dividing by a 2-digit number fluently

Divide.

1. $210 \div 80 =$ _____

2. $3,000 \div 70 =$ _____

3. $5,200 \div 90 =$ _____

4. $6,500 \div 80 =$ _____

Estimate the quotient. Then, divide.

5. $65 \div 18$

    Estimate = _____

    Quotient = _____

6. $92 \div 21$

    Estimate = _____

    Quotient = _____

7. $82 \div 16$

    Estimate = _____

    Quotient = _____

8. $69 \div 17$

    Estimate = _____

    Quotient = _____

Divide. Show your work.

9 $153 \div 27 =$ _____

10 $270 \div 39 =$ _____

11 $837 \div 67 =$ _____

12 $317 \div 21 =$ _____

13 $4{,}531 \div 50 =$ _____

14 $5{,}149 \div 56 =$ _____

Divide. Use an area model to help you.

15 $523 \div 12$

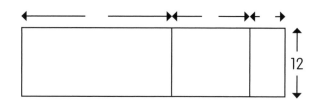

$523 \div 12 = (\underline{\hspace{1cm}} \div 12) + (\underline{\hspace{1cm}} \div 12) + (\underline{\hspace{1cm}} \div 12)$

$ = \underline{\hspace{1cm}} + \underline{\hspace{1cm}} + \underline{\hspace{1cm}} \text{ R } \underline{\hspace{1cm}}$

$ = \underline{\hspace{1cm}} \text{ R } \underline{\hspace{1cm}}$

16 $3,735 \div 28$

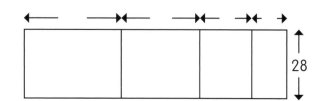

$3,735 \div 28 = (\underline{\hspace{1cm}} \div 28) + (\underline{\hspace{1cm}} \div 28) + (\underline{\hspace{1cm}} \div 28) + (\underline{\hspace{1cm}} \div 28)$

$ = \underline{\hspace{1cm}} + \underline{\hspace{1cm}} + \underline{\hspace{1cm}} + \underline{\hspace{1cm}} \text{ R } \underline{\hspace{1cm}}$

$ = \underline{\hspace{1cm}} \text{ R } \underline{\hspace{1cm}}$

INDEPENDENT PRACTICE

Multiply. Show your work. Estimate to check that each answer is reasonable.

1 56 × 32 = _____

2 26 × 76 = _____

3 68 × 93 = _____

4 89 × 77 = _____

5 235 × 21 = _____

6 548 × 85 = _____

7 $817 \times 69 =$ _____

8 $913 \times 54 =$ _____

9 $1,256 \times 45 =$ _____

10 $3,438 \times 81 =$ _____

11 $4,522 \times 38 =$ _____

12 $6,029 \times 58 =$ _____

Divide. Show your work. Estimate to check that each answer is reasonable.

13 $90 \div 40 =$ _____

14 $60 \div 40 =$ _____

15 $56 \div 34 =$ _____

16 $270 \div 20 =$ _____

17 $544 \div 16 =$ _____

18 $600 \div 73 =$ _____

19 $105 \div 12 =$ _____

20 $4{,}544 \div 71 =$ _____

21. $3,541 \div 20 = $ _____

22. $6,400 \div 51 = $ _____

23. $5,340 \div 15 = $ _____

24. $3,722 \div 45 = $ _____

Divide. Use an area model to help you.

25. $981 \div 81$

26. $5,283 \div 36$

27. $8,206 \div 24$

5 Order of Operations

Learning Objectives:
- Use order of operations to evaluate a numeric expression.
- Evaluate numeric expressions with parentheses.

**THINK**

Ana and Mason calculated the value of the expression $(8 + 12) \times 2 - 6$. Ana's answer was 34, and Mason's answer was 26. Who is correct?

ENGAGE

Write an expression to represent each situation. Jack subtracts 5 from 18, and multiplies the result by 3. Jill multiplies 3 by 5, and subtracts the result from 18. Are the two expressions the same? How about the answers? Use to explain your reasoning.

LEARN Order of operations

1 Ava and Justin solved the following problems differently. Who is correct?

a Leah had 10 stickers. She gave away 4 and bought 5 more. How many stickers did Leah have in the end?

$10 - 4 + 5 = ?$

Ava's solution:	Justin's solution:
$10 - 4 = 6$	$4 + 5 = 9$
$6 + 5 = 11$	$10 - 9 = 1$
Leah had 11 stickers in the end.	Leah had 1 sticker in the end.

Use  to check the answer.

given away   bought

$10 - 4 + 5$

$= 6 + 5$

$= 11$

Ava is correct.
She carried out the addition and subtraction from left to right.

Leah had 11 stickers in the end.

© 2020 Marshall Cavendish Education Pte Ltd

b Rachel divided 16 markers equally among 4 boys. 2 of the boys lost their markers. How many markers did the boys lose in all?

$16 \div 4 \times 2 = ?$

Ava's solution:
$4 \times 2 = 8$
$16 \div 8 = 2$
The boys lost 2 markers in all.

Justin's solution:
$16 \div 4 = 4$
$4 \times 2 = 8$
The boys lost 8 markers in all.

Use 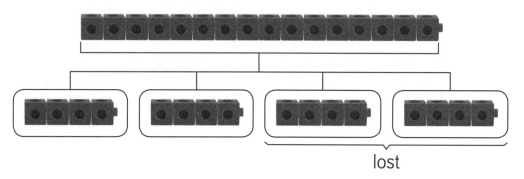 to check the answer.

lost

$16 \div 4 \times 2$

$= 4 \times 2$
$= 8$

The boys lost 8 markers in all.

Justin is correct.
He carried out the multiplication and division from left to right.

c Richard had 9 apples. He gave away 3 bags of 2 apples. How many apples did Richard have left?

$9 - 3 \times 2 = ?$

Ava's solution:
$3 \times 2 = 6$
$9 - 6 = 3$
Richard had 3 apples left.

Justin's solution:
$9 - 3 = 6$
$6 \times 2 = 12$
Richard had 12 apples left.

Use to check the answer.

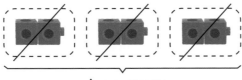

given away

$9 - 3 \times 2$

$= 9 - 6$

$= 3$

Richard had 3 apples left.

Ava is correct. She carried out the multiplication first before subtraction.

d Jack baked 12 cookies. His sister gave him another 8 cookies.
Jack divided the cookies equally among 4 people. How many cookies
did each person receive?

$(12 + 8) \div 4 = ?$

Ava's solution:
$8 \div 4 = 2$
$12 + 2 = 14$
Each person received 14 cookies.

Justin's solution:
$12 + 8 = 20$
$20 \div 4 = 5$
Each person received 5 cookies.

from Jack's sister

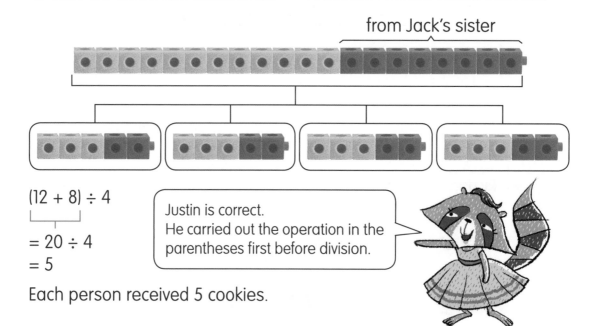

$(12 + 8) \div 4$

$= 20 \div 4$
$= 5$

Justin is correct.
He carried out the operation in the
parentheses first before division.

Each person received 5 cookies.

STEP **1** Carry out operations within parentheses.

STEP **2** Multiply and/or divide from left to right.

STEP **3** Add and/or subtract from left to right.

Activity 1

(1) Use a scientific calculator to find the value of 28 − 6 × 2.
Example:

Press 2 8 − 6 × 2 = 16

Then, find the value by working from left to right.

(2) Fill in the table.

		Using a scientific calculator	Working from left to right
a	28 − 6 × 2	16	
b	248 + 152 − 64		
c	58 × 63 ÷ 9		
d	40 + 64 ÷ 4 × 2		
e	684 − 208 ÷ 2 + 5		

(3) **Mathematical Habits 7** **Make use of structure**
Compare your answers in the table. What do you notice? Explain.

Activity 2

1 Use a scientific calculator to find the value of each expression without parentheses and with parentheses. Then, complete the table.

		Without parentheses		With parentheses
a	$34 + 96 \times 2$		$(34 + 96) \times 2$	
b	$68 + 120 \div 4$		$(68 + 120) \div 4$	
c	$900 - 25 \times 30$		$(900 - 25) \times 30$	
d	$82 + 64 \times 12 - 7$		$(82 + 64) \times 12 - 7$	
e	$520 + 248 \div 4 \times 2$		$520 + 248 \div (4 \times 2)$	
f	$965 - 480 \div 5 + 3$		$965 - 480 \div (5 + 3)$	

2 **Mathematical Habits 7** **Make use of structure**
Compare your answers in the table. What do you notice? Explain.

TRY Practice using order of operations

Find the value of each expression. Then, use your scientific calculator to check each answer.

1) 82 + 94 + 60 = _____

2) 78 + 125 – 50 = _____

3) 34 × 5 × 20 = _____

4) 756 ÷ 3 × 2 = _____

5) 43 + 20 × 17 = _____

6) 370 – 125 ÷ 5 = _____

Find the value of each expression. Then, use your scientific calculator to check each answer.

7) $274 - (180 - 90) =$ _____

8) $360 \div (5 \times 2) =$ _____

9) $15 \times (416 - 312) =$ _____

10) $510 + (42 + 38) \times 7 =$ _____

11) $18 \times 240 \div (10 \div 2) =$ _____

12) $(325 + 45) \div 5 \times 2 =$ _____

Find the value of each expression. Then, use your scientific calculator to check your answers.

13 $46 + 24 \times 6 - 120 \div 8 =$ _____

14 $26 \times 5 + 34 - 144 \div 6 =$ _____

15 $56 + (24 - 8) \times (10 + 2) =$ _____

16 $(38 - 15) \times 14 \times (2 + 5) =$ _____

17 $(45 - 37) \times (75 + 125 \div 5) =$ _____

18 $(36 + 15) \times 6 - (48 - 8) =$ _____

Mathematical Habits 2 Use mathematical reasoning

Look at the following numerical expression: 233 + 67.
Without evaluating the expression, share an expression with your partner that is:

a 4 times as great,

b 12 less than the given expression,

c one-third of (233 + 67),

d 18 more than 7 times of this expression,

e the product of this expression and 12,

f the quotient of this expression divided by 16.

INDEPENDENT PRACTICE

Find the value of each expression. Then, use your scientific calculator to check each answer.

1 96 – 50 + 65 = _____

2 175 + 25 – 95 = _____

3 6 × 40 ÷ 3 = _____

4 250 ÷ 5 × 53 = _____

5 79 + 27 × 2 = _____

6 280 – 72 ÷ 8 = _____

Find the value of each expression. Then, use your scientific calculator to check each answer.

7 $35 \times (560 \div 70) = \underline{\hspace{2cm}}$

8 $540 \div (293 - 203) = \underline{\hspace{2cm}}$

9 $(66 + 44) \div 5 + 12 = \underline{\hspace{2cm}}$

10 $71 - 6 \times 8 \div (43 - 27) = \underline{\hspace{2cm}}$

11 $148 + (75 - 59) \div 4 + 7 = \underline{\hspace{2cm}}$

12 $97 - 32 + 66 - (6 \times 4) = \underline{\hspace{2cm}}$

Real-World Problems: Four Operations of Whole Numbers

Learning Objective:
- Use different strategies to solve multi-step problems.

**THINK**

Ms. Lee was 6 times as old as her grandson 7 years ago. How old is Ms. Lee now if the sum of their present ages is 77 years? Use different strategies to solve this problem.

ENGAGE

Andy, Tiana, and Lex measured their heights. The total height of Andy and Tiana is 320 centimeters. This is twice that of Lex's height. Lex is 15 centimeters taller than Tiana. Tiana is 30 centimeters shorter than Andy. Draw a bar model to find how tall Andy is.

LEARN Solve real-world problems

1. Evelyn has a length of rope 250 centimeters long. She cuts it into pieces that are each 20 centimeters long. How many pieces does she cut? What is the length of the remaining rope?

    Understand the problem.

   Do I need all the information given?
   How much rope does Evelyn have?
   How long is each piece of rope she cuts?
   What do I need to find?

   STEP 2 Think of a plan.
   I can divide to find the quotient and remainder.

STEP 3 Carry out the plan.

250 ÷ 20 = 12 R 10

Eve cuts the rope into 12 pieces.

The length of the remaining rope is 10 centimeters.

$$
\begin{array}{r}
12\ \text{R}\ 10 \\
20\overline{)250} \\
\underline{20} \\
50 \\
\underline{40} \\
10
\end{array}
$$

STEP 4 Check the answer.

I can use estimation to check that my answer is reasonable.

240 is a multiple of 20 that is near 250.

240 ÷ 20 = 12

There should be about 12 pieces of rope.

My answer is reasonable.

2   120 fifth-graders are going on a field trip by bus. Each bus holds 35 students. How many buses are needed?

120 ÷ 35 = 3 R 15

The 15 remaining fifth-graders would need 1 more bus.

$$
\begin{array}{r}
3\ \text{R}\ 15 \\
35\overline{)120} \\
\underline{105} \\
15
\end{array}
$$

3 + 1 = 4

4 buses are needed.

3   Amy, Brian, and Carla had some basketball cards. Amy and Brian had 1,250 cards. Amy and Carla had 830 cards. Brian had 4 times as many cards as Carla. How many cards did Amy have?

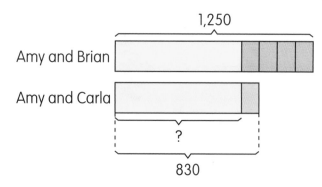

1,250 − 830 = 420

Brian had 420 more cards than Carla.

3 units = 420

  1 unit = 420 ÷ 3

        = 140

Carla had 140 cards.

830 − 140 = 690

Amy had 690 cards.

4 Pablo had 638 grams of cashew nuts and 594 grams of peanuts. He mixed the nuts and packed them into 7 packets. Each packet of nuts had a mass of 120 grams. How many grams of nuts did Pablo have left?

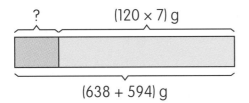

638 + 594 = 1,232

Pablo had a total of 1,232 grams of nuts at first.

120 × 7 = 840

Pablo packed 840 grams of nuts into 7 packets.

1,232 − 840 = 392

Pablo had 392 grams of nuts left.

1. Read the problem. Draw a bar model for the problem.
A salesman sold five vacuum cleaners. He sold two of the vacuum cleaners at $659 each and the rest at $478 each. How much money did the salesman receive from the sale of the five vacuum cleaners?

2. Estimate the answer.

3. **Mathematical Habits 2** Use mathematical reasoning
Solve the problem in ① and compare your answer with your estimate.
How do you know whether your answer is reasonable? Explain.

TRY Practice solving real-world problems

Solve. Show your work.

1. A load of potatoes weighs 100 pounds. The potatoes are packed into 15-pound bags. How many bags of potatoes are there? How many pounds of potatoes are left?

   _____ ÷ _____ = _____

   There are _____ bags of potatoes.

   There are _____ pounds of potatoes left.

2. Mary has 172 stamps. She wants to put them in an album. Each page of the album can hold up to 25 stamps. What is the least number of pages Mary will need to hold all her stamps?

   _____ ÷ _____ = _____

   Mary will need _____ more page/s to hold the remaining

   _____ stamps.

   _____ + _____ = _____

   Mary will need _____ pages to hold all her stamps.

3 Mr. Walker bought just enough gas to fill nine 250-gallon fuel tanks. The gas was sold at $3 per gallon. How much money did he pay in all?

_____ × _____ = _____

Mr. Walker bought _____ gallons of gas.

_____ × $_____ = $_____

He paid $_____.

4 A grocer bought 32 cartons of apples. There were 40 apples in each carton. She packed the apples into bags of 5 and sold each bag for $4. How much money did she make from selling all the apples?

_____ × _____ = _____

There were _____ apples.

_____ ÷ _____ = _____

There were _____ bags of apples.

_____ × $_____ = $_____

She made $_____ from selling all the apples.

5 The table shows the wages of workers in a plumbing company. Ms. Clark works Tuesday through Sunday. How much does Ms. Clark earn in the six days?

Weekdays	$170 per day
Saturdays and Sundays	$315 per day

_____ × $_____ = $_____

Ms. Clark earns $_____ for working on weekdays.

_____ × $_____ = $_____

Ms. Clark earns $_____ for working on Saturday and Sunday.

$_____ + $_____ = $_____

Ms. Clark earns $_____ in the six days.

Solve. Use the bar model to help you.

6 The cost of 4 belts and 5 ties is $247. Each tie costs 3 times as much as a belt. What is the total cost of a tie and a belt?

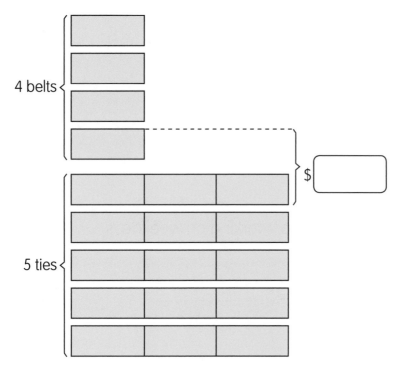

_____ units = $247

1 unit = $247 ÷ _____

= $_____

Each belt costs $_____.

3 units = $_____ × 3

= $_____

Each tie costs $_____.

$_____ + $_____ = $_____

The total cost of a belt and a tie is $_____.

7 A florist had an equal number of red and yellow tulips. She sold 624 red tulips. Then, she had 4 times as many yellow tulips as red tulips. How many tulips did the florist have at first?

Before

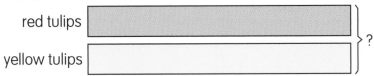

red tulips

yellow tulips

}?

After

624

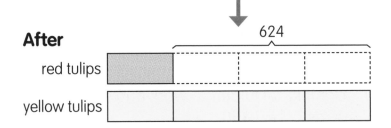

red tulips

yellow tulips

1 unit represents the number of red tulips left and 4 units represent the number of yellow tulips.

3 units = 624 tulips

1 unit = 624 ÷ 3
      = 208 tulips

8 units = 8 × _____

       = _____ tulips

She had _____ tulips at first.

1 Find the value of 1,350 × 27 ÷ 25.

2 Use a scientific calculator to work out 1,350 × 27 first. Then, divide the result by 25.

3 Next, use your scientific calculator to work out 27 ÷ 25 first. Then, multiply the result by 1,350.

What do you notice? Try with other numbers. Discuss your findings with your classmates.

Name: _____   Date: _____

Solve. Show your work.

1 A water tank contains 1,250 gallons of water. The water is used to fill 30-gallon barrels. How many barrels can be filled completely? How much water is left?

2 A grocer had 49 boxes of strawberries. Each box contained 75 strawberries. The strawberries were repacked into small boxes, each holding 15 strawberries. How many small boxes of strawberries did the grocer have?

3. A box of 12 granola bars costs $2. Mr. Perez bought some boxes and sold each granola bar for $0.50. In a week, he sold a total of 4,386 granola bars.

    a What was the least number of boxes of granola bars he bought?

    b How much did he pay for this number of boxes of granola bars?

    c How much money did he make after he sold 4,386 granola bars?

4. There is a total of 20 cars and motorcycles in a parking lot. The total number of wheels is 50. How many motorcycles are there?

5 Chris and Ella bought some beads from a hobby store. The table shows the cost of beads by weight.

Weight	Cost
First 2 ounces	70¢
Each additional ounce	30¢

a Chris bought 5 ounces of beads. How much did they cost?

b Ella paid $6.10 for her beads. What was the total weight of the beads that she bought?

6 A restaurant owner bought 245 cartons of candles. Each carton held 28 yellow and white candles. There were 2,198 yellow candles, and the remaining candles were white. She used the same number of white candles each month for 42 months. How many white candles did she use each month?

7 A farmer has some cows and chickens. The animals have a total of 40 heads and 112 legs. How many cows are there?

Solve. Draw a bar model to help you.

8 A stamp collector bought 112 packets of stamps. There were 60 stamps in each packet. He gave away 570 stamps and put the remainder equally into 25 albums. How many stamps did he put in each album?

9 A shopkeeper sold a total of 15 boxes of pencils on Monday and Tuesday. She sold 3 more boxes of pencils on Monday than on Tuesday. There were 12 pencils in each box. How many pencils did she sell on Monday?

10 The Evans family paid $1,800 for a new refrigerator, washer, and dryer. The refrigerator cost $250 more than the washer. The dryer cost half as much as the washer. How much did the washer cost?

11 Jessica had $7 and her sister had $2. After their parents gave each of them an equal amount of money, Jessica had twice as much money as her sister. How much money did their parents give each of them?

12 Maya is 12 years old and Sophia is 15 years older than Maya. In how many years will Sophia be twice as old as Maya?

Mathematical Habits **2** **Use mathematical reasoning**

Amanda wants to solve the problem **187 ÷ 31**.
Write the steps she should follow.

Problem Solving with Heuristics

1 **Mathematical Habits 1** **Persevere in solving problems**

Emma wants to solve a 7-digit secret code. Use the following clues to help her solve the secret code.

- All seven digits are different.
- The digit in the ten thousands place is 5.
- The digit in the thousands place is twice the digit in the hundred thousands place.
- The digit in the ones place is 2 more than the digit in the millions place.
- The digit in the millions place is 8 less than the digit in the hundreds place.
- The digit in the millions place is 1 less than the digit in the tens place.

What is the secret code?

2 **Mathematical Habits 8** **Look for patterns**

Without adding the 99s, find the value of each of the following:

99 + 99 =

99 + 99 + 99 + 99 + 99 + 99 =

What is the value of the digit in the ones place in each case?

What is the least number of 99s that must be added to get a 1 in the ones place?

Without multiplying 99 by 45, explain how you can find the sum of 45 groups of 99?

3 **Mathematical Habits 7** Make use of structure

The 9 key on your calculator is not working. Show two ways you can use the calculator to find 1,234 × 79.

4 **Mathematical Habits 8** Look for patterns

Lucas thought of a number less than 100. When he divided it by 8, the remainder was 1. When he divided it by 9, the remainder was 2. What was his number?

5 **Mathematical Habits 1** Persevere in solving problems

Ms. Wilson went to a store to buy some supplies. A water bottle cost $33, a keyboard cost $34, and a dictionary cost $35. She bought at least one of each item. She spent $235 to buy seven items. How many of each item did she buy?

CHAPTER WRAP-UP

Whole Numbers and the Four Operations

Numbers to 10,000,000

Multiplying by Tens, Hundreds, Thousands, and Powers of 10

Dividing by Tens, Hundreds, and Thousands

Order of Operations

Standard form:
3,569,214
Word form: Three million, five hundred sixty-nine thousand, two hundred fourteen
Expanded form:
3,569,214 = 3,000,000 + 500,000 + 60,000 + 9,000 + 200 + 10 + 4

Use a pattern to divide a number by 10, 100 and 1,000 and their multiples.
$56,000 \div 80 = 700$
$56,000 \div 800 = 70$
$56,000 \div 8,000 = 7$

Multiplying and Dividing by 2-Digit Numbers

Use a pattern to multiply a number by 10, 100 and 1,000 and their multiples.
$1,234 \times 20 = 24,680$
$1,234 \times 200 = 246,800$
$1,234 \times 2,000 = 2,468,000$

Use strategies to multiply or divide a 2-digit, 3-digit, or 4-digit number by a 2-digit number.

```
    2 4 1
    2 3 1
  5, 3 6 2
 ×      7 6
  3 2, 1 7 2
3 7 5, 3 4 0
4 0 7, 5 1 2
```

```
            3 4 7 R 8
   15 ) 5, 2 1 3
          4 5
          7 1
          6 0
          1 1 3
          1 0 5
              8
```

STEP 1 Carry out operations within parentheses.

STEP 2 Multiply and/or divide from left to right.

STEP 3 Add and/or subtract from left to right.

Name: _____   Date: _____

Write each number in standard form.

1 three million, seventy-six thousand, two hundred fourteen

   _____

2 seven million, four hundred fifty thousand, nine hundred eighty-six

   _____

Write each number in word form.

3 9,380,170 _____

   _____

4 5,872,649 _____

   _____

Complete each expanded form.

5 4,623,180 = _____ + 623,000 + 180

6 _____ + 10,000 + 600 + 8 = 210,608

Write each number in expanded form.

7 4,578,312 = _____

8 9,400,176 = _____

Multiply.

9 9 × 100 = _____   10 81 × 400 = _____

11 58 × 3,000 = _____   12 331 × 80 = _____

Find each product. Show your work.

13 672 and 300

14 3,102 and 1,000

Multiply. Show your work.

15 67×10^2

16 429×10^2

17 872×10^3

18 $5,462 \times 10^3$

Divide. Show your work.

19 $9,200 \div 100$

20 $64,000 \div 4,000$

21 $800 \div 200$

22 $1,740 \div 60$

23 $1,400 \div 100$

24 $270,000 \div 9,000$

Multiply. Show your work. Estimate to check that each answer is reasonable.

25 735 × 48 = _____

26 2,054 × 66 = _____

Divide. Show your work. Estimate to check that each answer is reasonable.

27 864 ÷ 36 = _____

28 8,036 ÷ 57 = _____

Use order of operations to solve each expression.

29 54 ÷ 3 × 2 = _____

30 3 + 4 × 8 = _____

31 96 − 24 ÷ 2 × 7 + 5 = _____

32 20 × (24 − 18) = _____

33 18 + (4 + 16) × 7 = _____

34 (72 + 18) ÷ (3 × 2) = _____

Solve. Draw a bar model to help you.

35 The cost of 6 refrigerators and 5 washing machines is $23,628. The cost of each refrigerator is $1,650 more than the cost of a washing machine. How much does a washing machine cost?

36 Mr. Jones was 4 times as old as his daughter 5 years ago. How old is Mr. Jones now if the sum of their present ages is 55 years?

37 A group of teachers, parents, and students attended a concert. The adults paid $1,200 altogether and the students paid $640 altogether for their tickets. The price of an adult ticket was $60, and there were 4 more teachers than parents. How many parents were there in the group?

38 Jade, Matthew, and Zane collect stamps. Jade and Matthew have 220 stamps more than Zane. Zane and Matthew have 140 stamps more than Jade. Jade and Zane have 500 stamps. How many stamps does Matthew have?

39 Henry bought 49 packs of red balloons, 66 packs of blue balloons, and 35 packs of yellow balloons. Each pack contained 12 balloons. He mixed them up and gave away some balloons. He then repacked the balance into packs of 25.

a   How many balloons were there altogether?

b   He gave away 225 balloons. How many large packs of 25 balloons were there?

c   Henry paid $3 for each pack of a dozen balloons. He sold each new pack of 25 balloons for $10. How much money did he make?

© 2020 Marshall Cavendish Education Pte Ltd

Assessment Prep

Answer each question.

40 Which expression matches the description "the quotient of 4,215 divided by 15, subtracted from the product of 31 and 12"?

Ⓐ $31 + 12 - 4,215 \div 15$

Ⓑ $31 \times 12 - 4,215 \div 15$

Ⓒ $4,215 \div 15 - 31 + 12$

Ⓓ $4,215 - 15 \times 31 - 12$

41 What is $9,954 \div 79$?
Write your answer in the answer grid.

42 This question has 2 parts.

Part A
Which **two** equations are true when the number 300 is written in the box?

(A) $\boxed{} \div 300 = 10$

(B) $45 \times \boxed{} = 1{,}350$

(C) $900 \div \boxed{} = 3$

(D) $6{,}000 \div 20 = \boxed{}$

(E) $\boxed{} \div 3 = 10$

(F) $300 \times 10 = \boxed{}$

Part B
Which **two** equations are true when the number 3,000 is written in the box?

(A) $\boxed{} \div 300 = 10$

(B) $45 \times \boxed{} = 13{,}500$

(C) $90{,}000 \div \boxed{} = 3$

(D) $60{,}000 \div 200 = \boxed{}$

(E) $\boxed{} \div 3 = 1{,}000$

(F) $300 \times 100 = \boxed{}$

43 Busy Pharmacy sold 3 bottles of vitamins for $84. Wally Pharmacy sold 5 bottles of the same vitamins for $100.
- Find the cost of a bottle of vitamin in each of the stores.
- Dan wants to buy 8 bottles with the least amount of money. Which store should he buy the vitamins from? Explain.

Write your answers and explanation in the space below.

© 2020 Marshall Cavendish Education Pte Ltd

Name: _____ Date: _____

Field Day

1 At a school's field day, students will throw table tennis balls and then measure the distance of their throws. There are 626 students in the school. There are 6 table tennis balls in one pack. What is the least number of packs needed so that each student gets to throw 1 table tennis ball? Explain your work.

2 The school coach decides to have each student throw 2 table tennis balls instead of one. Explain how this will affect the number of packs needed.

3 The vice principal decides to order a field day T-shirt for every student. The cost of each student's T-shirt is $14, so the total cost of the T-shirts for all the students will be:

```
        6  2  6
  ×        1  4
  2  4 , 8  2  4
     6 , 2  6  0
  3  1 , 0  8  4
```

Is this correct? If so, explain why. If not, identify the mistake and find the correct cost.

Rubric

Level	Point(s)	My Performance
4	7–8	• Most of my answers are correct. • I showed complete understanding of what I have learned. • I used the correct strategies to solve the problems. • I explained my answers and mathematical thinking clearly and completely.
3	5–6	• Some of my answers are correct. • I showed some understanding of what I have learned. • I used some correct strategies to solve the problems. • I explained my answers and mathematical thinking clearly.
2	3–4	• A few of my answers are correct. • I showed little understanding of what I have learned. • I used a few correct strategies to solve the problems. • I explained some of my answers and mathematical thinking clearly.
1	0–2	• A few of my answers are correct. • I showed little or no understanding of what I have learned. • I used a few strategies to solve the problems. • I did not explain my answers and mathematical thinking clearly.

Teacher's Comments

STEAM

The National Park Service

In 1872, President Ulysses S. Grant signed an act to make Yellowstone the country's first national park. Then, in 1916, Congress established the National Park Service. Today, Yellowstone National Park and more than 400 other parks, monuments, seashores, rivers, and trails belong to the National Park Service.

Task

Advertise a Park

Imagine working for a bus company that offers special fares to the national parks. Work in pairs or groups to promote a trip to a national park.

1. Visit the National Park Service online to choose and learn more about any park. Find answers to questions, such as:
   - How large is the park?
   - How many people visit the park each year?
   - When are the least and most crowded times of the year to visit?
   - What kinds of wildlife live in the park? How large are their populations?
   - What special things are there to see or do in the park?
   - How much does it cost to stay in hotels and campgrounds inside the park?

2. Think about how you can use the information you collect to encourage people to travel with your company to the park. Then, think about the best way to share that information. For example, you might want to record a radio spot, video a commercial, or design an advertisement to hang in travel offices and bus terminals.

Fractions and Mixed Numbers

I have painted $\frac{2}{5}$ of the wall blue. I want to paint $\frac{1}{2}$ of the wall green. Will there be any space left on the wall to be painted yellow?

There are 2 cans of white paint. I mixed $\frac{3}{4}$ of a can of white paint with $\frac{7}{8}$ of a can of navy blue paint to get light blue paint. I mixed $\frac{5}{7}$ of a can of white paint with $\frac{5}{6}$ of a can of dark green paint to get light green paint. How much white paint is left?

How are fractions and division related? How is adding and subtracting unlike fractions and mixed numbers similar to adding and subtracting like fractions?

Name: _____ Date: _____

Like and unlike fractions

a Robert had $\frac{2}{5}$ of a cracker.   Mariah had $\frac{3}{5}$ of a cracker.

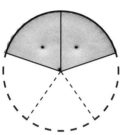

$\frac{2}{5}$ and $\frac{3}{5}$ are like fractions.

They have the same denominator, 5.

b In one tray, $\frac{3}{4}$ of a pie was left.

In another tray, $\frac{2}{5}$ of a pie was left.

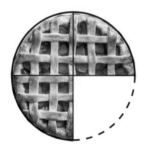

$\frac{3}{4}$ and $\frac{2}{5}$ are unlike fractions.

They have different denominators, 4 and 5.

▶ Quick Check

Circle the like fractions in each set.

1 $\frac{3}{4}, \ \frac{1}{2}, \ \frac{2}{5}, \ \frac{1}{4}$

2 $\frac{5}{6}, \ \frac{5}{9}, \ \frac{9}{10}, \ \frac{7}{9}$

Circle the unlike fractions that do not belong in each set.

3 $\frac{1}{8}, \ \frac{2}{7}, \ \frac{3}{8}, \ \frac{1}{2}$

4 $\frac{5}{9}, \ \frac{5}{12}, \ \frac{1}{10}, \ \frac{7}{9}$

Finding equivalent fractions

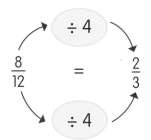

$$\frac{3}{4} \xrightarrow{\times 2}{\times 2} = \frac{6}{8}$$

$$\frac{8}{12} \xrightarrow{\div 2}{\div 2} = \frac{4}{6}$$

▶ Quick Check

Fill in each blank.

5 $\dfrac{3}{5} = \dfrac{\boxed{}}{10}$

6 $\dfrac{5}{6} = \dfrac{\boxed{}}{24}$

Expressing fractions in simplest form

$$\frac{6}{9} \xrightarrow{\div 3}{\div 3} = \frac{2}{3}$$

$$\frac{8}{12} \xrightarrow{\div 4}{\div 4} = \frac{2}{3}$$

Divide the numerator and denominator by their common factor.

▶ Quick Check

Express each fraction in simplest form.

7 $\dfrac{8}{10} =$ _____

8 $\dfrac{20}{100} =$ _____

Representing fractions on a number line

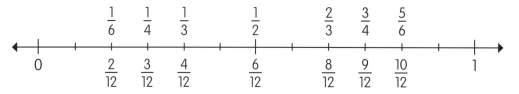

▶ Quick Check

Fill in each blank with the correct equivalent fraction.
Give your answer in simplest form.

9

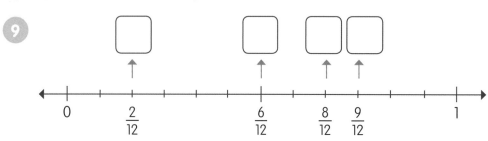

Understanding mixed numbers

1 whole

1 whole

1 half

$$2 \quad + \quad \frac{1}{2} \quad = \quad 2\frac{1}{2}$$

whole number   fraction   mixed number

▶ Quick Check

Find the number of wholes and parts that are shaded.
Then, write the mixed number.

10

_____ wholes _____ parts = _____

Expressing improper fractions as mixed numbers

Express $\frac{5}{3}$ as a mixed number.
Using models:

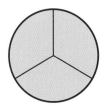 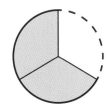

$\frac{5}{3} = 5$ thirds

$= 3$ thirds $+ 2$ thirds

$= \frac{3}{3} + \frac{2}{3}$

$= 1 + \frac{2}{3}$

$= 1\frac{2}{3}$

▶ **Quick Check**

Express the improper fraction as a mixed number.

⑪

$\frac{8}{3} = $ _____ thirds

$= $ _____ thirds $+ $ _____ thirds

$= $ _____ $+ $ _____

$= $ _____ $+ $ _____

$= $ _____

Express each improper fraction as a mixed number.

⑫ $\frac{13}{4} = $ _____

⑬ $\frac{19}{5} = $ _____

Expressing mixed numbers as improper fractions

Convert $3\frac{1}{2}$ to an improper fraction.

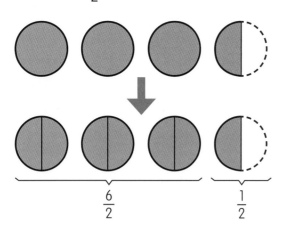

$$3\frac{1}{2} = \frac{6}{2} + \frac{1}{2}$$
$$= \frac{7}{2}$$

▶ **Quick Check**

Express each mixed number as an improper fraction in simplest form.

14 $2\frac{4}{6} =$ _____

15 $2\frac{1}{2} =$ _____

16 $1\frac{6}{10} =$ _____

Adding and subtracting like fractions

Add or subtract. Express the sum or difference in simplest form.

a $\frac{2}{9} + \frac{4}{9} = \frac{6}{9}$
$= \frac{2}{3}$

b $\frac{9}{10} - \frac{3}{10} = \frac{6}{10}$
$= \frac{3}{5}$

c $1\frac{1}{3} + 1\frac{1}{3} = 2\frac{1}{3} + \frac{1}{3}$
$= 2\frac{2}{3}$

d $1\frac{4}{5} - 1\frac{1}{5} = \frac{4}{5} - \frac{1}{5}$
$= \frac{3}{5}$

▶ **Quick Check**

Add or subtract. Express the sum or difference in simplest form.

17 $\frac{5}{8} + \frac{1}{8} =$ _____

18 $\frac{3}{10} - \frac{1}{10} =$ _____

19 $3\frac{1}{7} + 4\frac{2}{7} =$ _____

20 $6\frac{5}{8} - 2\frac{3}{8} =$ _____

Fractions, Mixed Numbers, and Division Expressions

Learning Objective:
- Understand and apply the relationships between fractions, mixed numbers, and division expressions.

> **New Vocabulary**
> division expression

 **THINK**

Ana bought some apples. She shared them equally among 7 children. Each child received more than 1 apple. Ana bought fewer than 12 apples. How is it possible?

ENGAGE

Divide two square pieces of paper into three equal parts each. Put the pieces into equal groups. How many ways can you do it? How can you name each group? Now, do the same in another way.

LEARN Rewrite division expressions as fractions

1 Share 2 fruit tarts equally among 3 children. What fraction of a fruit tart will each child receive?

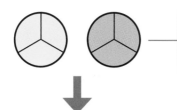

> Each tart is divided into 3 equal parts.
> Each child will get $\frac{2}{3}$ of each tart.

$2 \div 3 = \frac{2}{3}$ ——— $\frac{2}{3}$ is the same as 2 divided by 3.

$2 \div 3$ is a division expression. A division expression is an expression that contains only numbers and the division symbol.

Each child will receive $\frac{2}{3}$ of a fruit tart.

Hands-on Activity Dividing a whole number by a 1-digit whole number

Work in pairs.

1. Pick two cards from a set of 9. Write two division expressions to relate the two numbers and leave your answers as fractions.

2. Cut paper strips into equal pieces to represent the fractions in ①.

3. What can you say about the fractions and the division expressions?

TRY Practice rewriting division expressions as fractions

Solve.

1. Mr. Brown cuts 3 strawberry pies to share equally among 4 children. What fraction of a strawberry pie does each child receive?

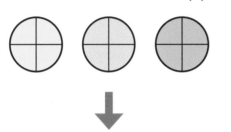

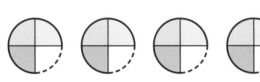

Each strawberry pie is divided into _____ equal parts. Each part is _____ of a strawberry pie.

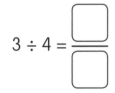

$3 \div 4 = \dfrac{\boxed{}}{\boxed{}}$

Each child receives _____ of a strawberry pie.

3 divided by 4 is the same as $\dfrac{\boxed{}}{\boxed{}}$.

Draw lines to divide each bar into equal pieces. Then, write the fraction.

2 **a** Share 2 granola bars equally among 3 children. What fraction of a granola bar does each child receive?

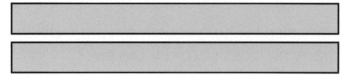

$2 \div 3 =$ _____

Each child receives _____ of a granola bar.

b Share 3 granola bars equally among 5 children. What fraction of a granola bar does each child receive?

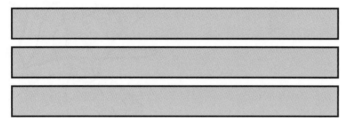

$3 \div 5 =$ _____

Each child receives _____ of a granola bar.

Rewrite each division expression as a fraction.

3 $4 \div 5 = \dfrac{\Box}{\Box}$

4 $7 \div 9 = \dfrac{\Box}{\Box}$

5 $5 \div 8 = \dfrac{\Box}{\Box}$

6 $7 \div 11 = \dfrac{\Box}{\Box}$

Rewrite each fraction as a division expression.

7 $\dfrac{3}{7} =$ _____ $\div$ _____

8 $\dfrac{8}{12} =$ _____ $\div$ _____

9 $\dfrac{3}{10} =$ _____ $\div$ _____

10 $\dfrac{5}{6} =$ _____ $\div$ _____

ENGAGE

a Take 5 quarters. Put them into wholes and parts. What fraction is formed? How can we write this fraction in two ways?

b Now, do the same with 7 halves.

LEARN Rewrite division expressions as mixed numbers

1 Mr. Davis made 5 pancakes. The pancakes were divided equally among his 4 children. How many pancakes did each child receive?

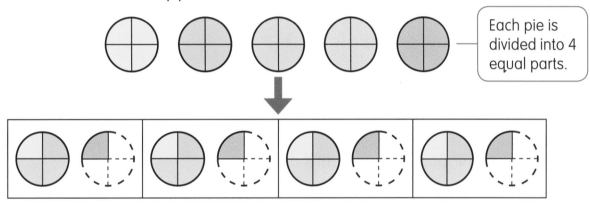

Each pie is divided into 4 equal parts.

▶ **Method 1**

$$5 \div 4 = \frac{5}{4}$$
$$= 1\frac{1}{4}$$

▶ **Method 2**

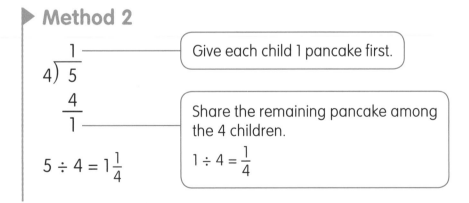

Give each child 1 pancake first.

Share the remaining pancake among the 4 children.

$$1 \div 4 = \frac{1}{4}$$

$$5 \div 4 = 1\frac{1}{4}$$

Each child received $1\frac{1}{4}$ pancakes.

Hands-on Activity

Activity 1 Using models to relate fractions and division

(1) Draw a bar model to show the division expression "12 ÷ 3."

(2) Write each part as a fraction of 12.

Activity 2 Relating fractions and division

(1) Share 2 pies equally among 5 people. Use to show the fraction of a pie that each person receives. Explain.

(2) Write a word problem to represent the following equation.

$$6 \div 4 = \frac{6}{4} = 1\frac{1}{2}$$

TRY Practice rewriting division expressions as mixed numbers and vice versa

Express the division expression as a fraction in simplest form. Then, rewrite the fraction as a mixed number.

1 $14 \div 4 = \dfrac{\boxed{} \div \boxed{}}{\boxed{} \div \boxed{}}$

$= \dfrac{\boxed{}}{\boxed{}}$

$= \boxed{} \dfrac{\boxed{}}{\boxed{}}$

Express each division expression as a fraction in simplest form. Then, rewrite the fraction as a mixed number.

2 $19 \div 2 =$ _____

   $=$ _____

   $=$ _____

3 $43 \div 4 =$ _____

   $=$ _____

   $=$ _____

4 $20 \div 8 =$ _____

   $=$ _____

   $=$ _____

5 $45 \div 10 =$ _____

   $=$ _____

   $=$ _____

Express each division expression as a fraction in simplest form. Then, rewrite the fraction as a mixed number.

6 $22 \div 4 =$ _____

$\quad\quad\quad\quad = $ _____

$\quad\quad\quad\quad = $ _____

7 $18 \div 6 =$ _____

$\quad\quad\quad\quad = $ _____

$\quad\quad\quad\quad = $ _____

Rewrite each fraction as a division expression.

8 $\frac{9}{4} =$ _____ $\div$ _____

9 $\frac{10}{7} =$ _____ $\div$ _____

10 $1\frac{1}{3} =$ _____ $\div$ _____

11 $1\frac{1}{5} =$ _____ $\div$ _____

12 $3\frac{3}{5} =$ _____ $\div$ _____

13 $4\frac{2}{9} =$ _____ $\div$ _____

INDEPENDENT PRACTICE

Express each division expression as a fraction in simplest form. Rewrite the fraction as a mixed number if necessary.

1 $4 \div 9 =$ _____

2 $2 \div 5 =$ _____

3 $6 \div 7 =$ _____

4 $18 \div 8 =$ _____

5 $7 \div 3 =$ _____

6 $11 \div 4 =$ _____

7 $25 \div 7 =$ _____

8 $57 \div 9 =$ _____

Rewrite each fraction as a division expression.

9 $\frac{4}{7}$ = _____ ÷ _____

10 $\frac{5}{11}$ = _____ ÷ _____

11 $\frac{9}{13}$ = _____ ÷ _____

12 $\frac{4}{3}$ = _____ ÷ _____

13 $1\frac{4}{5}$ = _____ ÷ _____

14 $2\frac{1}{4}$ = _____ ÷ _____

15 $1\frac{3}{7}$ = _____ ÷ _____

2 Adding Unlike Fractions and Mixed Numbers

Learning Objectives:
- Add two unlike fractions where one denominator may or may not be a multiple of the other.
- Add mixed numbers with or without renaming.
- Estimate sums of fractions and mixed numbers.

THINK

Recall that the sum of $\frac{2}{9}$ and $\frac{4}{9}$ is $\frac{6}{9}$. Landon says the sum of $\frac{2}{9}$ and $\frac{1}{3}$ is $\frac{3}{9}$.

Daniel says the sum is $\frac{3}{12}$, and Evelyn says the sum is $\frac{3}{3}$. Who is correct? Why?

ENGAGE

Fold a piece of paper into fourths. Color $\frac{1}{4}$ of the piece of paper red.

Now, fold the same paper into eighths and color $\frac{1}{8}$ of the piece of paper green.

What fraction of the whole is colored red and green? What addition equation can you write?

LEARN Use a common denominator to add unlike fractions

1 A fence is painted $\frac{1}{2}$ red and $\frac{1}{3}$ green. The rest is painted yellow.
   What fraction of the fence is painted red and green?

   > $\frac{1}{2}$ and $\frac{1}{3}$ are unlike fractions. To add, rewrite $\frac{1}{2}$ and $\frac{1}{3}$ as like fractions.

   List the multiples of the denominators, 2 and 3.
   Multiples of 2: 2, 4, ⑥, 8, ...
   Multiples of 3: 3, ⑥, 9, 12, ...
   The first common multiple of 2 and 3 is 6.

   So, 6 is a common denominator of $\frac{1}{2}$ and $\frac{1}{3}$.

$\frac{1}{2}$ and $\frac{3}{6}$ are equivalent fractions.

$\frac{1}{3}$ and $\frac{2}{6}$ are equivalent fractions.

Rewrite $\frac{1}{2}$ and $\frac{1}{3}$ as like fractions.

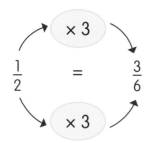

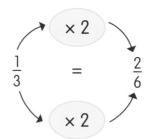

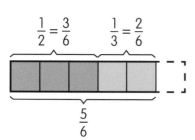

$$\frac{1}{2} + \frac{1}{3} = \frac{3}{6} + \frac{2}{6}$$
$$= \frac{5}{6}$$

$\frac{5}{6}$ of the fence is painted red and green.

Work in pairs.

1. Draw a bar model to show each pair of fractions. Then, find the sum.

   a $\dfrac{1}{2} + \dfrac{1}{4}$

   b $\dfrac{1}{5} + \dfrac{3}{4}$

   c $\dfrac{1}{4} + \dfrac{2}{3}$

TRY Practice using a common denominator to add unlike fractions

Add each fraction.

1 $\dfrac{1}{3} + \dfrac{2}{9} = \dfrac{\boxed{}}{\boxed{}} + \dfrac{\boxed{}}{\boxed{}}$

$= \dfrac{\boxed{}}{\boxed{}}$

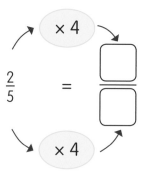

$\dfrac{1}{3} = \dfrac{\boxed{}}{\boxed{}}$ ×3 ... ×3

2 $\dfrac{2}{5} + \dfrac{1}{4} = \dfrac{\boxed{}}{\boxed{}} + \dfrac{\boxed{}}{\boxed{}}$

$= \dfrac{\boxed{}}{\boxed{}}$

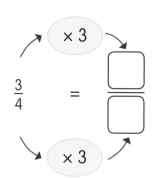 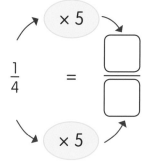

$\dfrac{2}{5} = \dfrac{\boxed{}}{\boxed{}}$ ×4 ... ×4 $\dfrac{1}{4} = \dfrac{\boxed{}}{\boxed{}}$ ×5 ... ×5

3 $\dfrac{3}{4} + \dfrac{2}{3} = \dfrac{\boxed{}}{\boxed{}} + \dfrac{\boxed{}}{\boxed{}}$

$= \dfrac{\boxed{}}{\boxed{}}$

$= \dfrac{\boxed{}}{\boxed{}} + \dfrac{\boxed{}}{\boxed{}}$

$= \boxed{}\dfrac{\boxed{}}{\boxed{}}$

$\dfrac{3}{4} = \dfrac{\boxed{}}{\boxed{}}$ ×3 ... ×3 $\dfrac{2}{3} = \dfrac{\boxed{}}{\boxed{}}$ ×4 ... ×4

Mathematical Habit 3 **Construct viable arguments**

One of the three models shows the sum of $\frac{1}{2}$ and $\frac{1}{7}$. The other two models are incorrect.

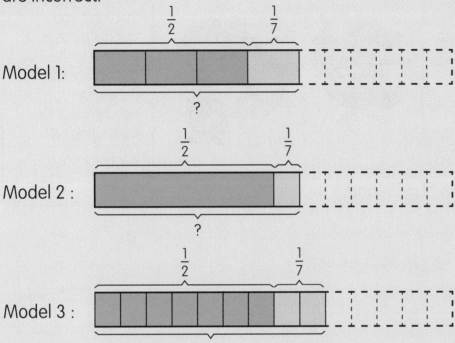

Model 1:

Model 2 :

Model 3 :

Which model is correct? Discuss why the other two are incorrect.

ENGAGE

1. Draw a number line and mark 0, $\frac{1}{2}$, and 1. Mark $\frac{4}{5}$ and $\frac{2}{3}$ on the number line. How do you use a benchmark to estimate the sum of $\frac{4}{5}$ and $\frac{2}{3}$? Explain your thinking to your partner.

2. Name two fractions with an estimated sum of 3.

LEARN Use benchmarks to estimate sums of fractions

1

Benchmarks are numbers that are easier to work with and to picture than others. They help you to compare numbers and estimate answers.

In estimating with fractions, you approximate each fraction to the closest benchmark. Common benchmarks for estimating with fractions are 0, $\frac{1}{2}$, and 1.

Estimate the sum of $\frac{11}{12}$, $\frac{2}{3}$, and $\frac{1}{6}$.

$\frac{11}{12}$ is about 1, $\frac{2}{3}$ is about $\frac{1}{2}$, and $\frac{1}{6}$ is about 0.

$$\frac{11}{12} + \frac{2}{3} + \frac{1}{6}$$
$$\downarrow \quad \downarrow \quad \downarrow$$
$$1 + \frac{1}{2} + 0 = 1\frac{1}{2}$$

The sum of $\frac{11}{12}$, $\frac{2}{3}$, and $\frac{1}{6}$ is about $1\frac{1}{2}$.

Math Talk

Samuel uses benchmarks to estimate the sum of $\frac{1}{9} + \frac{3}{5}$. He explains his process as follows:

Step 1: $\frac{1}{9}$ is about 0.

Step 2: $\frac{3}{5}$ is about $\frac{1}{2}$.

Step 3: $\frac{1}{9} + \frac{3}{5}$ is about $\frac{1}{2}$.

Do you agree with Samuel? Why?

TRY Practice using benchmarks to estimate sums of fractions

Use benchmarks to estimate each sum.

1 $\frac{1}{10} + \frac{2}{5}$

2 $\frac{8}{9} + \frac{9}{10}$

3 $\frac{1}{6} + \frac{7}{12} + \frac{5}{6}$

1 Show $\frac{1}{2}$ and $\frac{1}{3}$ using 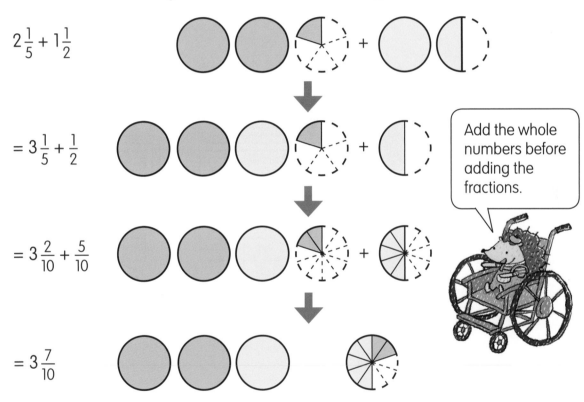. How can you represent $\frac{1}{2}$ and $\frac{1}{3}$ in the same denominator? Now, find the sum of $\frac{1}{2}$ and $\frac{1}{3}$.

2 Share with your partner how you can find the sum of $1\frac{1}{2}$ and $1\frac{1}{5}$.

LEARN Add mixed numbers without renaming

1 Sara bought $2\frac{1}{5}$ pounds of oranges. She also bought $1\frac{1}{2}$ pounds of grapes. What is the total weight of the fruit that she bought?

$2\frac{1}{5} + 1\frac{1}{2}$

$= 3\frac{1}{5} + \frac{1}{2}$

Add the whole numbers before adding the fractions.

$= 3\frac{2}{10} + \frac{5}{10}$

$= 3\frac{7}{10}$

The total weight of the fruit she bought is $3\frac{7}{10}$ pounds.

TRY Practice adding mixed numbers without renaming

Add.

1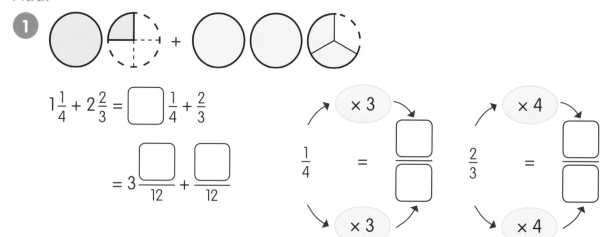

$$1\frac{1}{4} + 2\frac{2}{3} = \boxed{} \frac{1}{4} + \frac{2}{3}$$

$$= 3\frac{\boxed{}}{12} + \frac{\boxed{}}{12}$$

$$\frac{1}{4} \overset{\times 3}{\underset{\times 3}{=}} \frac{\boxed{}}{\boxed{}}$$

$$\frac{2}{3} \overset{\times 4}{\underset{\times 4}{=}} \frac{\boxed{}}{\boxed{}}$$

$$= \underline{\hspace{3cm}}$$

2 $5\frac{1}{6} + 3\frac{1}{12}$

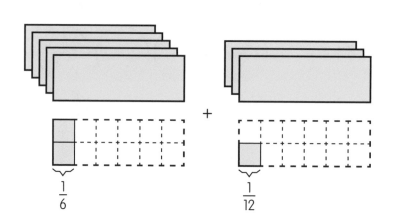

3 $2\frac{1}{7} + 4\frac{1}{5}$

ENGAGE

Show $\frac{3}{4}$ using 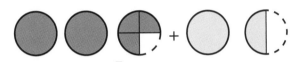. Then, use to show $\frac{1}{2}$ in fourths. Now, show how you add $1\frac{3}{4}$ and $1\frac{1}{2}$. Draw a sketch to explain your thinking. Create a story to represent the problem. Share it with your partner.

LEARN Add mixed numbers with renaming wholes

1. Timothy jogged $2\frac{3}{4}$ miles and walked $1\frac{1}{2}$ miles. How many miles did he jog and walk altogether?

$2\frac{3}{4} + 1\frac{1}{2}$

$= 3\frac{3}{4} + \frac{1}{2}$

$= 3\frac{3}{4} + \frac{2}{4}$

$= 3\frac{5}{4}$

$= 4\frac{1}{4}$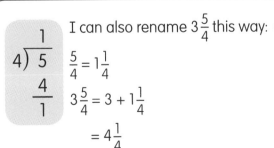

I can also rename $3\frac{5}{4}$ this way:

$$4 \overline{)5} \quad \frac{5}{4} = 1\frac{1}{4}$$
$$\underline{4} \qquad 3\frac{5}{4} = 3 + 1\frac{1}{4}$$
$$1 \qquad\qquad = 4\frac{1}{4}$$

He jogged and walked $4\frac{1}{4}$ miles altogether.

TRY Practice adding mixed numbers with renaming wholes

Find the sum of each pair of mixed numbers.

1 $2\frac{2}{3} + 3\frac{1}{2}$

$= \boxed{}\ \frac{2}{3} + \frac{1}{2}$

$= 5\ \frac{\boxed{}}{6} + \frac{\boxed{}}{6}$

$= 5\ \dfrac{\boxed{}}{\boxed{}}$

$= \rule{3cm}{0.4pt}$

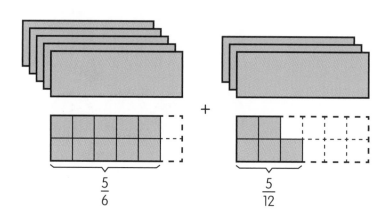

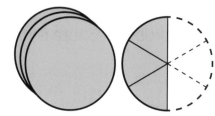

2 $5\frac{5}{6} + 3\frac{5}{12}$

$\dfrac{5}{6}$ $+$ $\dfrac{5}{12}$

3 $4\frac{2}{5} + 2\frac{3}{4}$

1. Draw a number line with benchmark fractions to model the problem.

   At a farm, Mr. Harris has about $2\frac{1}{4}$ crates of blueberries. Mr. Ortiz has about $2\frac{2}{3}$ crates of blueberries. About how many crates of blueberries do they have in all? Explain your thinking to your partner.

2. Mr. Harris and Mr. Ortiz shared the $6\frac{1}{2}$-acre piece of farm. What is the possible size of the land in acres that each person has?

LEARN Use benchmarks to estimate sums of mixed numbers

1. Estimate the sum $2\frac{1}{3}$ and $3\frac{2}{5}$.
   Compare the fractional part in each mixed number to the benchmarks $0, \frac{1}{2},$ and 1.

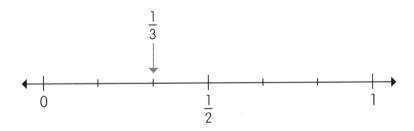

$\frac{1}{3}$ is about $\frac{1}{2}$.
So, $2\frac{1}{3}$ is about $2\frac{1}{2}$.

$\frac{2}{5}$ is about $\frac{1}{2}$.
So, $3\frac{2}{5}$ is about $3\frac{1}{2}$.

$$2\frac{1}{3} \quad + \quad 3\frac{2}{5}$$
$$\downarrow \qquad\qquad \downarrow$$
$$2\frac{1}{2} \quad + \quad 3\frac{1}{2} \quad = \quad 6$$

The sum of $2\frac{1}{3}$ and $3\frac{2}{5}$ is about 6.

TRY Practice using benchmarks to estimate sums of mixed numbers

Use benchmarks to estimate each sum.

1 $11\frac{5}{6} + 5\frac{5}{9}$

2 $8\frac{3}{7} + 10\frac{1}{9}$

3 $32\frac{1}{5} + 14\frac{9}{10}$

4 $16\frac{9}{11} + 37\frac{2}{5}$

INDEPENDENT PRACTICE

Find the part of the bar model that shows the fractions $\frac{1}{2}$, $\frac{2}{5}$, and $\frac{9}{10}$.
Then, use the fractions to write two addition equations.

1

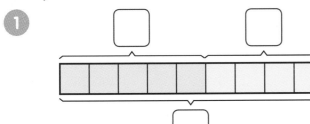

Draw a bar model to find each sum.

2 $\frac{1}{3}$ and $\frac{1}{4}$

3 $\frac{3}{5}$ and $\frac{1}{3}$

Add. Express each sum in simplest form.

4 $\frac{2}{3} + \frac{1}{12}$

5 $\frac{1}{5} + \frac{3}{10}$

6 $\dfrac{1}{4} + \dfrac{1}{6}$

7 $\dfrac{2}{3} + \dfrac{1}{8}$

8 $\dfrac{5}{9} + \dfrac{1}{2}$

9 $\dfrac{2}{5} + \dfrac{5}{6}$

10 $\dfrac{3}{4} + \dfrac{5}{12}$

11 $\dfrac{2}{3} + \dfrac{5}{6}$

Use benchmarks to estimate each sum.

12 $\dfrac{2}{5} + \dfrac{6}{7}$

13 $\dfrac{4}{9} + \dfrac{4}{10}$

14 $\dfrac{1}{8} + \dfrac{3}{5} + \dfrac{9}{10}$

Add. Express each sum in simplest form.

15 $1\dfrac{1}{4} + 2\dfrac{2}{5}$

16 $3\dfrac{3}{8} + 4\dfrac{1}{3}$

17 $1\frac{3}{5} + 2\frac{3}{8}$

18 $3\frac{3}{4} + 5\frac{2}{7}$

19 $5\frac{1}{6} + 2\frac{8}{9}$

Use benchmarks to estimate each sum.

20 $1\frac{3}{5} + 3\frac{4}{7}$

21 $5\frac{1}{8} + 7\frac{1}{12}$

22 $43\frac{5}{6} + 69\frac{5}{12}$

3 Subtracting Unlike Fractions and Mixed Numbers

Learning Objectives:
- Subtract two unlike fractions where one denominator may or may not be a multiple of the other.
- Subtract mixed numbers with or without renaming.
- Estimate differences of fractions and mixed numbers.

THINK

a Laila wrote the following $1\frac{4}{9} - \frac{5}{6} = 3$. Explain why Laila's answer is unreasonable.

b What is the missing number in the equation? _____ $- \frac{2}{3} = \frac{5}{6}$

ENGAGE

1 Charlotte is asked to subtract $\frac{1}{6}$ from $\frac{2}{3}$. Write down the first two steps she follows.

2 Find the missing fraction in the equation. _____ $- \frac{1}{2} = \frac{3}{8}$

LEARN Use a common denominator to subtract unlike fractions

1 A carton contains $\frac{3}{4}$ quart of milk. James pours $\frac{1}{3}$ quart of milk into a mug. How much milk is left in the carton?

List the multiples of the denominators, 3 and 4.

Multiples of 3: 3, 6, 9, ⑫, ...

Multiples of 4: 4, 8, ⑫, 16, ...

The first common multiple of 3 and 4 is 12.

So, 12 is a common denominator of $\frac{1}{3}$ and $\frac{3}{4}$.

$\frac{1}{3}$ and $\frac{3}{4}$ are unlike fractions.

To subtract, rewrite $\frac{1}{3}$ and $\frac{3}{4}$ as like fractions.

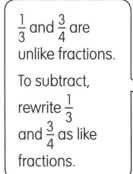

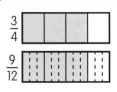

$\frac{3}{4}$ and $\frac{9}{12}$ are equivalent fractions.

$\frac{1}{3}$ and $\frac{4}{12}$ are equivalent fractions.

Rewrite $\frac{1}{3}$ and $\frac{3}{4}$ as like fractions.

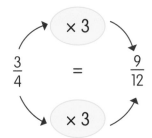

$$\frac{3}{4} \xrightarrow{\times 3} \frac{9}{12} \quad \frac{1}{3} \xrightarrow{\times 4} \frac{4}{12}$$

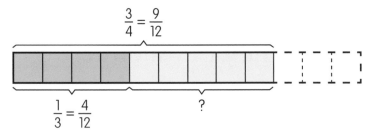

$$\frac{3}{4} - \frac{1}{3} = \frac{9}{12} - \frac{4}{12}$$
$$= \frac{5}{12}$$

$\frac{5}{12}$ quart of milk is left in the carton.

Hands-on Activity Using a common denominator to subtract unlike fractions

Work in pairs.

Draw a bar model to show each pair of fractions. Then, find the difference.

  a $\frac{1}{2} - \frac{2}{7}$

b $\frac{5}{6} - \frac{4}{9}$

c $\frac{3}{4} - \frac{3}{5}$

TRY Practice using a common denominator to subtract unlike fractions

Subtract. Express each difference in simplest form.

1 $\dfrac{5}{6} - \dfrac{1}{2} = \dfrac{\square}{\square} - \dfrac{\square}{\square}$

$= \dfrac{\square}{\square}$

$= \underline{\hspace{2cm}}$

$\dfrac{1}{2} \quad \overset{\times 3}{=} \quad \dfrac{\square}{\square} \quad \times 3$

2 $\dfrac{4}{5} - \dfrac{2}{3} = \dfrac{\square}{\square} - \dfrac{\square}{\square}$

$= \underline{\hspace{2cm}}$

$\dfrac{4}{5} \quad \overset{\times 3}{=} \quad \dfrac{\square}{\square} \quad \times 3$

$\dfrac{2}{3} \quad \overset{\times 5}{=} \quad \dfrac{\square}{\square} \quad \times 5$

3 $\dfrac{3}{4} - \dfrac{1}{5} = \dfrac{\square}{\square} - \dfrac{\square}{\square}$

$= \underline{\hspace{2cm}}$

$\dfrac{3}{4} \quad \overset{\times 5}{=} \quad \dfrac{\square}{\square} \quad \times 5$

$\dfrac{1}{5} \quad \overset{\times 4}{=} \quad \dfrac{\square}{\square} \quad \times 4$

ENGAGE

1 Draw a number line to estimate the difference between $\frac{11}{12}$ and $\frac{1}{4}$. Share your number line with your partner and explain your thinking.

2 What are two possible sets of fractions that will have an estimated difference of $1\frac{1}{12}$?

LEARN Use benchmarks to estimate differences between fractions

1 Estimate the difference between $\frac{8}{9}$ and $\frac{4}{10}$.

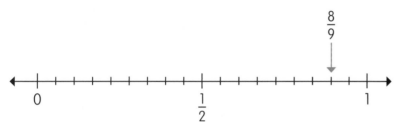

$\frac{8}{9}$ is about 1.

$\frac{4}{10}$ is about $\frac{1}{2}$.

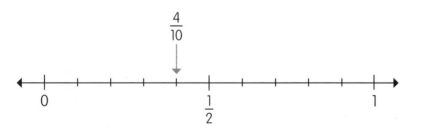

$$\frac{8}{9} \quad - \quad \frac{4}{10}$$
$$1 \quad - \quad \frac{1}{2} \quad = \quad \frac{1}{2}$$

The difference between $\frac{8}{9}$ and $\frac{4}{10}$ is about $\frac{1}{2}$.

TRY Practice using benchmarks to estimate differences between fractions

Use benchmarks to estimate each difference.

1 $\dfrac{5}{6} - \dfrac{2}{5}$

2 $\dfrac{9}{10} - \dfrac{1}{8}$

3 $\dfrac{7}{12} - \dfrac{4}{9}$

ENGAGE

1 Use to show $\dfrac{7}{8}$. Take away $\dfrac{1}{2}$ from $\dfrac{7}{8}$. What is the first step you follow to subtract? What equation can you write?

2 Find the missing fraction in the equation. _____ $- 1\dfrac{1}{2} = 1\dfrac{3}{4}$

LEARN Subtract mixed numbers without renaming

1 Demi had $2\dfrac{3}{4}$ pies. She gave away $1\dfrac{1}{8}$ pies. How many pies did she have left?

$2\dfrac{3}{4} - 1\dfrac{1}{8}$

$= 1\dfrac{3}{4} - \dfrac{1}{8}$

> Subtract the whole numbers before subtracting the fractions.

$= 1\dfrac{6}{8} - \dfrac{1}{8}$

$= 1\dfrac{5}{8}$

She had $1\dfrac{5}{8}$ pies left.

TRY Practice subtracting mixed numbers without renaming

Subtract.

1)

$$5\frac{5}{9} - 2\frac{1}{3} = \boxed{}\,\frac{5}{9} - \frac{1}{3}$$

$$= 3\frac{\boxed{}}{9} - \frac{\boxed{}}{9}$$

$$= \underline{\hspace{2cm}}$$

2) $3\frac{4}{5} - 2\frac{1}{2} = \boxed{}\,\dfrac{\boxed{}}{\boxed{}} - \boxed{}\,\dfrac{\boxed{}}{\boxed{}}$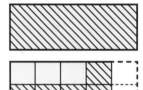

$\dfrac{4}{5}$

$$= \underline{\hspace{2cm}}$$

3) $4\frac{5}{6} - 3\frac{2}{5}$

Show $2\frac{2}{3}$ using 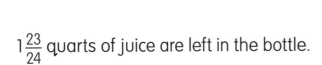. Write the first two steps you would follow to subtract $1\frac{5}{6}$ from $2\frac{2}{3}$.

LEARN Subtract mixed numbers with renaming

1. A bottle contains $3\frac{1}{3}$ quarts of juice. Julia uses $1\frac{3}{8}$ quarts of juice to make fruit punch. How much juice is left in the bottle?

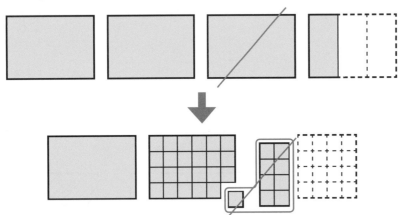

$$3\frac{1}{3} - 1\frac{3}{8} = 2\frac{1}{3} - \frac{3}{8}$$
$$= 2\frac{8}{24} - \frac{9}{24}$$
$$= 1\frac{32}{24} - \frac{9}{24}$$
$$= 1\frac{23}{24}$$

We cannot take away $\frac{9}{24}$ from $\frac{8}{24}$.

So, we rename $2\frac{8}{24}$.

$$2\frac{8}{24} = 1 + \frac{24}{24} + \frac{8}{24}$$
$$= 1\frac{32}{24}$$

$1\frac{23}{24}$ quarts of juice are left in the bottle.

TRY Practice subtracting mixed numbers with renaming

Find the difference between each pair of mixed numbers.

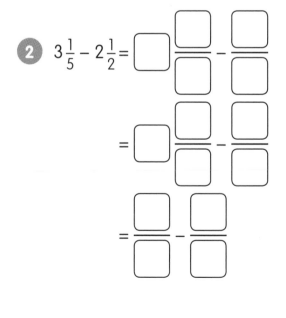

1 $4\frac{5}{9} - 3\frac{5}{6} = \boxed{}\dfrac{\boxed{}}{\boxed{}} - \dfrac{\boxed{}}{\boxed{}}$

$= \boxed{}\dfrac{\boxed{}}{\boxed{}} - \dfrac{\boxed{}}{\boxed{}}$

$= \dfrac{\boxed{}}{\boxed{}} - \dfrac{\boxed{}}{\boxed{}}$

$= \underline{}$

$\frac{5}{9} \overset{\times 2}{\underset{\times 2}{=}} \dfrac{\boxed{}}{18}$

$\frac{5}{6} \overset{\times 3}{\underset{\times 3}{=}} \dfrac{\boxed{}}{\boxed{}}$

2 $3\frac{1}{5} - 2\frac{1}{2} = \boxed{}\dfrac{\boxed{}}{\boxed{}} - \dfrac{\boxed{}}{\boxed{}}$

$= \boxed{}\dfrac{\boxed{}}{\boxed{}} - \dfrac{\boxed{}}{\boxed{}}$

$= \dfrac{\boxed{}}{\boxed{}} - \dfrac{\boxed{}}{\boxed{}}$

$= \underline{}$

3 $4\frac{1}{3} - 2\frac{5}{8} = \boxed{}\dfrac{\boxed{}}{\boxed{}} - \dfrac{\boxed{}}{\boxed{}}$

$= \boxed{}\dfrac{\boxed{}}{\boxed{}} - \dfrac{\boxed{}}{\boxed{}}$

$= \boxed{}\dfrac{\boxed{}}{\boxed{}} - \dfrac{\boxed{}}{\boxed{}}$

$= \underline{}$

ENGAGE

1 Draw a number line to estimate the difference between $3\frac{1}{5}$ and $2\frac{2}{3}$. Share your number line with your partner and explain your thinking.

2 Find the possible values of each missing fraction. _____ − _____ = $2\frac{1}{2}$

LEARN Use benchmarks to estimate differences between mixed numbers

1 Estimate the difference between $4\frac{7}{8}$ and $3\frac{5}{12}$.

Compare the fractional part in each mixed number to the benchmarks, 0, $\frac{1}{2}$, and 1.

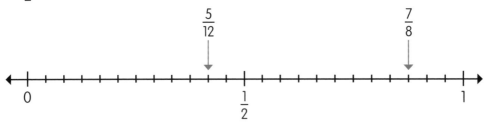

$\frac{7}{8}$ is about 1. So, $4\frac{7}{8}$ is about 5.

$\frac{5}{12}$ is about $\frac{1}{2}$. So, $3\frac{5}{12}$ is about $3\frac{1}{2}$.

$$4\frac{7}{8} \qquad - \qquad 3\frac{5}{12}$$
$$\downarrow \qquad\qquad\qquad \downarrow$$
$$5 \qquad - \qquad 3\frac{1}{2} \qquad = \qquad 1\frac{1}{2}$$

The difference between $4\frac{7}{8}$ and $3\frac{5}{12}$ is about $1\frac{1}{2}$.

TRY Practice using benchmarks to estimate differences between mixed numbers

Use benchmarks to estimate each sum.

1 $7\frac{7}{9} - 3\frac{4}{7}$

2 $23\frac{2}{5} - 17\frac{1}{6}$

INDEPENDENT PRACTICE

Find the part of the bar model that shows the fractions $\frac{1}{2}$, $\frac{3}{10}$, and $\frac{4}{5}$.
Then, use the fractions to write two subtraction equations.

1

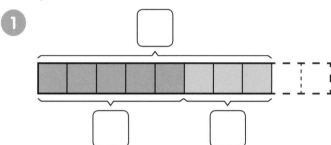

Draw a bar model to find each difference.

2 $\frac{5}{8} - \frac{1}{2}$

3 $\frac{4}{5} - \frac{1}{4}$

Subtract. Express each difference in simplest form.

4 $\frac{8}{9} - \frac{5}{6}$

5 $\frac{11}{12} - \frac{7}{8}$

6 $\frac{4}{5} - \frac{2}{7}$

7 $\frac{7}{9} - \frac{3}{4}$

8 $\frac{4}{7} - \frac{1}{6}$

9 $\frac{2}{3} - \frac{3}{8}$

10 $2 - \frac{1}{3} - \frac{9}{10}$

11 $4 - \frac{5}{6} - \frac{3}{8}$

Use benchmarks to estimate each difference.

12 $\frac{4}{5} - \frac{3}{7}$

13 $\frac{5}{8} - \frac{1}{9}$

14 $\frac{11}{12} - \frac{5}{6}$

Subtract. Express each difference in simplest form.

15 $3\frac{3}{4} - 1\frac{1}{3}$

16 $4\frac{5}{6} - 3\frac{5}{8}$

17 $7\frac{2}{3} - 4\frac{1}{2}$

18 $9\frac{4}{7} - 2\frac{1}{3}$

19 $6\frac{1}{10} - 3\frac{4}{5}$

20 $4\frac{1}{2} - 1\frac{7}{8}$

21 $5\frac{1}{4} - 2\frac{1}{3}$

22 $12\frac{7}{12} - 5\frac{8}{9}$

Use benchmarks to estimate each difference.

23 $6\frac{7}{10} - 4\frac{3}{5}$

24 $39\frac{4}{5} - 13\frac{5}{9}$

4 Real-World Problems: Fractions and Mixed Numbers

Learning Objective:
• Solve real-world problems involving fractions and mixed numbers.

THINK

Bruno had a longer piece of string than Ella. The total length of their pieces of string was 2 meters. After Bruno cut off some of his string, it had the same length as Ella's piece of string. How do you find the length of Bruno's piece of string at first? What are the possible answers?

ENGAGE

Sebastian's school is 4 miles from home. He walked $\frac{5}{8}$ mile to the bus stop. He then rode the rest of the way on the bus. How far did he ride on the bus? Draw a sketch of Sebastian's trip to show your thinking.

LEARN Solve one-step real-world problems

1. Ian used $1\frac{3}{8}$ kilograms of flour to make muffins. He used $1\frac{1}{4}$ kilograms less flour than Lily. How much flour did Lily use?

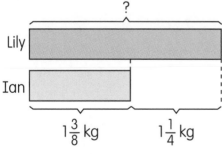

$$1\frac{3}{8} + 1\frac{1}{4} = 2\frac{5}{8}$$

Lily used $2\frac{5}{8}$ kilograms of flour.

2 Alex expected to complete his homework in $\frac{4}{5}$ hour. He completed it in $\frac{3}{4}$ hour. How much faster did Alex complete his homework than he expected?

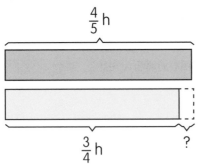

$$\frac{4}{5} - \frac{3}{4} = \frac{16}{20} - \frac{15}{20}$$
$$= \frac{1}{20}$$

Alex completed his homework $\frac{1}{20}$ hour faster.

Math Talk

Amy and Bailey drew bar models to solve the following problem.

Chris drank $1\frac{2}{3}$ quarts of water. Jack drank $\frac{2}{5}$ quart less water than Chris. How many quarts of water did Jack drink?

Amy's bar model:

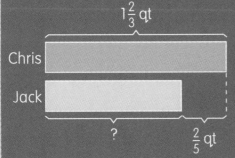

Bailey's bar model:

Whose bar model is correct? Explain.

TRY Practice solving one-step real-world problems

Solve. Use the bar model to help you.

1. Trinity has $1\frac{2}{9}$ pounds of peaches. She buys another $2\frac{1}{6}$ pounds of peaches. How many pounds of peaches does Trinity have now?

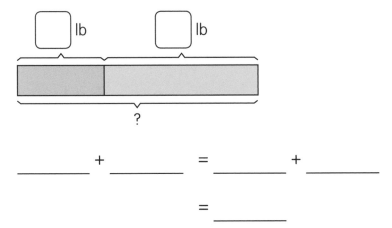

_____ + _____ = _____ + _____

= _____

Trinity has _____ pounds of peaches now.

2. Ms. Young had 3 kilograms of flour. She used $\frac{3}{4}$ kilogram of the flour to bake a loaf of bread. How much flour did she have left?

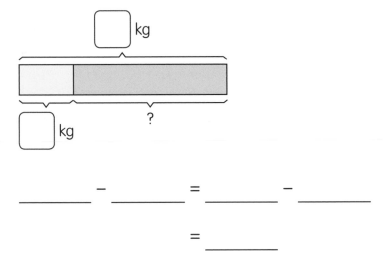

_____ – _____ = _____ – _____

= _____

She had _____ kilograms of flour left.

ENGAGE

On Monday, Mr. Turner used $\frac{7}{10}$ kilogram of flour. On Tuesday, he used $\frac{1}{5}$ kilogram less flour than on Monday. Draw a bar model to find the amount of flour Mr. Turner used over the two days. Share your bar model with your partner.

LEARN Solve two-step real-world problems

1 Ms. Clark baked 2 pies. She sold $\frac{4}{9}$ of a pie in the morning and $\frac{1}{3}$ of a pie in the afternoon.

a How much of a pie did Ms. Clark sell?
b How much of a pie did Ms. Clark have left?

STEP 1 Understand the problem.

STEP 2 Think of a plan.
I can draw a bar model.

How many pies did Ms. Clark bake?
How much of a pie did she sell in the morning?
How much of a pie did she sell in the afternoon?
What do I need to find?

STEP 3 Carry out the plan.

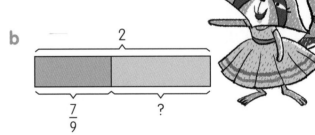

a

$$\frac{1}{3} = \frac{3}{9} \qquad \frac{4}{9}$$

$$\frac{4}{9} + \frac{1}{3} = \frac{4}{9} + \frac{3}{9}$$
$$= \frac{7}{9}$$

Ms. Clark sold $\frac{7}{9}$ of a pie.

b

$$\frac{7}{9} \qquad ?$$

$$2 - \frac{7}{9} = 1\frac{2}{9}$$

Ms. Clark had $1\frac{2}{9}$ pies left.

STEP 4 Check the answer
I can work backwards to check my answers.

a $\frac{7}{9} - \frac{4}{9} = \frac{3}{9} = \frac{1}{3}$

b $1\frac{2}{9} + \frac{7}{9} = 2$

My answers are correct.

2 A bottle contained $\frac{3}{4}$ liter of water. A pail contained $\frac{1}{8}$ liter more water than the bottle. What was the total amount of water in both containers?

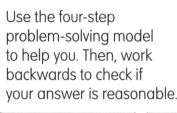

Use the four-step problem-solving model to help you. Then, work backwards to check if your answer is reasonable.

$$\frac{3}{4} + \frac{1}{8} = \frac{6}{8} + \frac{1}{8}$$
$$= \frac{7}{8}$$

The pail contained $\frac{7}{8}$ liter of water.

$$\frac{7}{8} + \frac{3}{4} = \frac{7}{8} + \frac{6}{8}$$
$$= \frac{13}{8}$$
$$= 1\frac{5}{8}$$

The total amount of water in both containers was $1\frac{5}{8}$ liters.

3 The total mass of a box and a parcel was $\frac{9}{10}$ kilogram. The mass of the parcel was $\frac{1}{4}$ kilogram. How much lighter was the parcel than the box?

$$\frac{9}{10} - \frac{1}{4} = \frac{18}{20} - \frac{5}{20}$$
$$= \frac{13}{20}$$

The mass of the box was $\frac{13}{20}$ kilogram.

$$\frac{13}{20} - \frac{1}{4} = \frac{13}{20} - \frac{5}{20}$$
$$= \frac{8}{20}$$
$$= \frac{2}{5}$$

The parcel was $\frac{2}{5}$ kilogram lighter than the box.

Hands-on Activity Solving real-world problems

Work in groups.

① Use the following fractions and words to complete the word problems.

| $\frac{1}{3}$ | $\frac{1}{4}$ | $\frac{1}{6}$ | $\frac{1}{12}$ | more | fewer |

a Grace bought 3 tarts. She ate _____ of a tart.
How many tarts did she have left?

b Hayden cycled $\frac{5}{9}$ kilometer. Kayla cycled _____ kilometers

_____ than Hayden.

Jason cycled _____ kilometers _____ than Kayla.
How far did Jason cycle?

② Use the following words and fractions to write a word problem.

| $\frac{3}{10}$ | pie | $\frac{2}{5}$ | $\frac{1}{10}$ | Molly | Avery | ate | Ethan |

③ **Mathematical Habit 1** Persevere in solving problems
Ask your classmates to solve the word problems in ① and ②, and explain their work. Explain the method.

TRY Practice solving two-step real-world problems

Solve. Use the bar model to help you.

1 Alan cut a pole into three shorter poles. The first pole was $1\frac{1}{5}$ meters long

and the second pole was $1\frac{1}{10}$ meters long. The third pole was as long as

the first pole and the second pole put together.

  a How long was the third pole?

  b How long was the original pole?

a $1\frac{1}{5}$ m $1\frac{1}{10}$ m

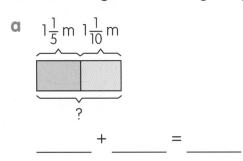

?

_____ + _____ = _____

The third pole was _____
meters long.

b $1\frac{1}{5}$ m $1\frac{1}{10}$ m $2\frac{3}{10}$ m

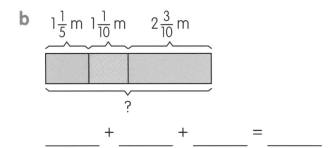

?

_____ + _____ + _____ = _____

The original pole was _____
meters long.

2 Mr. Hall spent $\frac{1}{6}$ of his money on food and $\frac{5}{8}$ of his money on a new suit.
What fraction of Mr. Hall's money did he have left?

$\frac{1}{6} = \boxed{}$ $\frac{5}{8} = \boxed{}$

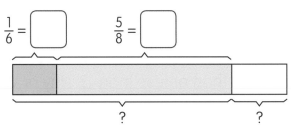

?   ?

First, find the amount
of money Mr. Hall
spent on food and
the new suit.

_____ + _____ = _____

_____ − _____ = _____

Mr. Hall spent _____ of his
money on food and the new suit.

_____ of Mr. Hall's money
was left.

3 Irene took $2\frac{3}{4}$ hours to read a book. Her brother Jackson took $\frac{2}{3}$ hour less to read his book. How much time did they spend reading in all?

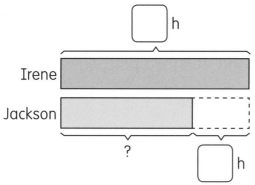

First, find the time Jackson took to read his book.

$2\frac{3}{4} - \frac{2}{3} = $ _____

Jackson read his book in _____ hours.

$2\frac{3}{4} + $ _____ = _____

Irene and Jackson spent _____ hours reading in all.

© 2020 Marshall Cavendish Education Pte Ltd

LET'S EXPLORE

Without solving, do you think the sum of $\frac{1}{3}$ and $\frac{3}{8}$ is less than 1? Explain your reasoning.

Do you think the sum of $\frac{5}{9}$ and $\frac{6}{11}$ is greater than 1? Why?

Can you tell if the sum of $\frac{5}{11}$ and $\frac{4}{7}$ is greater than or less than 1? Why or why not?

Without solving, do you think the difference between 1 and $\frac{3}{7}$ is greater than $\frac{1}{2}$? Explain your reasoning.

Do you think the difference between 1 and $\frac{7}{12}$ is less than $\frac{1}{2}$? Why?

Can you tell if the difference between $\frac{11}{12}$ and $\frac{1}{4}$ is greater than or less than $\frac{1}{2}$? Why or why not?

INDEPENDENT PRACTICE

Solve. Show your work.

1. Mr. Garcia spent $\frac{1}{4}$ of a day at his office on Monday and $\frac{7}{10}$ of a day at the office on Tuesday. What fraction of a day did he spend at the office in the two days?

Solve. Draw a bar model to help you.

2. The total mass of a book and a water bottle was $\frac{4}{5}$ kilogram. The mass of the water bottle was $\frac{1}{2}$ kilogram. What was the mass of the book?

3 Mr. Martin has $2\frac{1}{2}$ pints of apple juice. He used $\frac{7}{8}$ pint of the juice to make a fruit punch and drank another $\frac{5}{6}$ pint of the juice. How many pints of apple juice did he have left?

4 A grocer sold $5\frac{2}{3}$ pounds of blueberries in the morning. In the afternoon, the grocer sold $\frac{11}{12}$ fewer pound of blueberries than he sold in the morning. How many pounds of blueberries did he sell in all?

Mathematical Habit 3 Construct viable arguments

Jocelyn, Megan, and Diego each added these fractions.

$$\frac{5}{6} + \frac{7}{9} = ?$$

Jocelyn's answer: $\frac{12}{15}$ Megan's answer: $2\frac{9}{18}$ Diego's answer: $1\frac{11}{18}$

Two of the three answers are incorrect.
Whose answers are incorrect? Explain.

Problem Solving with Heuristics

1 **Mathematical Habit 2** Use mathematical reasoning

Complete the equation with + or −.

$$5\frac{2}{5} \bigcirc 3\frac{1}{10} \bigcirc 2\frac{1}{2} = 6$$

2 **Mathematical Habit 2** Use mathematical reasoning

Use the digits 1, 2, 3, 4, 5, and 6 only once to fill in the boxes so that they make the equation correct.

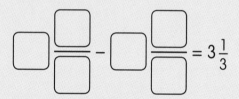

3 **Mathematical Habit 8** Make use of structure

Use each of the following numbers and fractions only once to complete the

table so that the sum of each horizontal, vertical, and diagonal line is $7\frac{1}{2}$.

$$\frac{1}{2}, 1, 2, 3, 4, 1\frac{1}{2}, 3\frac{1}{2}, 4\frac{1}{2}$$

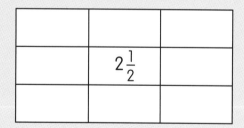

4 **Mathematical Habit 1** Persevere in solving problems

Luis has two equal-sized bottles. The first bottle contains 1 quart of water. The second bottle contains $\frac{5}{9}$ quart of water. What amount of water must Luis pour from the first bottle into the second bottle so that both bottles contain the same amount of water? Express your answer as a fraction. Use a bar model to explain your answers.

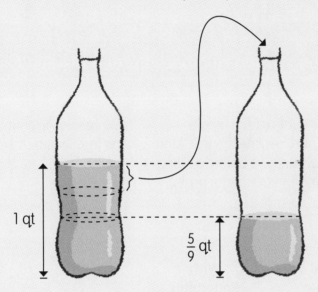

1 qt

$\frac{5}{9}$ qt

How are fractions and division related? How is adding and subtracting unlike fractions, and mixed numbers similar to adding and subtracting like fractions?

Fractions and Mixed Numbers

Adding and Subtracting Unlike Fractions

Find the first common multiple of their denominators. Use it to rewrite the fractions as like fractions. Then, add or subtract.

$\frac{1}{4} + \frac{1}{6} = ?$

Multiples of 4: 4, 8, 12, ...
Multiples of 6: 6, 12, ...
12 is the first common multiple of 4 and 6.

$\frac{1}{4} + \frac{1}{6} = \frac{3}{12} + \frac{2}{12}$

$= \frac{5}{12}$

Adding and Subtracting Mixed Numbers

First, add or subtract the whole numbers. Then, rewrite the fractional parts as like fractions before adding or subtracting the fractional parts.

Without Renaming

$3\frac{1}{2} + 1\frac{1}{3}$

$= 4\frac{1}{2} + \frac{1}{3}$

$= 4\frac{3}{6} + \frac{2}{6}$

$= 4\frac{5}{6}$

With Renaming

$3\frac{1}{3} - 1\frac{1}{2}$

$= 2\frac{1}{3} - \frac{1}{2}$

$= 1\frac{4}{3} - \frac{1}{2}$

$= 1\frac{8}{6} - \frac{3}{6}$

$= 1\frac{5}{6}$

Fractions, Mixed Numbers, and Division Expressions

Express division expressions as fractions or mixed numbers.

$10 \div 6 = \frac{10 \div 2}{6 \div 2}$

$= \frac{5}{3}$

$= 1\frac{2}{3}$

Express fractions as division expressions.

$\frac{4}{5} = 4 \div 5$

Use Benchmarks to Estimate Sums and Differences

$\frac{4}{9} - \frac{5}{12}$

$\downarrow \quad \downarrow$

$\frac{1}{2} - \frac{1}{2} = 0$

$2\frac{7}{8} + 2\frac{3}{5}$

$\downarrow \quad \downarrow$

$3 + 2\frac{1}{2} = 5\frac{1}{2}$

Name: _____ Date: _____

Express each division expression as a fraction or mixed number in simplest form.

1 $6 \div 8 =$ _____

2 $10 \div 3 =$ _____

Write each fraction as a division expression.

3 $\frac{4}{11} =$ _____ $\div$ _____

4 $\frac{6}{7} =$ _____ $\div$ _____

Add or subtract. Express each sum or difference in simplest form.

5 $\frac{1}{2} + \frac{3}{7}$

6 $\frac{1}{6} + \frac{3}{10}$

7 $\frac{7}{8} - \frac{1}{2}$

8 $\frac{7}{9} - \frac{1}{4}$

Use benchmarks to estimate each sum or difference.

9 $\dfrac{4}{9} - \dfrac{3}{7}$

10 $\dfrac{7}{9} + \dfrac{4}{7} + \dfrac{1}{6}$

Add. Express each answer as a mixed number in simplest form.

11 $7 + 2\dfrac{5}{6}$

12 $3\dfrac{3}{8} + 2\dfrac{1}{4}$

13 $6\dfrac{1}{3} + 4\dfrac{3}{4}$

14 $2\dfrac{1}{6} + 3\dfrac{9}{10}$

Subtract. Express each answer as a mixed number in simplest form.

15 $7\dfrac{1}{3} - 2$

16 $4\dfrac{1}{2} - 1\dfrac{1}{4}$

17 $6\frac{4}{5} - 5\frac{3}{4}$

18 $5\frac{1}{6} - 3\frac{3}{10}$

19 $5 - 2\frac{3}{8}$

20 $12 - 7\frac{5}{10}$

Use benchmarks to estimate each sum or difference.

21 $4\frac{3}{5} + 2\frac{3}{8}$

22 $8\frac{11}{12} - 2\frac{11}{20}$

23 Jacob spent $\frac{1}{5}$ of an hour cleaning the table and $\frac{3}{10}$ of an hour mopping the floor. After he finished the housework, he spent $\frac{2}{3}$ of an hour reading a book. How much more time did he spend reading than doing housework?

24 Ivan bought 7 pounds of apples and gave them to his 4 friends. His friends shared the apples equally among themselves.

a How many pounds of apples did each person receive?

b Two of the friends put their apples together. How many pounds of apples did two of his friends receive in all?

c The two friends used $1\frac{2}{3}$ pounds of the apples they received to make applesauce and the remaining to make apple pies. How many pounds of apples did they use to make apple pies?

Assessment Prep

Answer each question.

25 Which expression shows the possible next step to adding the fractions $\frac{4}{5} + \frac{3}{4}$? Choose all the correct answers.

Ⓐ $\frac{8}{10} + \frac{6}{8}$

Ⓑ $\frac{4}{5} + \frac{6}{8}$

Ⓒ $\frac{16}{20} + \frac{15}{20}$

Ⓓ $\frac{4}{20} + \frac{3}{20}$

Ⓔ $\frac{32}{40} + \frac{30}{40}$

26 Which expression is equal to $\frac{2}{7}$?

Ⓐ $2 + 7$

Ⓑ 2×7

Ⓒ $\frac{7}{2}$

Ⓓ $2 \div 7$

27 Without solving, estimate the sum of $2\frac{1}{5}$ and $3\frac{7}{9}$.
Show your work and explain your answer.

28 Kevin estimated the difference between $\frac{11}{12}$ and $\frac{4}{7}$ as less than $\frac{1}{2}$.

- Estimate the two fractions using benchmarks.
- Explain whether Kevin is correct.

Show your work and explanation in the space below.

Building a Tree House

Maya and her friends build and paint a tree house. On Monday, they painted $\frac{2}{5}$ of the tree house. On Tuesday, they painted $\frac{3}{7}$ of the tree house.

1 The children must finish painting the tree house by Wednesday. How much more do Maya and her friends need to paint? Show your work.

2 Maya and her friends used $1\frac{3}{4}$ quarts of paint on Monday and $1\frac{7}{8}$ quarts of paint on Tuesday. How much paint did Maya and her friends use on Monday and Tuesday in all? Express your answer as a mixed number.

3 How much paint will Maya and her friends need to finish the job on Wednesday? Show your work.

4 If Maya and her friends have $\frac{4}{5}$ quart of paint left, do they have enough paint to finish the job on Wednesday? Justify your answer.

Rubric

Point(s)	Level	My Performance
7–8	4	• Most of my answers are correct. • I showed complete understanding of what I have learned. • I used the correct strategies to solve the problems. • I explained my answers and mathematical thinking clearly and completely.
5–6.5	3	• Some of my answers are correct. • I showed some understanding of what I have learned. • I used some correct strategies to solve the problems. • I explained my answers and mathematical thinking clearly.
3–4.5	2	• A few of my answers are correct. • I showed little understanding of what I have learned. • I used a few correct strategies to solve the problems. • I explained some of my answers and mathematical thinking clearly.
0–2.5	1	• A few of my answers are correct. • I showed little or no understanding of what I have learned. • I used a few strategies to solve the problems. • I did not explain my answers and mathematical thinking clearly.

Teacher's Comments

School Carnivals

Many schools host annual school carnivals, which often include game booths. Planning fun and attractive game booths needs a lot of work. Designers must decide what the booths will look like, the purpose of each game, the instructions players will need, and how prizes will be awarded.

Task

Design a game booth

You and your friends have been asked to design and operate a game booth at a school carnival.

Draw a design for the game booth. List the rules players must follow. Award points in fractions, and require players to earn a score of 10 points before they win prizes.

Chapter 3
Multiplying and Dividing Fractions and Mixed Numbers

Creamy Salmon Pasta (serves 4)

350 g dried spaghetti

$\frac{1}{2}$ cup shelled broad beans

1 cup fresh garden peas

$\frac{4}{5}$ cup double cream

$\frac{4}{5}$ cup Greek yoghurt

2 large free-range egg yolks

$\frac{1}{4}$ cup grated Parmesan cheese

3 salmon fillets

Zest of 1 unwaxed lemon

A small bunch of fresh chives

This recipe serves 4. How can I find the amount of each ingredient for 3 servings?

How do we multiply and divide fractions, mixed numbers, and whole numbers? How do the factors affect the product if one of the factors is a fraction?

Name: _____ Date: _____

Finding equivalent fractions

Find the equivalent fraction of $\frac{3}{4}$.

$\frac{3}{4}$ is the same as $\frac{6}{8}$.

$\frac{3}{4} = \frac{3 \times 2}{4 \times 2}$

$\quad = \frac{6}{8}$

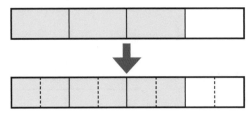

▶ Quick Check

Write an equivalent fraction for each fraction.

1 $\frac{2}{3}$ _____

2 $\frac{1}{4}$ _____

3 $\frac{5}{6}$ _____

4 $\frac{3}{5}$ _____

Simplifying fractions

Express $\frac{6}{8}$ in simplest form.

$\frac{6}{8} = \frac{6 \div 2}{8 \div 2}$ ← Divide the numerator and denominator by their common factor.

$\quad = \frac{3}{4}$

▶ Quick Check

Simplify each fraction.

5 $\frac{5}{10}$ _____

6 $\frac{15}{25}$ _____

7 $\frac{18}{32}$ _____

8 $\frac{4}{16}$ _____

Expressing improper fractions as mixed numbers and mixed numbers as improper fractions in simplest form

a $\frac{10}{3} = \frac{9}{3} + \frac{1}{3}$

$= 3 + \frac{1}{3}$

$= 3\frac{1}{3}$

b $3\frac{1}{2} = 3 + \frac{1}{2}$

$= \frac{6}{2} + \frac{1}{2}$

$= \frac{7}{2}$

▶ Quick Check

Express each improper fraction as a mixed number in simplest form.

9 $\frac{17}{4}$

10 $\frac{22}{6}$

11 $\frac{40}{9}$

Express each mixed number as an improper fraction.

12 $3\frac{3}{7}$

13 $6\frac{5}{9}$

14 $8\frac{2}{5}$

Expressing fractions as decimals

$$\frac{1}{4} = \frac{1 \times 25}{4 \times 25}$$

$$= \frac{25}{100}$$

$$= 0.25$$

▶ **Quick Check**

Express each fraction as a decimal.

15 $\frac{3}{4}$ _____

16 $\frac{3}{5}$ _____

17 $\frac{1}{2}$ _____

Finding the number of units to solve a problem

7 tickets cost $49. How much do 6 tickets cost?

7 units = $49

1 unit = $49 ÷ 7

= $7

6 units = $7 × 6

= $42

6 tickets cost $42.

▶ **Quick Check**

Solve.

18 A store sells 5 notebooks for $15. How much do 3 notebooks cost?

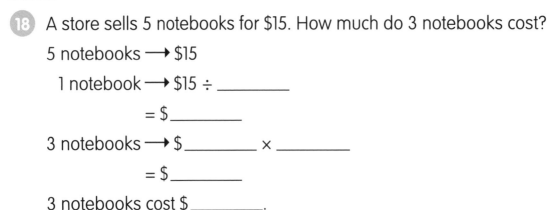

5 notebooks ⟶ $15

1 notebook ⟶ $15 ÷ _____

= $ _____

3 notebooks ⟶ $ _____ × _____

= $ _____

3 notebooks cost $ _____.

Drawing a bar model to represent the problem

Three friends share a foot-long turkey sandwich. Richard eats $\frac{1}{2}$ of the sandwich. Emma eats $\frac{1}{3}$ of the sandwich. Kevin eats the rest.

Find a common multiple: $2 \times 3 = 6$

$$\frac{1}{2} = \frac{3}{6} \qquad \frac{1}{3} = \frac{2}{6} \qquad 1 - \frac{3}{6} - \frac{2}{6} = \frac{1}{6}$$

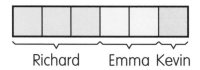

Richard   Emma Kevin

▶ Quick Check

19 Mía has some trading cards. $\frac{1}{2}$ of the cards are baseball cards, $\frac{2}{5}$ are soccer cards, and the rest are basketball cards.

Draw a bar model to represent the problem.

Using order of operations to simplify expressions

Simplify $(32 + 40) - 8 \times 6$.

First expression $\qquad$ **(32 + 40)** $- 8 \times 6$ ⎯⎯⎯ Perform all operations in the parentheses first.

Second expression $\qquad$ **72 $- 8 \times 6$** ⎯⎯⎯ Then, multiply.

Third expression $\qquad$ $72 - \textbf{48}$ ⎯⎯⎯ Finally, subtract.

24

▶ Quick Check

Solve each problem.

20 $(60 + 6 \times 80) \div 20$

21 $27 \div (1 + 2) \times 5 - 9$

22 $(6 - 3) \times (4 + 2) \div 9$

Name: _____ Date: _____

Multiplying Fractions and Whole Numbers

Learning Objectives:
• Multiply proper fractions by whole numbers.
• Multiply improper fractions by whole numbers.

THINK

When we multiply 2 by $\frac{1}{2}$, is the product greater than any of its factors? When you multiply 2 by $\frac{3}{2}$, is the product greater than any of its factors? Explain.

ENGAGE

1. Use  to regroup 9 groups of $\frac{2}{3}$ into wholes and parts. How many wholes and parts are there? What is $9 \times \frac{2}{3}$?

2. Find the missing number. _____ $\times \frac{1}{2} = 4\frac{1}{2}$

LEARN Multiply a fraction by a whole number

1. Destiny bought 16 stamps. She gave $\frac{3}{4}$ of the stamps to her brother. How many stamps did Destiny give to her brother?

Is $\frac{3}{4} \times 16$ the same as $16 \times \frac{3}{4}$?

$$\frac{3}{4} \text{ of } 16 = \frac{3}{4} \times 16$$
$$= \frac{3 \times 16}{4}$$
$$= \frac{48}{4}$$
$$= 12$$

Destiny gave 12 stamps to her brother.

2 Find the product of $\frac{5}{2}$ and 3.

$$\frac{5}{2} \times 3 = \frac{5 \times 3}{2}$$
$$= \frac{15}{2}$$
$$= 7\frac{1}{2}$$

Hands-on Activity Relating fractions of a set to multiplication

Work in pairs.

1 Count 15 ◯ and show $\frac{2}{5}$ of 15. Explain your reasoning.

2 Find the product of $\frac{2}{5}$ and 15. Show your work.

3 **Mathematical Habits 2** Use mathematical reasoning

What do you notice about the answers in ① and ②? Explain.

TRY Practice multiplying a fraction by a whole number

Fill in each blank.

1 $\frac{6}{5}$ of 20 = $\frac{6}{5} \times \boxed{}$

$= \dfrac{\boxed{} \times \boxed{}}{\boxed{}}$

$= \dfrac{\boxed{}}{\boxed{}}$

$= \underline{}$

2 There are 12 apples in a basket. $\frac{5}{6}$ of the apples are red. How many red apples are there in the basket?

$\frac{5}{6}$ of 12 = $\frac{5}{6} \times \boxed{}$

$= \dfrac{5 \times \boxed{}}{6}$

$= \dfrac{\boxed{}}{6}$

$= \underline{}$

There are _____ red apples in the basket.

Multiply. Express each product in simplest form.

3 $\frac{4}{7}$ of 35

4 $\frac{7}{12}$ of 50

5 $\frac{11}{8}$ of 48

6 $\frac{9}{4}$ of 62

MATH SHARING

Mathematical Habit 3 Construct viable arguments

Molly used the following method to find $\frac{4}{7} \times 35$.

$$\frac{4}{7} \times 35 = \frac{4 \times \overset{5}{\cancel{35}}}{\underset{1}{\cancel{7}}}$$
$$= 4 \times 5$$
$$= 20$$

Explain if her work is correct. Use her method to find $\frac{8}{3} \times 24$.

INDEPENDENT PRACTICE

Find each product.

1 $\frac{2}{3}$ of 18

2 $\frac{3}{5}$ of 15

3 $\frac{3}{7}$ of 15

4 $\frac{5}{9}$ of 48

5 $\frac{8}{3}$ of 42

6 $\frac{5}{2}$ of 28

7 $\frac{11}{6}$ of 10

8 $\frac{7}{4}$ of 22

Solve.

9 Ryan had 24 stickers. He gave $\frac{1}{4}$ of the stickers away. How many stickers did he give away?

10 Carla needs $\frac{3}{2}$ cups of flour to bake some cupcakes. How many cups of flour does she need to bake 3 times as many cupcakes?

 Multiplying Proper Fractions

Learning Objective:
• Multiply proper fractions.

 THINK

The product of 2 and 3 is greater than both of its factors. Explain whether the product of $\frac{1}{2}$ and $\frac{1}{3}$ is greater than any of its factors. Why do you think so?

ENGAGE

1 Color $\frac{3}{4}$ of a square yellow. Color $\frac{1}{2}$ of the yellow parts green. Show at least two different ways to do it. What fraction of the square is colored green? Explain.

2 Sydney colored $\frac{3}{4}$ of a square blue. If she colored $\frac{1}{4}$ of the blue colored parts red, what fraction of the square did she color red?

LEARN Use models to multiply fractions

1 Alex has $\frac{1}{2}$ of a granola bar. He eats $\frac{1}{3}$ of that piece of granola bar. What fraction of the whole granola bar does he eat?

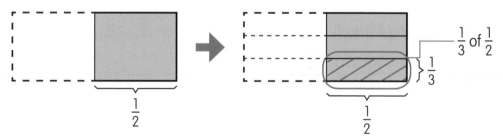

$$\frac{1}{3} \text{ of } \frac{1}{2} = \frac{1}{3} \times \frac{1}{2}$$
$$= \frac{1}{6}$$

He eats $\frac{1}{6}$ of the granola bar.

2 Evelyn has $\frac{1}{3}$ of a pie. She eats $\frac{1}{2}$ of that piece of pie. What fraction of the whole pie does she eat?

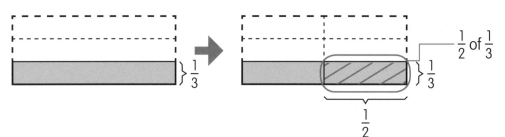

$\frac{1}{2}$ of $\frac{1}{3} = \frac{1}{2} \times \frac{1}{3}$

$\qquad = \frac{1}{6}$

She eats $\frac{1}{6}$ of the whole pie.

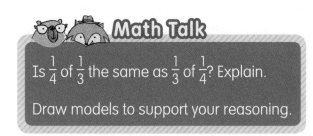

Math Talk

Is $\frac{1}{4}$ of $\frac{1}{3}$ the same as $\frac{1}{3}$ of $\frac{1}{4}$? Explain.

Draw models to support your reasoning.

Hands-on Activity **Modeling the commutative law using fractions**

Work in pairs.

1 Draw a 4 × 4 square on the grid. Then, do the following.

a Use the horizontal grid lines to divide the square into four equal parts. Color $\frac{3}{4}$ of the parts yellow.

b Use the vertical grid lines to divide the square into four equal parts. Draw blue lines on $\frac{1}{4}$ of the yellow parts.

c Use the model to complete:

$\frac{1}{4} \times \frac{3}{4} =$ _____

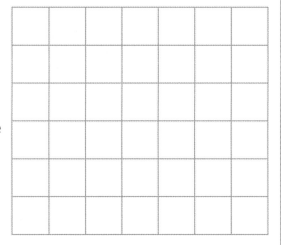

2 Draw a 4 × 4 square on the grid. Then, do the following.

a Use the horizontal grid lines to divide the square into four equal parts. Color $\frac{1}{4}$ of it blue.

b Use the vertical grid lines to divide the square into four equal parts. Draw yellow lines on $\frac{3}{4}$ of the blue parts.

c Use the model to complete: $\frac{3}{4} \times \frac{1}{4} =$ _____

3 Are the answers in ① and ② the same? What can you say about $\frac{3}{4} \times \frac{1}{4}$ and $\frac{1}{4} \times \frac{3}{4}$?

TRY Practice using models to multiply fractions

Draw a model to find each product.

1 $\frac{1}{2} \times \frac{1}{4}$

2 $\frac{1}{2} \times \frac{3}{4}$

3 $\frac{3}{5} \times \frac{1}{2}$

$\frac{1}{2}$ of $\frac{1}{4}$

$\frac{1}{2} \times \frac{1}{4} = \dfrac{\boxed{} \times 1}{\boxed{} \times 4}$

$= \underline{}$

ENGAGE

Find $\frac{1}{2}$ of $\frac{2}{3}$. Explain by coloring $\frac{2}{3}$ of a piece of paper green and $\frac{1}{2}$ of the green part yellow. What fraction is the overlapping part?

LEARN Multiply fractions by simplifying

1 Find $\frac{2}{3} \times \frac{5}{6}$.

▶ **Method 1**

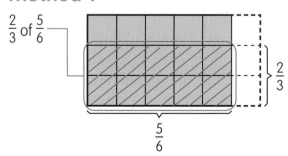

$\frac{2}{3}$ of $\frac{5}{6}$

$\frac{2}{3}$

$\frac{5}{6}$

$\frac{2}{3} \times \frac{5}{6} = \frac{2 \times 5}{3 \times 6}$ ——— Multiply the numerators.
Multiply the denominators.

$= \frac{10}{18}$ ——— Simplify the fraction.

$= \frac{5}{9}$

▶ **Method 2**

$\frac{2}{3} \times \frac{5}{6} = \frac{\overset{1}{2}}{3} \times \frac{5}{\underset{3}{6}}$ ——— 2 is a common factor of 2 and 6.
Divide 2 and 6 by their common factor, 2, to simplify the fractions before multiplying.

$= \frac{1 \times 5}{3 \times 3}$

$= \frac{5}{9}$ ——— Multiply the numerators.
Multiply the denominators.

| When divided by itself, any number other than zero will have a quotient of 1. So, $3 \div 3 = 1$ $4 \div 4 = 1$ | When multiplied by 1, any number will have a product equal to itself. So, $1 \times 2 = 2$ $1 \times 3 = 3$ |

Work in pairs.

1. Draw a model to solve $\frac{3}{4} \times \frac{2}{3}$.

2. Solve $\frac{3}{4} \times \frac{2}{3}$ by simplifying the fractions.

3. Compare the methods in ① and ②. Which method do you prefer? Explain.

TRY Practice multiplying fractions by simplifying

Multiply. Express each product in simplest form.

1 $\dfrac{3}{8} \times \dfrac{8}{9}$

2 $\dfrac{5}{6} \times \dfrac{3}{10}$

3 $\dfrac{3}{10} \times \dfrac{5}{12}$

4 $\dfrac{5}{9} \times \dfrac{3}{10}$

INDEPENDENT PRACTICE

Draw a model to find each product.

1 $\frac{1}{3}$ of $\frac{2}{7}$

2 $\frac{3}{4}$ of $\frac{1}{5}$

3 $\frac{2}{3}$ of $\frac{2}{3}$

4 $\frac{2}{7}$ of $\frac{4}{5}$

Multiply. Express each product in simplest form.

5 $\dfrac{1}{3} \times \dfrac{6}{7}$

6 $\dfrac{6}{8} \times \dfrac{4}{9}$

7 $\dfrac{10}{15} \times \dfrac{3}{4}$

8 $\dfrac{7}{10}$ of $\dfrac{5}{10}$

9 $\dfrac{3}{8}$ of $\dfrac{4}{6}$

10 $\dfrac{7}{12}$ of $\dfrac{9}{14}$

3 Real-World Problems: Multiplying Proper Fractions

Learning Objective:
• Solve real-world problems involving multiplication of proper fractions.

THINK

Leah has $\frac{4}{5}$ liter of water. She drinks $\frac{1}{3}$ of the water and offers some to Riley.

What is the greatest amount of water Riley can drink so that in the end,

Leah has $\frac{4}{15}$ of the water she had at first? Explain.

ENGAGE

Nicholas had $\frac{6}{7}$ pound of blueberry jam. He used $\frac{1}{3}$ of the jam.

How much jam was left? Draw a bar model to record your thinking.

LEARN Multiply fractions to solve real-world problems

1   Mr. Martin has $\frac{3}{4}$ quart of chicken stock. He uses $\frac{2}{3}$ of the stock to make some soup.

   a   How much chicken stock does he use to make the soup?

   b   How much chicken stock does he have left?

   STEP 1   Understand the problem.

   > How much chicken stock does Mr. Martin have?
   > How much of the stock does he use? What do I need to find?

   STEP 2   Think of a plan.
   Method 1: I can draw a bar model.
   Method 2: I can multiply fractions.

STEP 3 Carry out the plan.

▶ Method 1

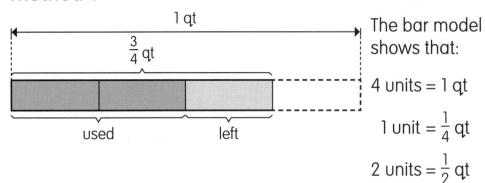

The bar model shows that:

4 units = 1 qt

1 unit = $\frac{1}{4}$ qt

2 units = $\frac{1}{2}$ qt

a Mr. Martin uses $\frac{1}{2}$ quart of chicken stock to make the soup.

b He has $\frac{1}{4}$ quart of chicken stock left.

▶ Method 2

a $\frac{2}{3} \times \frac{3}{4} = \frac{6}{12}$

$= \frac{1}{2}$

Mr. Martin uses $\frac{1}{2}$ quart of chicken stock to make the soup.

b $\frac{3}{4} - \frac{1}{2} = \frac{3}{4} - \frac{2}{4}$

$= \frac{1}{4}$

He has $\frac{1}{4}$ quart of chicken stock left.

STEP 4 Check the answer.
I can work backwards to check my answer.

Add $\frac{1}{4}$ to $\frac{1}{2}$. The answer is $\frac{3}{4}$.

My answers are correct.

TRY Practice multiplying fractions to solve real-world problems

Solve. Use the bar model to help you.

1. Mariah has $\frac{4}{5}$ gallon of paint. She uses $\frac{3}{4}$ of the paint to paint a door.
   a   How much paint does she use?
   b   How much paint is left?

▶ **Method 1**

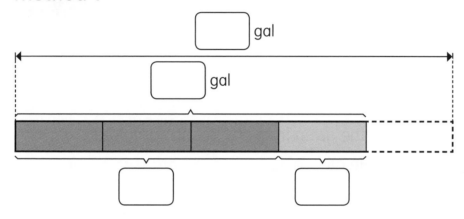

The bar model shows that:

_____ units = _____ gal

_____ unit = _____ gal

_____ units = _____ gal

a   Mariah uses _____ gallon of paint.

b   There is _____ gallon of paint left.

▶ Method 2

a $\frac{3}{4} \times$ _____ = _____

   = _____

   Mariah uses _____ gallon of paint.

b $\frac{4}{5} -$ _____ = _____

   There is _____ gallon of paint left.

ENGAGE

Draw a model to show all the given fractions in each problem.

1 Sean had $\frac{5}{6}$ of a pie. He ate $\frac{1}{5}$ of it.

2 Color $\frac{1}{5}$ of a rectangle. Divide the remaining rectangle into parts in a way such that the fraction $\frac{3}{10}$ can be shown. Color the parts that show the fraction $\frac{3}{10}$.

3 Larry had $\frac{1}{3}$ of a cake. He ate $\frac{1}{3}$ of it and gave $\frac{1}{4}$ of the remainder to Minah. Show the parts that Minah had. What fraction did she have?

LEARN Solve real-world problems with fractional remainder

1 Cole earned some money at a summer job. He saved $\frac{1}{4}$ of his earnings, spent $\frac{4}{9}$ of the remainder to download two movies, and used the rest to buy a T-shirt.

   a What fraction of his earnings did Cole spend on the downloads?

   b What fraction of his earnings did he spend on the T-shirt?

▶ Method 1

$1 - \frac{1}{4} = \frac{3}{4}$

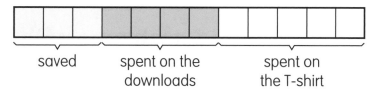

Remainder ⟶ 3 parts   saved remainder

To show $\frac{4}{9}$ of the remainder which is spent on the downloads,

I have to further divide the remainder into 9 parts.
First common multiple of 3 and 9 = 9
By equivalent fractions:

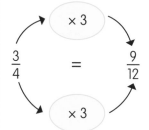

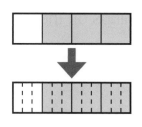

$\frac{3}{4} = \frac{9}{12}$

I need to draw a bar model with 12 equal units to show the problem.

saved   spent on the   spent on
              downloads   the T-shirt

The bar model shows that:
Number of units spent on the downloads = 4
Number of units spent on the T-shirt = 5
Total number of units in 1 whole = 12

$\frac{1}{4}$ of 12 units = 3 units

$\frac{4}{9}$ of 9 units = 4 units

a $\frac{4}{12} = \frac{1}{3}$

Cole spent $\frac{1}{3}$ of his earnings on the downloads.

b   Cole spent $\frac{5}{12}$ of his earnings on the T-shirt.

▶ Method 2

a $1 - \frac{1}{4} = \frac{3}{4}$

$\frac{3}{4}$ of Cole's earnings was left after he saved $\frac{1}{4}$ of it.

$\frac{4}{9} \times \frac{3}{4} = \frac{12}{36}$

$= \frac{1}{3}$

Cole spent $\frac{1}{3}$ of his earnings on the downloads.

b $\frac{3}{4} - \frac{1}{3} = \frac{9}{12} - \frac{4}{12}$

$= \frac{5}{12}$

Cole spent $\frac{5}{12}$ of his earnings on the T-shirt.

TRY Practice solving real-world problems with fractional remainder

Solve. Use the bar model to help you.

1 Layla picks some strawberries. She uses $\frac{3}{5}$ of the strawberries to make jam.

She gives $\frac{3}{4}$ of the remaining strawberries to her neighbor.

a   What fraction of the strawberries does she give to her neighbor?

b   What fraction of the strawberries does she have left?

▶ Method 1

$1 - \frac{3}{5} = \frac{2}{5}$

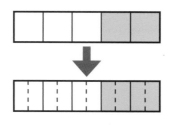

Remainder ⟶ 2 parts

jam   remainder

To show $\frac{3}{4}$ of the remainder which is given to Layla's neighbor,

I have to further divide the remainder into 4 parts.
First common multiple of 2 and 4 = 4
By equivalent fractions:

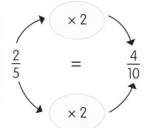

$\frac{2}{5}$ = $\frac{4}{10}$

× 2

× 2

I need to draw a bar model with 10 equal units to show the problem.

$\frac{3}{5}$ of 10 units = 6 units

$\frac{3}{4}$ of 4 units = 3 units

jam

The bar model shows that:

Number of units given to the neighbor = _____

Total number of units in 1 whole = _____

a   She gives _____ of the strawberries to her neighbor.

b   She has _____ of the strawberries left.

▶ Method 2

a $1 - \underline{\hspace{2cm}} = \underline{\hspace{2cm}}$

$\underline{\hspace{2cm}}$ of Layla's strawberries are left after she makes jam with $\frac{3}{5}$ of them.

$\frac{3}{4} \times \underline{\hspace{2cm}} = \frac{6}{20}$

$= \underline{\hspace{2cm}}$

She gives $\underline{\hspace{2cm}}$ of the strawberries to her neighbor.

b $\underline{\hspace{2cm}} - \underline{\hspace{2cm}} = \underline{\hspace{2cm}} - \underline{\hspace{2cm}}$

$= \underline{\hspace{2cm}}$

She has $\underline{\hspace{2cm}}$ of the strawberries left.

Name: _____ Date: _____

Solve. Draw a bar model to help you.

1 Constance has a garden. She plants flowers to cover $\frac{3}{4}$ of the garden. $\frac{2}{3}$ of the flowers are sunflowers. What fraction of the garden is planted with sunflowers?

2 Blake spends $\frac{7}{9}$ of his homework time on math and social studies.

He spends $\frac{4}{7}$ of this time on math. What fraction of the total time does he

spend on social studies?

3 Molly has a piece of string $\frac{5}{6}$ yard long. She uses $\frac{3}{5}$ of the piece of string to tie a present. What is the length of string left?

4 Ms. Carter spends $\frac{1}{2}$ of her salary. She gives $\frac{1}{3}$ of the remainder to charity and saves the rest. What fraction of her salary does Ms. Carter save?

5 Michael uses $\frac{1}{3}$ of a stick of butter in a sauce. He then uses $\frac{5}{8}$ of the remaining butter to make garlic bread. What fraction of the stick of butter is left?

6 Paula spends $\frac{2}{5}$ of her money on a blouse. She spends $\frac{4}{9}$ of her remaining money on a pair of shoes. What fraction of her money does Paula have left?

7 $\frac{7}{12}$ of the pottery Mr. Lopez made are cups and plates. Of the remaining pottery, $\frac{3}{5}$ are vases and the rest are bowls. What fraction of the pottery are bowls?

4 Multiplying Improper Fractions

Learning Objectives:
• Multiply improper fractions by proper fractions.
• Multiply improper fractions by improper fractions.

THINK

Do you agree that when you multiply an improper fraction by a proper fraction, the product is always less than 1? Give examples to support your explanation.

ENGAGE

Color $\frac{3}{2}$ of two strips of paper. Cut out $\frac{1}{2}$ of what you have colored. Paste the pieces on a new strip of paper. What fraction of the strip of paper is the colored pieces?

LEARN Multiply a proper fraction by an improper fraction

1 Find the product of $\frac{6}{5}$ and $\frac{3}{4}$.

▶ **Method 1**

$$\frac{6}{5} \times \frac{3}{4} = \frac{6 \times 3}{5 \times 4}$$

$$= \frac{18}{20}$$

$$= \frac{9}{10}$$

$\frac{3}{4} \times \frac{6}{5}$

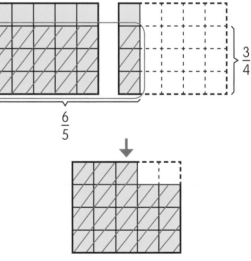

Is $\frac{6}{5} \times \frac{3}{4}$ the same as $\frac{3}{4} \times \frac{6}{5}$?

▶ **Method 2**

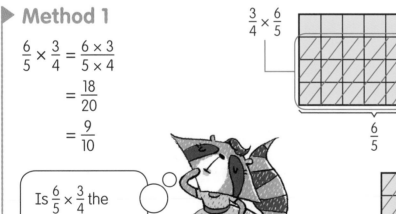

$$\frac{6}{5} \times \frac{3}{4} = \frac{\overset{3}{\cancel{6}}}{5} \times \frac{3}{\underset{2}{\cancel{4}}}$$

2 is a common factor of 6 and 4.
Divide 6 and 4 by their common factor, 2.

$$= \frac{3 \times 3}{5 \times 2}$$

Multiply the numerators.
Multiply the denominators.

$$= \frac{9}{10}$$

2 Find the product of $\frac{9}{4}$ and $\frac{2}{3}$.

▶ **Method 1**

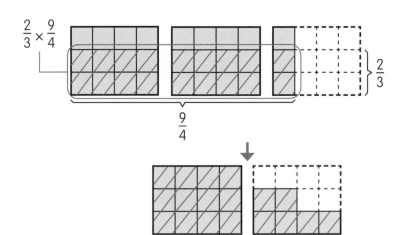

$\frac{9}{4} \times \frac{2}{3} = \frac{9 \times 2}{4 \times 3}$

$= \frac{18}{12}$

$= \frac{3}{2}$

$= 1\frac{1}{2}$

▶ **Method 2**

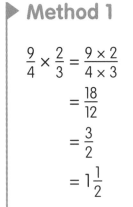

$\frac{9}{4} \times \frac{2}{3} = \frac{\overset{3}{\cancel{9}}}{\underset{2}{\cancel{4}}} \times \frac{\overset{1}{\cancel{2}}}{\underset{1}{\cancel{3}}}$

Divide 2 and 4 by their common factor, 2.
Divide 9 and 3 by their common factor, 3.

$= \frac{3 \times 1}{2 \times 1}$

Multiply the numerators.
Multiply the denominators.

$= \frac{3}{2}$

$= 1\frac{1}{2}$

TRY Practice multiplying a proper fraction by an improper fraction

Multiply. Express each product in simplest form.

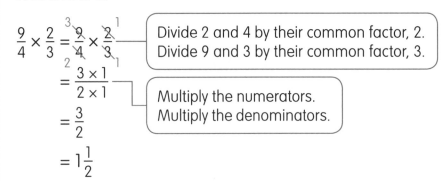

1 $\frac{8}{7} \times \frac{2}{3} = \dfrac{\boxed{} \times 2}{\boxed{} \times 3}$

$= \underline{}$

2 $\frac{8}{5} \times \frac{6}{7} = \dfrac{\boxed{} \times 6}{\boxed{} \times 7}$

$= \underline{}$

$= \underline{}$

3 $\frac{7}{6} \times \frac{3}{4}$

4 $\frac{5}{2} \times \frac{1}{5}$

5 $\frac{5}{2} \times \frac{4}{5}$

6 $\frac{9}{7} \times \frac{5}{6}$

ENGAGE

Draw a model to represent $\frac{5}{3}$. How do you use the model to find $\frac{3}{2} \times \frac{5}{3}$?

How do you find $\frac{5}{3} \times \frac{3}{2}$? Explain your reasoning.

LEARN Multiply two improper fractions

1 Find $\frac{6}{5} \times \frac{3}{2}$.

$$\frac{6}{5} \times \frac{3}{2} = \frac{\overset{3}{\cancel{6}}}{5} \times \frac{3}{\underset{1}{\cancel{2}}}$$

> Divide 6 and 2 by their common factor, 2.

$$= \frac{3 \times 3}{5 \times 1}$$

> Multiply the numerators.
> Multiply the denominators.

$$= \frac{9}{5}$$

$$= 1\frac{4}{5}$$

2 Find $\frac{4}{3} \times \frac{9}{8}$.

$$\frac{4}{3} \times \frac{9}{8} = \frac{\overset{1}{\cancel{4}}}{\underset{1}{\cancel{3}}} \times \frac{\overset{3}{\cancel{9}}}{\underset{2}{\cancel{8}}}$$

> Divide 4 and 8 by their common factor, 4.
> Divide 9 and 3 by their common factor, 3.

$$= \frac{1 \times 3}{1 \times 2}$$

> Multiply the numerators.
> Multiply the denominators.

$$= \frac{3}{2}$$

$$= 1\frac{1}{2}$$

TRY Practice multiplying two improper fractions

Multiply. Express each product in simplest form.

1. $\dfrac{8}{7} \times \dfrac{5}{2} = \dfrac{\overset{\square}{\cancel{8}}}{7} \times \dfrac{5}{\underset{\square}{\cancel{2}}}$

$$= \frac{\boxed{} \times 5}{7 \times \boxed{}}$$

$$= \boxed{}$$

$$= \boxed{}$$

2. $\dfrac{11}{4} \times \dfrac{8}{5}$

3. $\dfrac{9}{2} \times \dfrac{7}{3}$

4. $\dfrac{6}{5} \times \dfrac{10}{9}$

5. $\dfrac{12}{7} \times \dfrac{7}{6}$

6. $\dfrac{10}{3} \times \dfrac{9}{4}$

7. $\dfrac{16}{7} \times \dfrac{21}{2}$

8. $\dfrac{22}{9} \times \dfrac{3}{2}$

9. $\dfrac{14}{5} \times \dfrac{10}{7}$

10. $\dfrac{15}{8} \times \dfrac{16}{3}$

Name: _____ Date: _____

INDEPENDENT PRACTICE

Multiply. Express each product in simplest form.

1 $\dfrac{1}{3} \times \dfrac{7}{5}$

2 $\dfrac{3}{4} \times \dfrac{14}{5}$

3 $\dfrac{5}{9} \times \dfrac{24}{7}$

4 $\dfrac{2}{7} \times \dfrac{7}{4}$

5 $\dfrac{5}{2} \times \dfrac{4}{5}$

6 $\dfrac{7}{5} \times \dfrac{9}{2}$

7 $\dfrac{23}{10} \times \dfrac{11}{4}$

8 $\dfrac{15}{9} \times \dfrac{11}{3}$

9 $\dfrac{11}{3} \times \dfrac{3}{11}$

10 $\dfrac{15}{8} \times \dfrac{16}{5}$

11 $\dfrac{16}{3} \times \dfrac{9}{4}$

12 $\dfrac{21}{8} \times \dfrac{10}{7}$

13 $\dfrac{8}{3} \times \dfrac{15}{4}$

14 $\dfrac{28}{11} \times \dfrac{22}{6}$

15 $\dfrac{4}{3} \times \dfrac{13}{8}$

16 $\dfrac{24}{5} \times \dfrac{25}{8}$

5 Multiplying Mixed Numbers and Whole Numbers

Learning Objectives:
- Multiply a mixed number by a whole number.
- Multiply two mixed numbers.
- Compare the size of a product to the size of its factors.

THINK

Do you agree that when you multiply mixed numbers, the product is always greater than the factors? Give examples to support your explanation.

ENGAGE

1 Mr. Allen had some oranges. He gave a group of four students 2 oranges each. He also gave another four students $\frac{1}{3}$ of an orange each.

Use  to show the total number of oranges Mr. Allen gave to the eight students in all. Explain how you find your answer to your partner.

2 Mr. Allen then decided to give five students $2\frac{3}{4}$ oranges each. How many oranges did these five students receive altogether? Explain the steps you followed to solve the problem to your partner.

LEARN Multiply a mixed number by a whole number

1 3 students worked on a project. Each student worked $1\frac{1}{2}$ hours on the project. What was the total amount of time the students spent on the project?

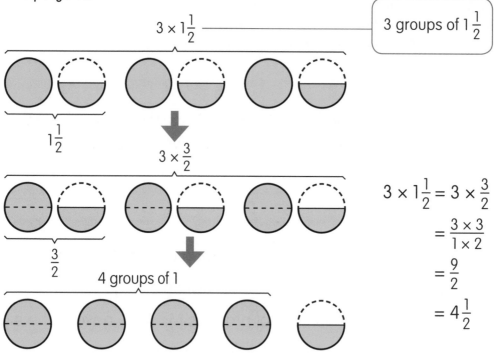

$3 \times 1\frac{1}{2}$ ——— 3 groups of $1\frac{1}{2}$

$3 \times \frac{3}{2}$

4 groups of 1

$$3 \times 1\frac{1}{2} = 3 \times \frac{3}{2}$$
$$= \frac{3 \times 3}{1 \times 2}$$
$$= \frac{9}{2}$$
$$= 4\frac{1}{2}$$

The students spent a total of $4\frac{1}{2}$ hours on the project.

2 Trevon picked 3 kilograms of berries. Karina picked $1\frac{1}{2}$ times as many berries as Trevon. How many kilograms of berries did Karina pick?

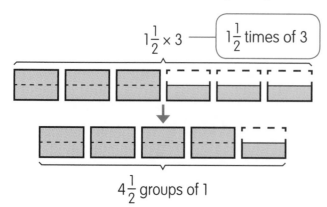

$1\frac{1}{2} \times 3$ ——— $1\frac{1}{2}$ times of 3

$4\frac{1}{2}$ groups of 1

$$1\frac{1}{2} \times 3 = \frac{3}{2} \times 3$$
$$= \frac{3 \times 3}{2 \times 1}$$
$$= \frac{9}{2}$$
$$= 4\frac{1}{2}$$

Karina picked $4\frac{1}{2}$ kilograms of berries.

Practice multiplying a mixed number by a whole number

1. Find $3 \times 2\frac{1}{3}$. Express the answer in simplest form.

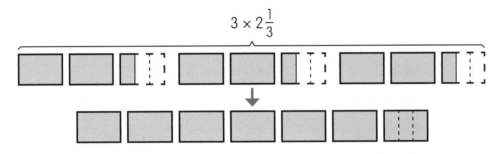

$$3 \times 2\frac{1}{3} = \underline{\hspace{3cm}}$$

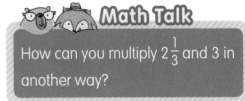

Math Talk

How can you multiply $2\frac{1}{3}$ and 3 in another way?

Multiply. Express each answer in simplest form. Use the bar model to help you.

2. $2 \times 2\frac{1}{3} = \underline{\hspace{2cm}}$

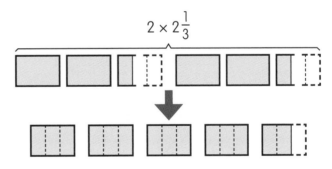

$$2 \times 2\frac{1}{3}$$

Multiply.

3. $1\frac{1}{4} \times 2 = \underline{\hspace{2cm}}$

4. $1\frac{1}{3} \times 3 = \underline{\hspace{2cm}}$

ENGAGE

A square paving stone measures $1\frac{1}{2}$ feet by $1\frac{1}{2}$ feet. Explain the steps you would follow to find the area of the paving stone. Draw diagrams to help you.

LEARN Multiply two mixed numbers

1 You can use square tiles to multiply two mixed numbers.

a A rectangle measures $2\frac{1}{2}$ inches by $1\frac{1}{2}$ inches. Find the area of the rectangle.

Both fractions have the same denominator, 2. You can use squares measuring $\frac{1}{2}$ inch by $\frac{1}{2}$ inch to tile the rectangle.

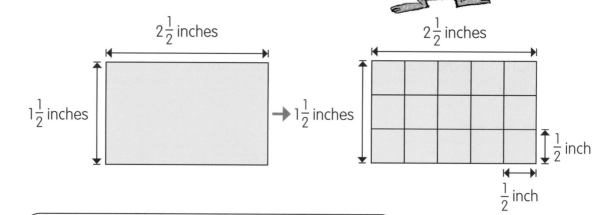

Each square measures $\frac{1}{2}$ inch by $\frac{1}{2}$ inch.

Area of each square $= \frac{1}{2} \times \frac{1}{2}$

$= \frac{1}{4}$ in.²

Area of the rectangle $= 15 \times \frac{1}{4}$

$= \frac{15}{4}$

$= 3\frac{3}{4}$ in.²

b A rectangle measures $1\frac{1}{2}$ inches by $1\frac{1}{4}$ inches. Find the area of the rectangle.

$1\frac{1}{2} = \frac{3}{2}$

$\quad = \frac{6}{4}$

You can use squares measuring $\frac{1}{4}$ inch by $\frac{1}{4}$ inch to tile the rectangle.

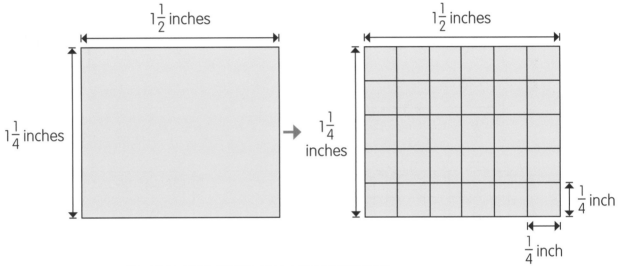

$1\frac{1}{2}$ inches

$1\frac{1}{4}$ inches

$1\frac{1}{2}$ inches

$1\frac{1}{4}$ inches

$\frac{1}{4}$ inch

$\frac{1}{4}$ inch

Each square measures $\frac{1}{4}$ inch by $\frac{1}{4}$ inch.

Area of each square $= \frac{1}{4} \times \frac{1}{4}$

$\quad = \frac{1}{16}$ in.^{2}

$\frac{1}{4}$ inch

$\frac{1}{4}$ inch

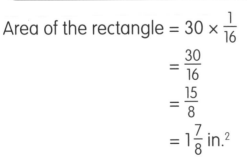

Area of the rectangle $= 30 \times \frac{1}{16}$

$\quad = \frac{30}{16}$

$\quad = \frac{15}{8}$

$\quad = 1\frac{7}{8}$ in.^{2}

2 You can also use area models to multiply two mixed numbers.

a Find the product of $1\frac{2}{3}$ and $1\frac{1}{2}$.

> The first common multiple of 2 and 3 is 6.
>
> $1\frac{2}{3} = \frac{5}{3}$ $\qquad\qquad$ $1\frac{1}{2} = \frac{3}{2}$
>
> $\quad = \frac{10}{6}$ $\qquad\qquad\qquad = \frac{9}{6}$
>
> You can draw a rectangle measuring $1\frac{2}{3}$ units by $1\frac{1}{2}$ units and
>
> use squares measuring $\frac{1}{6}$ unit by $\frac{1}{6}$ unit to tile the rectangle.
>
> Area of each square $= \frac{1}{6} \times \frac{1}{6}$
>
> $\qquad\qquad\qquad\quad = \frac{1}{36}$ square unit

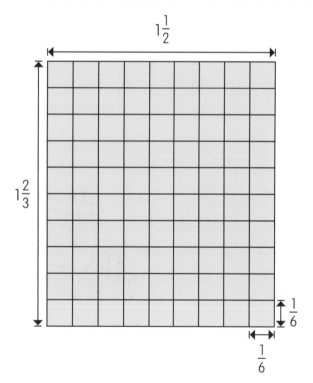

	1	$\frac{1}{2}$
1	36 squares $= 36 \times \frac{1}{36}$ $= 1$	18 squares $= 18 \times \frac{1}{36}$ $= \frac{18}{36} = \frac{1}{2}$
$\frac{2}{3}$	24 squares $= 24 \times \frac{1}{36}$ $= \frac{24}{36} = \frac{2}{3}$	12 squares $= 12 \times \frac{1}{36}$ $= \frac{12}{36} = \frac{1}{3}$

$$1\frac{2}{3} \times 1\frac{1}{2} = (1 \times 1) + \left(1 \times \frac{2}{3}\right) + \left(1 \times \frac{1}{2}\right) + \left(\frac{1}{2} \times \frac{2}{3}\right)$$

$$= 1 + \frac{2}{3} + \frac{1}{2} + \frac{1}{3}$$

$$= 2\frac{1}{2}$$

Math Talk

Discuss other ways to multiply two mixed numbers.

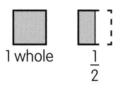

Hands-on Activity Multiplying fractions and comparing the product with its factors

Work in pairs.

1. Use a sheet of paper to represent 1 whole. Next, fold another sheet of paper in half and cut it into two equal pieces. Use one of these pieces to represent $\frac{1}{2}$. Do this with several pieces.

1 whole $\frac{1}{2}$

2. Use the pieces of paper in ① to show each of the following.

   a $3\frac{1}{2}$

   b $4 \times 3\frac{1}{2}$

   c $3\frac{1}{2} \times 5$

   d Rearrange the pieces representing $4 \times 3\frac{1}{2}$.

   How many wholes are there in $4 \times 3\frac{1}{2}$?

3. **Mathematical Habit 2** Use mathematical reasoning

   Consider $3\frac{1}{2} \times 4\frac{1}{2}$. Use the results of ② to predict, without multiplying, whether the product is greater than or less than $3\frac{1}{2}$. Explain your reasoning.

④ **Mathematical Habit 2** Use mathematical reasoning

Suppose you multiply $3\frac{1}{2}$ by any number greater than 1. Will the product be greater than or less than $3\frac{1}{2}$? Explain your reasoning.

⑤ Draw horizontal lines on some of the pieces as shown. Shade an amount equal to each product.

a $2\frac{1}{2} \times \frac{1}{2}$

b $\frac{1}{4} \times 2\frac{1}{2}$

⑥ **Mathematical Habit 2** Use mathematical reasoning

Consider $2\frac{1}{2} \times \frac{3}{4}$. Use the results of ⑤ to predict, without multiplying, whether the product is greater than or less than $2\frac{1}{2}$. Explain your reasoning.

⑦ **Mathematical Habit 2** Use mathematical reasoning

Suppose you multiply $2\frac{1}{2}$ by any number greater than 1. Will the product be greater than or less than $2\frac{1}{2}$? Explain your reasoning.

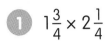 **Practice multiplying two mixed numbers**

Use square tiles to multiply each pair of mixed numbers. Express each answer in simplest form.

1 $1\frac{3}{4} \times 2\frac{1}{4}$

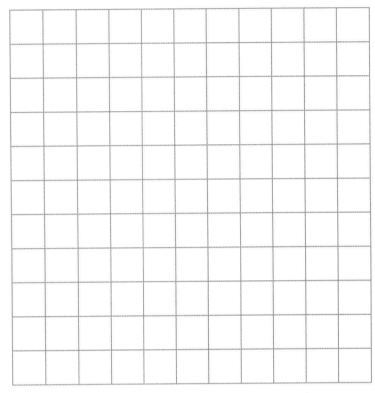

2 $1\frac{1}{6} \times 1\frac{1}{3}$

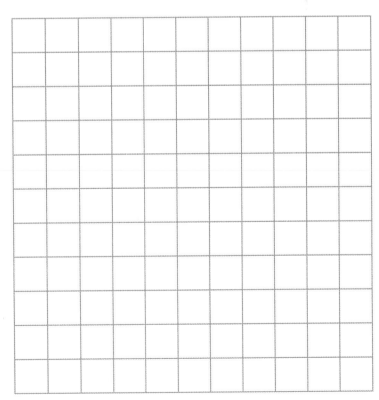

Draw an area model to multiply each pair of mixed numbers. Express each answer in simplest form.

3 $1\frac{5}{7} \times 2\frac{3}{5}$

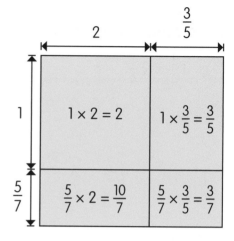

4 $2\frac{1}{8} \times 4\frac{1}{6}$

5 $5\frac{1}{4} \times 3\frac{4}{5}$

Name: _____   Date: _____

INDEPENDENT PRACTICE

Multiply. Express each answer in simplest form. Use the bar model to help you.

1 $4 \times 1\frac{1}{2} = $ _____

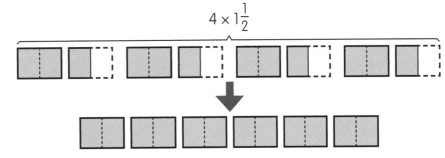

2 $2 \times 1\frac{3}{4} = $ _____

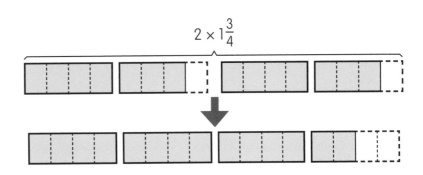

3 $2\frac{1}{4} \times 2 = $ _____

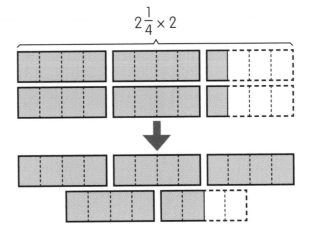

Multiply. Express each answer in simplest form.

4 $2\frac{5}{9} \times 16$

5 $3\frac{9}{11} \times 33$

6 $12 \times 7\frac{9}{10}$

7 $14 \times 1\frac{7}{8}$

Use square tiles to multiply each pair of mixed numbers. Express each product in simplest form.

8 $1\frac{1}{3} \times 2\frac{2}{3}$

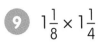 $1\frac{1}{8} \times 1\frac{1}{4}$

Draw an area model to multiply each pair of mixed numbers. Express each product in simplest form.

10 $2\frac{1}{3} \times 3\frac{2}{5}$

11 $6\frac{1}{2} \times 5\frac{3}{7}$

Solve.

12 Name a whole number that you can multiply $4\frac{3}{4}$ by to get a product greater than $4\frac{3}{4}$. Write a mixed number that would give a similar result.

13 Write a number you can multiply $3\frac{5}{6}$ by to get a product less than $3\frac{5}{6}$.

 **Real-World Problems: Multiplying Mixed Numbers**

Learning Objective:
• Solve real-world problems involving multiplication of whole numbers and mixed numbers.

THINK

Cameron wants to make 4 shirts. He needs $3\frac{1}{4}$ feet of cloth for a shirt. He can purchase cloth only in whole feet. How much cloth must he buy? How much cloth will he have left after he has sewn all of the shirts?

ENGAGE

Victor uses $\frac{1}{2}$ cup of flour to make a big loaf of bread and $\frac{1}{4}$ cup to make a small loaf of bread. How many cups of flour are needed to make 2 small loaves of bread and 4 big loaves of bread? Draw a bar model to represent the problem and explain your thinking.

LEARN Multiply a mixed number by a whole number to solve real-world problems

1. There are 40 guests at a party. Each guest eats $2\frac{3}{4}$ mini pies. How many mini pies do the guests eat in all?

40 guests

$2\frac{3}{4}$ mini pies

1 guest $\longrightarrow 2\frac{3}{4}$ mini pies

40 guests $\longrightarrow 40 \times 2\frac{3}{4}$ mini pies

$$= 40 \times \frac{11}{4}$$
$$= \frac{440}{4}$$
$$= 110$$

The guests eat 110 mini pies.

2 Ella has 5 ribbons, each $2\frac{1}{4}$ feet long. What is the total length of the ribbons? Express the product as a decimal.

5 ribbons

$2\frac{1}{4}$ ft

$$2\frac{1}{4} \times 5 = \frac{9}{4} \times 5$$
$$= \frac{45}{4}$$
$$= 11\frac{1}{4}$$
$$= 11\frac{25}{100}$$
$$= 11.25$$

The total length of the ribbons is 11.25 feet.

TRY Practice multiplying a mixed number by a whole number to solve real-world problems

Solve. Use the bar model to help you.

1 A fresh coconut contains $1\frac{1}{2}$ cups of juice. How many cups of juice are in 6 identical coconuts?

$1\frac{1}{2}$ cups

?

_____ unit = $\square\begin{array}{c}\square\\\hline\square\end{array}$

_____ units = $\square\begin{array}{c}\square\\\hline\square\end{array} \bigcirc \square$

$= \begin{array}{c}\square\\\hline\square\end{array} \bigcirc \square$

$= $ _____

6 similar coconuts contain _____ cups of juice.

Solve.

2 Alan's rectangular backyard has a length of $12\frac{3}{4}$ yards and a width of 7 yards. Find the area of Alan's backyard. Express your answer as a decimal.

Area of Alan's rectangular backyard = Length × Width

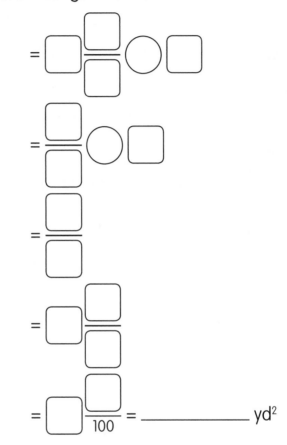

The area of Alan's backyard is _____ square yards.

A rectangular wall in Alexis's room measures $1\frac{1}{2}$ meters by $2\frac{1}{2}$ meters. She bought some wallpaper for \$4 per square meter. How much did Alexis pay for her wallpaper?

Draw a model to show the following:

a the amount of wallpaper needed for the wall

b the cost of the wallpaper needed

Share your model with your partner.

LEARN Solve two-step real-world problems involving multiplication of mixed numbers

1 Ms. Lee buys 4 packages of chicken. Each package has a mass of $2\frac{3}{5}$ pounds. The price of the chicken is $2 per pound. How much does Ms. Lee pay for the four packages of chicken?

STEP 1 Understand the problem.

How many packages of chicken does Ms. Lee buy? What is the mass of each package of chicken? What do I need to find?

STEP 2 Think of a plan.
I can draw a bar model.

STEP 3 Carry out the plan.

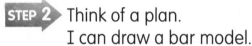

4 packages

$2\frac{3}{5}$ lb

1 package of chicken ⟶ $2\frac{3}{5}$ lb

4 packages of chicken ⟶ $4 \times 2\frac{3}{5}$

$= 10\frac{2}{5}$ lb

$$4 \times 2\frac{3}{5} = 4 \times \frac{13}{5}$$
$$= \frac{52}{5}$$
$$= 10\frac{2}{5}$$

The weight of the 4 packages of chicken is $10\frac{2}{5}$ pounds.

1 pound of chicken ⟶ $2

$10\frac{2}{5}$ pounds of chicken ⟶ $10\frac{2}{5} \times \$2$

$$= \$20\frac{4}{5}$$
$$= \$20\frac{8}{10}$$
$$= \$20.80$$

$$10\frac{2}{5} \times 2 = \frac{52}{5} \times 2$$
$$= \frac{104}{5}$$
$$= 20\frac{4}{5}$$

STEP 4 Check the answer.
I can work backwards to check my answer.

$20.8 \div 2 = 10.4$ $10.4 \div 4 = 2.6$
$= 10\frac{2}{5}$ $= 2\frac{3}{5}$

My answer is correct.

2 A tiler bought some tiles to tile a bathroom measuring $9\frac{1}{4}$ feet by $9\frac{1}{2}$ feet. The tiles were sold at \$4 per square foot. How much did he pay for the tiles?

Area of the bathroom $= 9\frac{1}{4} \times 9\frac{1}{2}$

$$= (9 \times 9) + \left(9 \times \frac{1}{2}\right) + \left(9 \times \frac{1}{4}\right) + \left(\frac{1}{4} \times \frac{1}{2}\right)$$

$$= 81 + \frac{9}{2} + \frac{9}{4} + \frac{1}{8}$$

$$= 87\frac{7}{8} \text{ ft}^2$$

$87\frac{7}{8} \times \$4 = \$351\frac{1}{2}$

$\qquad\qquad = \$351.50$

He paid \$351.50 for the tiles.

TRY Practice solving two-step real-world problems involving multiplication of mixed numbers

Solve. Use the bar model to help you.

1 A chef uses 3 bottles of olive oil to make salad dressing. Each bottle contains $1\frac{1}{2}$ quarts of oil. The cost of a quart of olive oil is \$5. Find the total cost of the oil she uses.

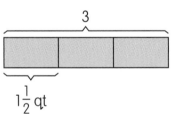

$1\frac{1}{2}$ qt

1 bottle $\longrightarrow$ _____ qt

3 bottles $\longrightarrow$ 3 × _____

$\qquad\qquad =$ _____ qt

3 bottles contain _____ quarts of olive oil.

1 qt of olive oil $\longrightarrow$ \$5

_____ qt of olive oil $\longrightarrow$ _____ × \$5

$\qquad\qquad\qquad = $ _____ × \$5

$\qquad\qquad\qquad = \$$ _____

The total cost of the olive oil is

\$ _____.

Solve.

2 Ms. Walker was carpeting the floor of a bedroom. The bedroom measured $3\frac{1}{2}$ meters by $2\frac{3}{4}$ meters. The carpet was sold at $8 per square meter. How much did Ms. Walker pay for the carpeting?

Area of the bedroom = $\boxed{}\,\boxed{\dfrac{\boxed{}}{\boxed{}}}\;\bigcirc\;\boxed{}\,\boxed{\dfrac{\boxed{}}{\boxed{}}}$

$= \left(\boxed{}\,\bigcirc\,\boxed{}\right)\bigcirc\left(\boxed{}\,\bigcirc\,\boxed{\dfrac{\boxed{}}{\boxed{}}}\right)$

$\bigcirc\left(\boxed{}\,\bigcirc\,\boxed{\dfrac{\boxed{}}{\boxed{}}}\right)\bigcirc\left(\boxed{\dfrac{\boxed{}}{\boxed{}}}\,\bigcirc\,\boxed{\dfrac{\boxed{}}{\boxed{}}}\right)$

$= \boxed{}\,\bigcirc\,\boxed{\dfrac{\boxed{}}{\boxed{}}}\,\bigcirc\,\boxed{}\,\bigcirc\,\boxed{\dfrac{\boxed{}}{\boxed{}}}$

$= \underline{}$ m^2

Cost of carpeting = $\boxed{}\,\boxed{\dfrac{\boxed{}}{\boxed{}}}\;\bigcirc\;\$\boxed{}$

$= \$\underline{}$

Ms. Walker paid $\$\underline{}$ for the carpeting.

INDEPENDENT PRACTICE

Solve.

1 There were 6 children at a birthday party. The party's host prepared $2\frac{1}{3}$ cups of fruit punch for each child. How many cups of fruit punch did the host prepare?

2 Aiden cuts a ball of string into 14 equal pieces. The length of each piece of string is $2\frac{1}{4}$ yards. What is the original length of the ball of string?

3 At a zoo, a zookeeper feeds an adult elephant $70\frac{1}{4}$ pounds of bananas each day. The zoo keeps 5 adult elephants. How many pounds of bananas does the zookeeper feed all 5 adult elephants in a day?

4 Mr. Evans hung wallpaper on a wall measuring $3\frac{1}{2}$ meters by $2\frac{4}{5}$ meters. He bought the wallpaper at $15 per square meter. How much did he pay for the wallpaper?

7 Dividing Fractions and Whole Numbers

Learning Objectives:
- Divide a fraction by a whole number.
- Divide a whole number by a unit fraction.

New Vocabulary
reciprocal

THINK

Steven colors $\frac{1}{3}$ of a rectangular piece of paper blue. He then cuts the remaining part of the paper into six equal pieces. What fraction of the whole is each piece?

ENGAGE

Audrey had $\frac{1}{3}$ of a pie. She shared the pie she had equally with her brother. Use ⊘ to show how much of a pie each of them received. Draw a sketch to explain your thinking.

LEARN Divide a unit fraction by a whole number

1. Jessica cuts a rectangular piece of clay in half. She then divides one half into three equal parts. What fraction of the whole piece of clay is each of the three parts?

▶ **Method 1**

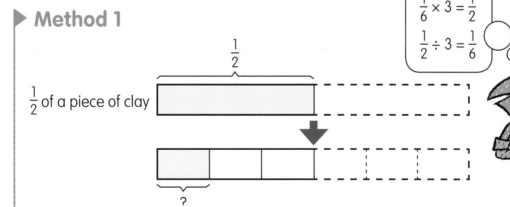

$$\frac{1}{6} \times 3 = \frac{1}{2}$$
$$\frac{1}{2} \div 3 = \frac{1}{6}$$

$$\frac{1}{2} \div 3 = \frac{1}{6}$$

The bar model shows that each part is $\frac{1}{6}$ of the whole piece of clay.

Method 2

$$\frac{1}{2} \div 3 = \frac{1}{3} \text{ of } \frac{1}{2}$$

$$= \frac{1}{3} \times \frac{1}{2}$$

$$= \frac{1}{6}$$

Each part is $\frac{1}{6}$ of the whole piece of clay.

Each part is $\frac{1}{3}$ of $\frac{1}{2}$ of the piece of clay.

Method 3

$$\frac{1}{2} \div 3 = \frac{1}{2} \div \frac{3}{1}$$

$$= \frac{1}{2} \times \frac{1}{3}$$

$$= \frac{1}{6}$$

Each part is $\frac{1}{6}$ of the whole piece of clay.

$\frac{1}{3}$ is the reciprocal of $\frac{3}{1}$ or 3. Dividing by a number is the same as multiplying by the reciprocal of the number.

Hands-on Activity Relating division of a unit fraction by a whole number to multiplication

Work in pairs.

① Use the following method to find $\frac{1}{4} \div 3$.

STEP 1 Use a piece of paper to represent 1 whole. Fold the paper into fourths and keep it folded.

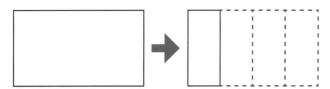

STEP 2 Now fold the folded paper into thirds. Color one side.

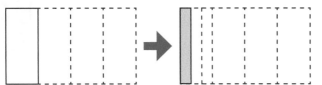

Unfold the paper to reveal the total number of parts.

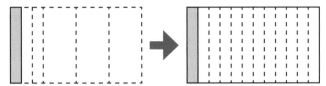

Count:
a   the total number of parts
b   the number of colored parts

$\frac{1}{4} \div 3 =$ _____

Check

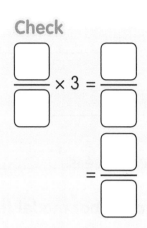

(2) Use the method in (1) to divide $\frac{1}{4}$ by 4.

TRY **Practice dividing a unit fraction by a whole number**

Solve. Use the bar model to help you.

(1) A piece of wire $\frac{1}{5}$ foot long is cut into 2 equal smaller pieces. How long is each small piece?

▶ **Method 1**

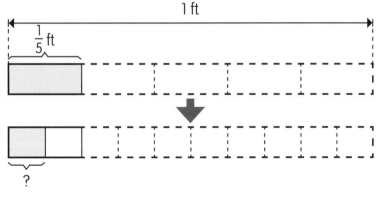

$\frac{1}{5} \div 2 =$ _____

The bar model shows that each piece is _____ foot long.

$$\frac{1}{5} \div 2 = \frac{1}{2} \text{ of } \frac{1}{5}$$

$$= \underline{\hspace{2cm}} \times \underline{\hspace{2cm}}$$

$$= \underline{\hspace{2cm}}$$

Each piece is _____ foot long.

$$\frac{1}{5} \div 2 = \frac{1}{5} \div \frac{2}{1}$$

$$= \frac{1}{5} \times \underline{\hspace{2cm}}$$

$$= \underline{\hspace{2cm}}$$

Each piece is _____ foot long.

Divide. Draw a bar model to help you.

2 $\frac{1}{8} \div 3$

3 $\frac{1}{3} \div 6$

ENGAGE

1 Color $\frac{2}{5}$ of a rectangle. Draw a line to divide the colored part into 2 equal parts. Show at least two different ways to do it. What fraction of the rectangle is each part? Explain.

2 Landon colored $\frac{2}{5}$ of another rectangle. He divides the colored part equally into some parts. If each part is $\frac{1}{10}$ of the rectangle, how many equal colored parts are there?

LEARN Divide a proper fraction by a whole number

1 $\frac{4}{5}$ of a fruit tart was shared equally between 2 children. What fraction of the fruit tart did each child receive?

▶ **Method 1**

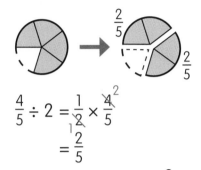

$$\frac{4}{5} \div 2 = \frac{1}{\cancel{2}_1} \times \frac{\cancel{4}^2}{5}$$
$$= \frac{2}{5}$$

Each child received $\frac{2}{5}$ of the fruit tart.

▶ **Method 2**

$$\frac{4}{5} \div 2 = \frac{\cancel{4}^2}{5} \times \frac{1}{\cancel{2}_1}$$
$$= \frac{2}{5}$$

Each child received $\frac{2}{5}$ of the fruit tart.

Hands-on Activity Dividing a proper fraction by a whole number

Work in pairs.

1 Divide $\frac{2}{3}$ equally into two groups. Use 🔵 to show the fraction in each group. Then, find $\frac{2}{3} \div 2$.

2 Ask your partner to find $\frac{2}{3} \times \frac{1}{2}$.

3 〔Mathematical Habit **2**〕 Use mathematical reasoning

Compare your answers in ① and ②. What do you notice?

TRY Practice dividing a proper fraction by a whole number

Solve.

1 $\frac{3}{4}$ of a block of clay was cut into 6 equal pieces. What fraction of the block was each piece?

▶ **Method 1**

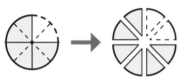

$\frac{3}{4} \div 6 = $ _____ $\times \frac{3}{4}$

$= $ _____

Each piece was _____ of the block of clay.

▶ **Method 2**

$\frac{3}{4} \div 6 = \frac{3}{4} \times$ _____

$= $ _____

Each piece was _____ of the block of clay.

Divide.

2 $\frac{4}{7} \div 8$

3 $\frac{3}{8} \div 9$

ENGAGE

1 A chef bakes 3 cakes. She cuts the cake into slices that are each $\frac{1}{4}$ of a cake. Use to show how many slices of cake there are. Draw a sketch to record your thinking.

2 Sam bakes 4 cakes. He cuts each cake into some equal slices. After cutting, he has a total of 36 equal slices. What fraction of a cake is each slice?

LEARN Divide a whole number by a unit fraction

1 Jacob uses $\frac{1}{3}$ yard of ribbon to decorate a greetings card. How many similar greetings cards can he decorate with 4 yards of ribbon?

Number of greetings cards = $4 \div \frac{1}{3}$

The bar model shows that:

Number of $\frac{1}{3}$ yard pieces in 1 yard = 3

Number of $\frac{1}{3}$ yard pieces in 4 yards = 4 × 3

So, $4 \div \frac{1}{3} = 4 \times 3$ —— Rewrite as a multiplication expression using the reciprocal of the divisor.

$= 12$ —— Then, multiply.

Jacob can decorate 12 similar greetings cards with 4 yards of ribbon.

Check

$12 \times \frac{1}{3} = \frac{12 \times 1}{3}$

$= \frac{12}{3}$

$= 4$

In general, dividing by a number is the same as multiplying by the reciprocal of the number.

$4 \div \frac{1}{3} = 4 \times 3$

$\frac{1}{3}$ and 3 are reciprocals.

7 Dividing Fractions and Whole Numbers **247**

TRY Practice dividing a whole number by a unit fraction

Solve. Use the bar model to help you.

1 Jack uses $\frac{1}{5}$ kilogram of butter to bake a loaf of bread. How many loaves of bread can he bake with 3 kilograms of butter?

Number of loaves of bread = $\boxed{} \div \dfrac{\boxed{}}{\boxed{}}$

= _____ × _____

= _____

He can bake _____ loaves of bread with 3 kilograms of butter.

Divide. Draw a bar model to help you.

2 $7 \div \frac{1}{3}$

INDEPENDENT PRACTICE

Divide. Express each quotient in simplest form.

1 $\dfrac{1}{7} \div 2$

2 $\dfrac{1}{5} \div 7$

3 $\dfrac{1}{11} \div 3$

4 $\dfrac{1}{9} \div 4$

Divide. Express each quotient in simplest form.

5 $\dfrac{2}{7} \div 9$

6 $\dfrac{3}{8} \div 10$

7 $\dfrac{5}{6} \div 3$

8 $\dfrac{4}{5} \div 8$

9 $\frac{5}{9} \div 10$

10 $\frac{2}{7} \div 6$

Divide.

11 $3 \div \frac{1}{8}$

12 $6 \div \frac{1}{10}$

13 $8 \div \frac{1}{12}$

14 $10 \div \frac{1}{9}$

8 Real-World Problems: Multiplying and Dividing with Fractions

Learning Objective:
- Solve real-world problems involving multiplication and division of fractions and whole numbers.

 THINK

A decorator had some paint. She used $\frac{2}{5}$ of the paint on Saturday and $\frac{4}{9}$ of the rest on Sunday. She bought another 10 liters of paint. Together with the paint she had left, she had a total of 25 liters of paint. How much paint did the decorator have at first? Discuss how you would solve the problem with your partner.

ENGAGE

Charles had 120 apples in his store. He sold $\frac{1}{3}$ of the apples in the morning.
a   Draw a bar model to represent the problem. Then, write an equation to find the number of apples sold in the morning.
b   He sold 15 fewer apples in the afternoon. What fraction of apples were not sold?

LEARN Find parts of a whole to solve real-world problems

1   A vendor at a farmers' market has 240 pieces of fruit. She sells $\frac{1}{2}$ of the fruit to one customer and $\frac{1}{3}$ of the fruit to another customer.
   a   How many pieces of fruit does the vendor sell?
   b   How many pieces of fruit does she have left?

   STEP 1 Understand the problem.

   How many pieces of fruit does the vendor have?
   What fraction of the fruit does she sell to each customer?
   What do I need to find?

   STEP 2 Think of a plan.
   I can draw a bar model.

STEP 3 Carry out the plan.

▶ Method 1

The first common
multiple of 2 and 3
is 6. Draw a
bar model with
6 equal units.

$\frac{1}{2}$ of 6 units $= \frac{1}{2} \times 6$
$= 3$ units

$\frac{1}{3}$ of 6 units $= \frac{1}{3} \times 6$
$= 2$ units

240 pieces of fruit

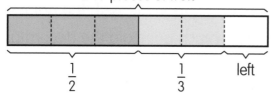

$\frac{1}{2}$ $\frac{1}{3}$ left

The bar model shows that:

6 units = 240 pieces of fruit

1 unit = 240 ÷ 6

= 40 pieces of fruit

5 units = 5 × 40

= 200 pieces of fruit

a The vendor sells 200 pieces
of fruit.

b She has 40 pieces of fruit left.

▶ Method 2

$\frac{1}{2} = \frac{3}{6}$ $\frac{1}{3} = \frac{2}{6}$

Fraction of fruit sold:

$\frac{3}{6} + \frac{2}{6} = \frac{5}{6}$

$\frac{5}{6} \times 240 = 200$

a The vendor sells 200 pieces
of fruit.
240 − 200 = 40

b She has 40 pieces of fruit left.

▶ Method 3

$\frac{1}{2} \times 240 = 120$

$\frac{1}{3} \times 240 = 80$

120 + 80 = 200

a The vendor sells 200 pieces
of fruit.
240 − 200 = 40

b She has 40 pieces of fruit left.

Check the answer.
I can work backwards to check my answers.

a Divide 200 by 5, then multiply the quotient by 6 to find the number of pieces of fruit at first.
200 ÷ 5 = 40   40 × 6 = 240

b Add to find the number of pieces of fruit at first.
40 + 200 = 240
The vendor has 240 pieces of fruit at first.
My answers are correct.

TRY Practice finding parts of a whole to solve real-world problems

Solve. Use the bar model to help you.

1 Amanda has 48 plants in her vegetable garden. Of the 48 plants, $\frac{2}{3}$ are carrots and $\frac{1}{4}$ are tomatoes. The rest of the plants are pumpkins. How many pumpkin plants are in the garden?

The first common multiple of 3 and 4 is 12. Draw a bar model with 12 equal units.

$\frac{2}{3}$ of 12 units = _____ × _____

= _____

$\frac{1}{4}$ of 12 units = _____ × _____

= _____

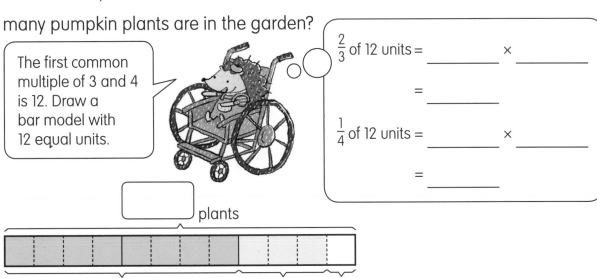

_____ plants

The bar model shows that:

_____ units = _____ plants

1 unit = _____ ÷ _____ = _____ plants

Amanda has _____ pumpkin plants.

ENGAGE

a   Rachel collected some seashells. She painted $\frac{1}{5}$ of the seashells blue and $\frac{1}{2}$ of the remaining seashells red. There were 48 unpainted seashells. Draw a bar model to represent the problem. Then, write an equation to find the total number of painted seashells.

b   Rachel collected more seashells and painted some of them. If $\frac{3}{4}$ of all the seashells were unpainted and 96 were painted, how many of the seashells were unpainted?

LEARN Find fractional parts to solve real-world problems

1   Ms. Nelson had $480. She used $\frac{1}{3}$ of the money to buy a winter coat and $\frac{1}{4}$ of the remainder on a pair of winter boots. How much money did Ms. Nelson have left?

▶ **Method 1**

$1 - \frac{1}{3} = \frac{2}{3}$

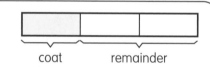
coat   remainder

Remainder ⟶ 2 parts

To show $\frac{1}{4}$ of the remainder which is spent on the boots, I have

to further divide the remainder into 4 parts.
First common multiple of 2 and 4 = 4
By equivalent fractions:

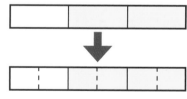

$$\frac{2}{3} = \frac{4}{6}$$

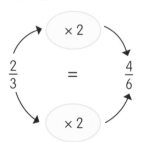

I need to draw a bar model with 6 equal units to show the problem.

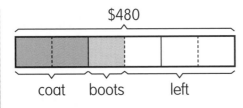

$480

$\frac{1}{3}$ of 6 units = 2 units

$\frac{1}{4}$ of 4 units = 1 unit

coat   boots   left

The bar model shows that:

6 units = $480

1 unit = $480 ÷ 6

= $80

3 units = 3 × $80

= $240

Ms. Nelson had $240 left.

▶ **Method 2**

$\frac{1}{3}$ of $480 = $\frac{1}{3}$ × $480

= $160

Ms. Nelson spent $160 on the coat.

$480 − $160 = $320

After buying the coat, she had $320 left.

$1 - \frac{1}{4} = \frac{3}{4}$

$\frac{3}{4}$ of $320 = $\frac{3}{4}$ × $\overset{80}{\cancel{$320}}$

= $240

Ms. Nelson had $240 left.

2 Noah took a test with three sections A, B, and C. He spent $\frac{1}{5}$ of his time on Section A and $\frac{1}{3}$ of the remaining time on Section B. He spent 48 minutes on Section C. How much time did Noah take to complete the test?

▶ **Method 1**

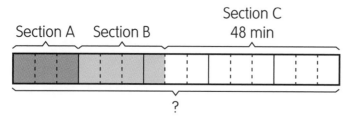

8 units = 48 min
1 unit = 48 ÷ 8
     = 6 min
15 units = 6 × 15
     = 90 min

Noah took 90 minutes to complete the test.

▶ **Method 2**

$\frac{1}{3} \times \frac{4}{5} = \frac{4}{15}$

Noah spent $\frac{4}{15}$ of the total time on Section B.

$\frac{1}{5} + \frac{4}{15} = \frac{7}{15}$

Noah spent $\frac{7}{15}$ of the total time on Sections A and B.

$1 - \frac{7}{15} = \frac{8}{15}$

Noah spent $\frac{8}{15}$ of the total time on Section C.

$\frac{8}{15}$ of the total time = 48 min

$\frac{1}{15}$ of the total time = 48 ÷ 8
               = 6 min

Total time = 6 × 15
        = 90 min

Noah took 90 minutes to complete the test.

TRY Practice finding fractional parts to solve real-world problems

Solve. Use the bar model to help you.

1 Kylie prepared a mixture of apple, carrot, and strawberry juices. Of the total amount, $\frac{1}{3}$ of the mixture was apple juice. $\frac{2}{5}$ of the remainder was strawberry juice. Kylie used 315 milliliters of strawberry juice in the mixture. How many milliliters of carrot juice were in the mixture?

$1 - \frac{1}{3} = $ _____

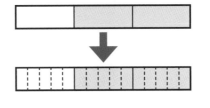

apple juice   remainder

Remainder ⟶ _____ parts

To show $\frac{2}{5}$ of the remainder which was strawberry juice, I have to further divide the remainder into _____ units.

First common multiple of _____ and _____ = _____

By equivalent fractions:

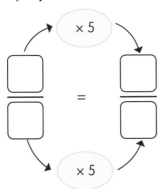

I need to draw a bar model with _____ equal units to show the problem.

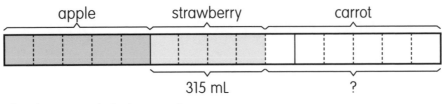

The bar model shows that:

4 units = 315 mL
1 unit = 315 ÷ 4

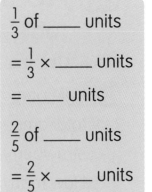

$\dfrac{1}{3}$ of _____ units

$= \dfrac{1}{3} \times$ _____ units

= _____ units

$\dfrac{2}{5}$ of _____ units

$= \dfrac{2}{5} \times$ _____ units

= _____ units

$$= \dfrac{\boxed{}}{\boxed{}} \text{ mL}$$

$$6 \text{ units} = 6 \times \dfrac{\boxed{}}{\boxed{}}$$

= _____ mL

_____ milliliters of the mixture were carrot juice.

2 Diego collects stamps as a hobby. He gives his cousin $\dfrac{1}{3}$ of his stamp collection. He then gives his sister $\dfrac{5}{6}$ of the remainder and has 80 stamps left. How many stamps did he have at first?

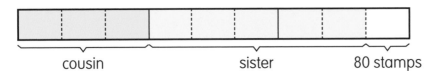

The bar model shows that:

1 unit = _____ stamps

_____ units = 9 × _____

= _____ stamps

Diego had _____ stamps at first.

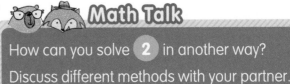

Math Talk

How can you solve 2 in another way?
Discuss different methods with your partner.

ENGAGE

Mr. Parker had $\frac{3}{4}$ of a gallon of juice. He used $\frac{1}{2}$ of the juice to make punch.

a   Draw a bar model to represent the problem. Then, write an equation to find the amount of juice used to make punch.

b   He poured the remaining juice equally into 3 glasses. What fraction of juice was in each glass?

LEARN Find fractional parts of a remainder to solve real-world problems

1   Ana makes $\frac{4}{5}$ gallon of lemonade. She pours $\frac{1}{4}$ of the lemonade equally into two glasses and the remaining lemonade into a jug. How much lemonade is in each glass?

▶ Method 1

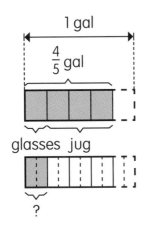

The bar model shows that:

10 units = 1 gal

1 unit = $\frac{1}{10}$ gal

There is $\frac{1}{10}$ gallon of lemonade in each glass.

▶ **Method 2**

Fraction of lemonade poured into 2 glasses $= \dfrac{4}{5} \times \dfrac{1}{4}$

$\qquad\qquad\qquad\qquad\qquad\qquad\qquad\qquad = \dfrac{1}{5}$

Amount of lemonade in 1 glass $= \dfrac{1}{5} \div 2$

$\qquad\qquad\qquad\qquad\qquad\quad = \dfrac{1}{5} \times \dfrac{1}{2}$

$\qquad\qquad\qquad\qquad\qquad\quad = \dfrac{1}{10}$

There is $\dfrac{1}{10}$ gallon of lemonade in each glass.

TRY Practice finding fractional parts of a remainder to solve real-world problems

Solve. Use the bar model to help you.

1 Brian buys $\dfrac{3}{4}$ pound of nuts. $\dfrac{1}{6}$ of the weight of the nuts are from walnuts and the rest are from almonds. Brian packs the almonds equally into 10 jars. What is the weight of the almonds in each jar?

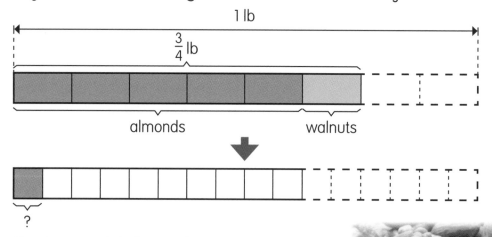

The bar model shows that:

16 units = _____ lb

1 unit = $\dfrac{\boxed{}}{\boxed{}}$ lb

There is _____ pound of almonds in each jar.

a A farmer had 4 kilograms of strawberries. He sold 2 kilograms to a fruit seller. He then packed the remaining strawberries into boxes of $\frac{2}{5}$ kilogram each. Draw a bar model to represent the problem. Then, write an equation to find the number of boxes the farmer packed.

b If he harvested another 3 kilograms of strawberries, how many more $\frac{2}{5}$-kilogram boxes of strawberries could he pack?

LEARN Divide fractions and whole numbers to solve real-world problems

1 Matthew buys 5 square yards of wrapping paper to wrap a large gift box and some small gift boxes. He uses 2 square yards of paper to wrap the large box, and uses the rest to wrap the small boxes. He uses $\frac{1}{2}$ square yard of paper for each small box. How many small gift boxes does Matthew wrap?

▶ **Method 1**

Wrapping paper used for the small gift boxes
= 5 − 2
= 3 square yards

Number of small gift boxes = number of $\frac{1}{2}$ square yards in 3 square yards

2 yd² of wrapping paper
for the large gift box   3 yd² of wrapping paper
                                for the small gift boxes

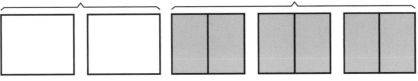

The model shows that:
Number of $\frac{1}{2}$ square yards in 3 square yards = 6
Matthew wraps 6 small gift boxes.

▶ Method 2

Wrapping paper used for the small gift boxes
$= 5 - 2$
$= 3$ square yards

Number of small gift boxes $= 3 \div \dfrac{1}{2}$
$= 3 \times 2$
$= 6$

Matthew wraps 6 small gift boxes.

Hands-on Activity ▶ Creating word problems

Work in pairs.

(1) Write a word problem to represent the expression.

$$\dfrac{1}{5} \div 6$$

(2) Ask your partner to draw a bar model for the problem and solve it.

(3) Trade places and repeat (1) and (2) using the expression $6 \div \frac{1}{5}$.

Word problem:

Bar model and solution:

TRY Practice dividing fractions and whole numbers to solve real-world problems

Solve. Use the bar model to help you.

① Bruno is watering some plants. He has 7 gallons of water. He uses 2 gallons of water to water the plants in his backyard, and uses the rest to water some potted plants. If he uses $\frac{1}{6}$ gallon of water for each potted plant, how many potted plants can he water?

Water used to water potted plants

= _____ − _____

= _____ gallons

Number of potted plants = Number of _____ gallon of water

in _____ gallons

⬜ gallons of water for the plants in his backyard

⬜ gallons of water for the potted plants

The bar model shows that:

Number of _____ gallon of water in _____ gallons

= _____ × _____

= _____

He can water _____ potted plants.

Math Talk
Discuss with your partner different methods to solve the problem.

INDEPENDENT PRACTICE

Solve. Draw a bar model to help you.

1. Hana has 324 tickets to sell for charity. She sells $\frac{2}{9}$ of the tickets to her family. She sells $\frac{1}{3}$ of the remaining tickets to her friends.

   a   How many tickets does Hana sell in all?

   b   How many tickets does she have left?

2 It took Henry 1 hour 40 minutes to run 3 laps in a road race. He ran the first lap in $\frac{1}{4}$ of the time and the second lap in $\frac{1}{5}$ of the time. Henry ran the last lap in the time that was left.

a How many minutes did it take Henry to complete the race?

b How many minutes did he take to run the third lap of the race?

3 Melanie had 3 pounds of dried fruit. She packed the dried fruit into bags of $\frac{3}{8}$ pound each.

    a How many bags of dried fruit did she pack?

    b In each bag, $\frac{1}{4}$ of the pieces of dried fruit were raisins. $\frac{1}{2}$ of the remaining pieces of fruit were bananas. There were 48 slices of dried banana. The remaining pieces of dried fruit were raspberries. How many pieces of raisins and dried raspberries were there in each bag?

Solve.

④ Clara has 3 bottles of paint. She buys 5 more bottles of paint. If she uses $\frac{1}{4}$ bottle of paint to paint a picture, how many similar paintings can she paint with all of the paint?

Mathematical Habit 3 **Construct viable arguments**

Luna and David were each given a problem to solve.

1 Luna: $\frac{1}{9} \div 3$

2 David: $\frac{1}{9} \times \frac{4}{11}$

They obtained answers to the problems as follows:

1 Luna: $\frac{1}{9} \div 3 = \frac{1}{3}$

2 David: $\frac{1}{9} \times \frac{4}{11} = \frac{5}{20}$

However, their answers are incorrect. Give explanations as to how they could have possibly arrived at these incorrect answers. Write the correct way to solve each problem.

$\frac{1}{9} \div 3 = \frac{1}{3}$

$9 \bigcirc 3 = 3$

Luna found the answer $\frac{1}{3}$ by

_____.

The correct way to solve the problem should have been:

$\frac{1}{9} \div 3 = \frac{1}{9} \bigcirc \dfrac{1}{\boxed{}}$

$= \underline{\hspace{2cm}}$

$\frac{1}{9} \times \frac{4}{11} = \frac{5}{20}$

$1 \bigcirc 4 = 5$

$9 \bigcirc 11 = 20$

David found the answer $\frac{5}{20}$ by

_____.

The correct way to solve the problem should have been:

$\frac{1}{9} \times \frac{4}{11} = \dfrac{\boxed{} \times \boxed{}}{\boxed{} \times \boxed{}}$

$= \underline{\hspace{2cm}}$

Problem Solving with Heuristics

1 | Mathematical Habit 8 | Look for patterns

a One of the masses in the pattern below is wrong. Can you find the correct mass?

7,000 g $\frac{5}{6}$ kg $\frac{1}{2}$ of 38 kg 31 kg $1\frac{1}{4}$ of 37,600 g

b Look at the pattern below and fill in the blank.

2,000 g $\frac{1}{3}$ of 18 kg 18,000 g _____ kg $\frac{1}{3}$ of 486 kg

2 | Mathematical Habit 2 | Use mathematical reasoning

Use some of the fractions or whole numbers below to complete the equation.

$\frac{3}{8}$, 120, $\frac{7}{8}$, 105

_____ × _____ = _____

3 **Mathematical Habit 7** **Make use of structure**

Find the value of the expression.

$$\left(1-\frac{1}{100}\right)\times\left(1-\frac{1}{101}\right)\times\left(1-\frac{1}{102}\right)\cdots\left(1-\frac{1}{200}\right)=\underline{\hspace{2cm}}$$

4 **Mathematical Habit 1** **Persevere in solving problems**

Ivan was the 31st person in line. His position in line was just behind $\frac{5}{9}$ of the total number of people in line. How many people were in line?

5 **Mathematical Habit 1** **Persevere in solving problems**

Franco bought 10 model cars. Sophie bought $1\frac{1}{2}$ times as many of the same model cars as Franco. All of the cars had the same price. Altogether, Franco and Sophie paid $75 for the model cars. What was the cost of each model car?

How do we multiply and divide fractions, mixed numbers, and whole numbers? How do the factors affect the product if one of the factors is a fraction?

Multiplying and Dividing Fractions and Mixed Numbers

Multiplying Fractions and Whole Numbers

$$\frac{3}{4} \text{ of } 16 = \frac{3}{4} \times 16$$

$$= \frac{3 \times 16}{4}$$

$$= \frac{48}{4}$$

$$= 12$$

$$\frac{5}{2} \times 3 = \frac{5 \times 3}{2}$$

$$= \frac{15}{2}$$

$$= 7\frac{1}{2}$$

Multiplying Proper Fractions

$$\frac{3}{5} \times \frac{1}{2}$$

$$= \frac{3 \times 1}{5 \times 2}$$

$$= \frac{3}{10}$$

Simplify the fractions before multiplying the numerators and denominators.

$$\frac{2}{3} \times \frac{5}{6} = \frac{2}{3} \times \frac{5}{\overset{}{6}_{3}}^{1}$$

$$= \frac{1 \times 5}{3 \times 3}$$

$$= \frac{5}{9}$$

Multiplying Improper Fractions

Method 1
Multiply the numerators and denominators. Then, simplify.

$$\frac{6}{5} \times \frac{3}{4} = \frac{6 \times 3}{5 \times 4}$$

$$= \frac{18}{20}$$

$$= \frac{9}{10}$$

$$\frac{6}{5} \times \frac{3}{2} = \frac{6 \times 3}{5 \times 2}$$

$$= \frac{18}{10}$$

$$= \frac{9}{5}$$

$$= 1\frac{4}{5}$$

Method 2
Simplify the fractions before multiplying the numerators and denominators.

$$\frac{9}{4} \times \frac{2}{3} = \frac{\overset{3}{\cancel{9}}}{\underset{2}{\cancel{4}}} \times \frac{\overset{1}{\cancel{2}}}{\underset{1}{\cancel{3}}}$$

$$= \frac{3 \times 1}{2 \times 1}$$

$$= \frac{3}{2}$$

$$= 1\frac{1}{2}$$

$$\frac{4}{3} \times \frac{9}{8} = \frac{\overset{1}{\cancel{4}}}{\underset{1}{\cancel{3}}} \times \frac{\overset{3}{\cancel{9}}}{\underset{2}{\cancel{8}}}$$

$$= \frac{1 \times 3}{1 \times 2}$$

$$= \frac{3}{2}$$

$$= 1\frac{1}{2}$$

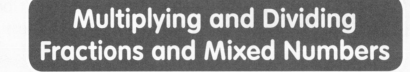

Multiplying and Dividing Fractions and Mixed Numbers

Multiplying Mixed Numbers and Whole Numbers

$12 \times 3\frac{5}{9}$

$= 12 \times \frac{32}{9}$

$= \frac{12 \times 32}{9}$

$= \frac{384}{9}$

$= 42\frac{6}{9}$

$= 42\frac{2}{3}$

$1\frac{1}{2} \times 3 = \frac{3}{2} \times 3$

$= \frac{3 \times 3}{2}$

$= \frac{9}{2}$

$= 4\frac{1}{2}$

Dividing a Fraction by a Whole Number

$\frac{1}{7} \div 8$

$= \frac{1}{7} \div \frac{8}{1}$

$= \frac{1}{7} \times \frac{1}{8}$

$= \frac{1}{56}$

$\frac{4}{7} \div 2$

$= \frac{\overset{2}{\cancel{4}}}{7} \div \frac{1}{\underset{1}{\cancel{2}}}$

$= \frac{2}{7}$

Dividing a Whole Number by a Unit Fraction

$4 \div \frac{1}{3}$

$= 4 \times 3$

$= 12$

You can use square tiles or area models to multiply two mixed numbers.

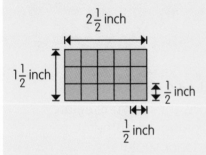

$2\frac{1}{2}$ inch

$1\frac{1}{2}$ inch

$\frac{1}{2}$ inch

$\frac{1}{2}$ inch

$1\frac{1}{2} \times 2\frac{1}{2} = 15 \times \frac{1}{4}$

$= \frac{15}{4}$

$= 3\frac{3}{4}$

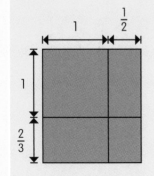

$1 \qquad \frac{1}{2}$

1

$\frac{2}{3}$

$1\frac{2}{3} \times 1\frac{1}{2} = (1 \times 1) + \left(1 \times \frac{2}{3}\right) + \left(1 \times \frac{1}{2}\right) + \left(\frac{1}{2} \times \frac{2}{3}\right)$

$= 1 + \frac{2}{3} + \frac{1}{2} + \frac{1}{3}$

$= 2\frac{1}{2}$

Name: _____ Date: _____

Multiply. Express each product in simplest form.

1 $\frac{2}{3} \times 24$

2 $\frac{5}{8} \times 32$

3 $\frac{4}{3} \times 12$

4 $\frac{7}{4} \times 28$

Multiply. Express each product in simplest form.

5 $\frac{1}{2} \times \frac{4}{7}$

6 $\frac{3}{8} \times \frac{2}{5}$

7 $\frac{4}{5} \times \frac{7}{8}$

8 $\frac{2}{3} \times \frac{9}{10}$

Multiply. Express each product in simplest form.

9 $\dfrac{8}{15} \times \dfrac{5}{4}$

10 $\dfrac{10}{3} \times \dfrac{12}{7}$

11 $\dfrac{16}{9} \times \dfrac{3}{2}$

12 $\dfrac{18}{4} \times \dfrac{28}{3}$

13 $5\dfrac{1}{4} \times 8$

14 $14 \times 3\dfrac{5}{6}$

15 $6 \times 2\dfrac{3}{8}$

16 $3\dfrac{5}{6} \times 4$

Use square tiles to multiply the pair of mixed numbers. Express each product in simplest form.

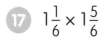 $1\frac{1}{6} \times 1\frac{5}{6}$

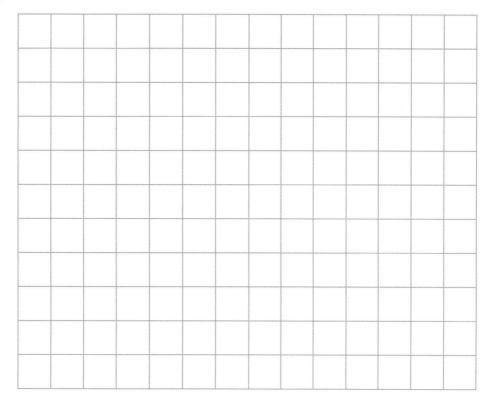

Draw an area model to multiply the pair of mixed numbers. Express each product in simplest form.

18 $3\frac{3}{5} \times 6\frac{1}{9}$

Divide. Express each quotient in simplest form.

19 $\frac{1}{5} \div 6$

20 $\frac{1}{6} \div 3$

21 $4 \div \frac{1}{6}$

22 $14 \div \frac{1}{8}$

Solve. Draw a bar model to help you.

23 A store sells T-shirts. $\frac{1}{4}$ of the T-shirts are pink, $\frac{1}{2}$ of the remaining T-shirts are white, and the rest are purple. What fraction of the T-shirts are purple?

Solve.

24 Chris works $1\frac{3}{4}$ hours a day at a bookstore. If he is paid $9 an hour, how much money does he earn in 5 days?

25 Sofia has a rectangular piece of fabric $1\frac{7}{8}$ yards long and $1\frac{4}{5}$ yards wide. What is the area of the piece of fabric?

26 Of the total number of people on a cruise ship, $\frac{1}{4}$ were child passengers. $\frac{2}{5}$ of the remaining people were crew. There were 1,320 crew onboard. How many adult passengers were there?

Assessment Prep

Answer each question.

27 What is the product of $\frac{9}{4}$ and $\frac{12}{5}$?

Ⓐ $\frac{45}{48}$

Ⓑ $\frac{21}{9}$

Ⓒ $\frac{27}{45}$

Ⓓ $\frac{27}{5}$

28 Choose the **two** correct statements.

A) The product of $3\frac{1}{4}$ and $1\frac{2}{5}$ is less than $1\frac{2}{5}$.

B) The product of $3\frac{1}{4}$ and $1\frac{2}{5}$ is greater than $3\frac{1}{4}$.

C) The product of 5 and $\frac{6}{7}$ is less than $\frac{6}{7}$.

D) The product of 5 and $\frac{6}{7}$ is greater than 5.

E) The product of $\frac{9}{2}$ and $\frac{7}{3}$ is less than $\frac{9}{2}$.

F) The product of $\frac{9}{2}$ and $\frac{7}{3}$ is greater than $\frac{7}{3}$.

29 Lucas made a poster measuring $\frac{3}{5}$ meter long and $\frac{3}{4}$ meter wide. What is the area of the poster in square meters?

30 Valery spent $\frac{1}{5}$ of her money buying 8 pencils and 2 markers. Each marker cost twice as much as each pencil. She used $\frac{5}{8}$ of her remaining money buying more markers. How many markers did Valery buy in all?

Show your working and explanation in the space below.

Name: _____ Date: _____

Summer Job

1 Owen earned some money at a summer job. He saved $\frac{1}{4}$ of the money and spent $\frac{1}{3}$ of the rest on a T-shirt. He then spent the remaining money on downloading some songs. What fraction of the money did he spend on the downloads? Show your work.

2 If the T-shirt cost $20, how much money did Owen earn at the summer job? Show your work.

3 Owen played a list of songs without repeating the same song twice.

He listened to $\frac{1}{3}$ of the list of songs before he began studying.

After studying, he listened to $\frac{1}{3}$ of the remaining songs in the list.

He wondered what fraction of the songs he had yet to listen to.

He thought that $1 - \frac{1}{3} - \frac{1}{3}$ would give him the answer. Is that correct?

If so, explain why and solve. If not, show his mistake and find the

correct fraction.

4 Owen's summer job was selling newspapers. One morning, he sold 24 newspapers. In the afternoon, he sold $\frac{2}{7}$ of the remaining newspapers. The number of newspapers left was $\frac{1}{2}$ of the number of newspapers he started with. How many newspapers did Owen start with? Use a diagram and/or equations to show your work.

Rubric

Point(s)	Level	My Performance
7–8	4	• Most of my answers are correct. • I showed complete understanding of what I have learned. • I used the correct strategies to solve the problems. • I explained my answers and mathematical thinking clearly and completely.
5–6.5	3	• Some of my answers are correct. • I showed some understanding of what I have learned. • I used some correct strategies to solve the problems. • I explained my answers and mathematical thinking clearly.
3–4.5	2	• A few of my answers are correct. • I showed little understanding of what I have learned. • I used a few correct strategies to solve the problems. • I explained some of my answers and mathematical thinking clearly.
0–2.5	1	• A few of my answers are correct. • I showed little or no understanding of what I have learned. • I used a few strategies to solve the problems. • I did not explain my answers and mathematical thinking clearly.

Teacher's Comments

Boy's 50-Meter Butterfly Race

Athlete	Times (in seconds)
Bennett	51.211
Diego	51.44
Ang	51.801
Luke	51.81
Zachary	51.82

Who is the fastest?
How do you compare the times?

What is the value of the second decimal place? What will be the value of the third decimal place?

Name: _____   Date: _____

Understanding tenths

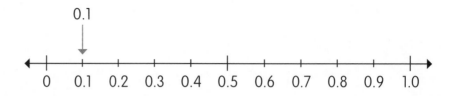

$\frac{1}{10}$ is 0.1 or 1 tenth.

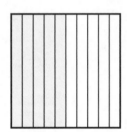
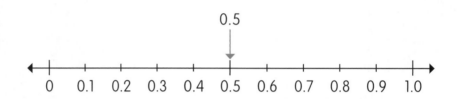

$\frac{5}{10}$ is 0.5 or 5 tenths.

▶ **Quick Check**

Find the decimal represented by the shaded parts.

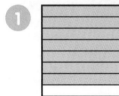

1   _____

Find the decimal represented by the labeled point.

2

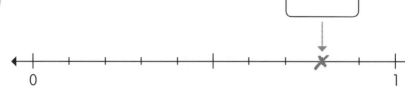

Understanding hundredths

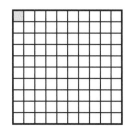

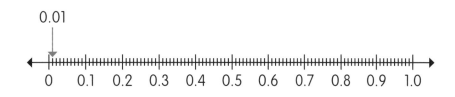

$\frac{1}{100}$ is 0.01 or 1 hundredth.

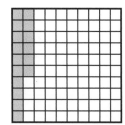

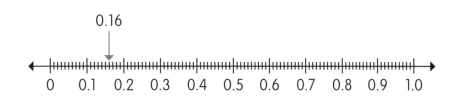

$\frac{16}{100}$ is 0.16 or 16 hundredths.

▶ Quick Check

Find the decimal represented by the shaded parts.

③

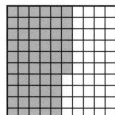

_____

Find the decimal represented by the labeled point.

④

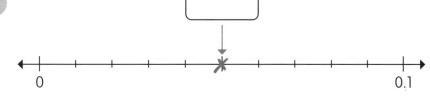

Understanding tenths and hundredths

10 tenths = 1 one

$$\frac{10}{10} = 1$$

10 hundredths = 1 tenth

$$\frac{10}{100} = \frac{1}{10}$$

0.23 = 23 hundredths

= 2 tenths 3 hundredths

$$= \frac{2}{10} + \frac{3}{100}$$

$$= \frac{23}{100}$$

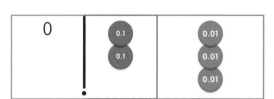

▶ Quick Check

Write each decimal.

 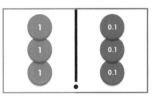

_____

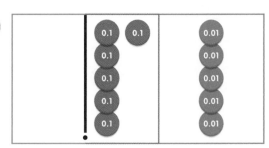

_____

Comparing decimals

Ones	Tenths	Hundredths
2	3	
2	1	3

2.3 is greater than 2.13.

▶ Quick Check

Which decimal is greater?

7   1.28 or 1.5 _____

Ones	Tenths	Hundredths
1	2	8
1	5	

8   5.63 or 5.68 _____

Ones	Tenths	Hundredths
5	6	3
5	6	8

Expressing fractions as decimals

Proper fractions

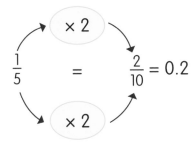

$$\frac{1}{5} = \frac{2}{10} = 0.2$$

Improper fractions

$$\frac{5}{4} = \frac{4}{4} + \frac{1}{4}$$
$$= 1 + \frac{1}{4}$$
$$= 1 + 0.25$$
$$= 1.25$$

▶ Quick Check

Express each fraction as a decimal.

9 $\frac{3}{4}$  _____

10 $\frac{12}{8}$ _____

Expressing mixed numbers as decimals

Express $1\frac{3}{5}$ as a decimal.

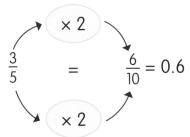

$$\frac{3}{5} = \frac{6}{10} = 0.6$$

$$1\frac{3}{5} = 1 + \frac{3}{5}$$
$$= 1 + \frac{6}{10}$$
$$= 1 + 0.6$$
$$= 1.6$$

▶ Quick Check

Express each mixed number as a decimal.

11 $1\frac{2}{5}$  _____

12 $2\frac{3}{4}$  _____

Rounding decimals to the nearest whole number

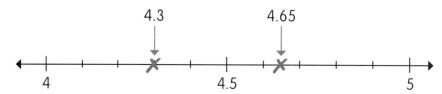

When the tenths digit is 0, 1, 2, 3, or 4, round to the lesser whole number.
4.**3** rounds to 4.

When the tenths digit is 5, 6, 7, 8, or 9, round to the greater whole number.
4.**6**5 rounds to 5.

▶ Quick Check

Round each decimal to the nearest whole number.

13 3.07 _____

14 6.5 _____

15 12.48 _____

16 88.63 _____

Rounding decimals to the nearest tenth

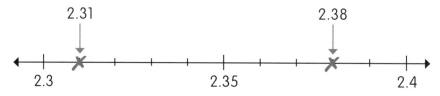

When the hundredths digit is 0, 1, 2, 3, or 4, round to the lesser tenth.
2.3**1** rounds to 2.3.

When the hundredths digit is 5, 6, 7, 8, or 9, round to the greater tenth.
2.3**8** rounds to 2.4.

▶ Quick Check

Round each decimal to the nearest tenth.

17 0.92 _____

18 4.86 _____

19 28.03 _____

20 56.34 _____

1 Understanding Thousandths

Learning Objective:
• Read and write thousandths in decimal and fractional form.

New Vocabulary
thousandth

THINK

A, B, C, and D represent the digits in the decimal A.BCD. The digit in the thousandths place is the greatest. The digit in the tenths place is one third of the digit in the thousandths place but greater than the digit in the hundredths place. The digit in the ones place is the least. What are the possible values of the decimal above?

ENGAGE

Find all possible values of A and B.

$$20.43 = 2 \times A + \frac{3}{10} + \frac{B}{100}$$

LEARN Express **thousandths** as decimals

1

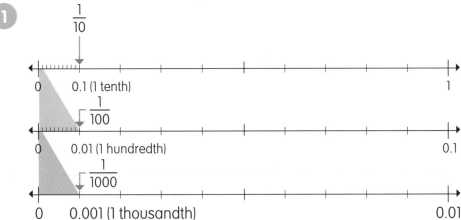

We write 1 thousandth as $\frac{1}{1,000}$ or 0.001.

> We read 0.001 as **zero point zero zero one**.

We write 2 thousandths as $\frac{2}{1,000}$ or 0.002.

> We read 0.002 as **zero point zero zero two**.

Math Talk

What is another way to read 0.002?

2 You can exchange 1 hundredth for 10 thousandths.

0.01 ⟷ (0.001 0.001 0.001 0.001 0.001 0.001 0.001 0.001 0.001 0.001)

1 hundredth = 10 thousandths

3 Express $2\frac{314}{1,000}$ as a decimal.

$2\frac{314}{1,000} = 2.314$

$\frac{314}{1,000}$ = 314 thousandths

= 3 tenths
  1 hundredth
  4 thousandths

Math Talk

We read 2.314 as two point three one four.
What is another way to read 2.314?

4 Represent 2.314 on a place-value chart.

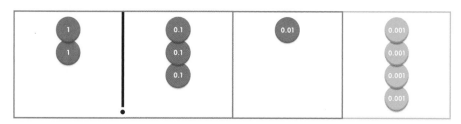

Ones	Tenths	Hundredths	Thousandths
2	3	1	4

stands for **2 ones**   stands for **3 tenths**   stands for **1 hundredth**   stands for **4 thousandths**

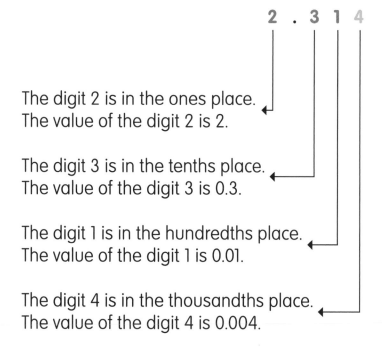

2 . 3 1 4

The digit 2 is in the ones place.
The value of the digit 2 is 2.

The digit 3 is in the tenths place.
The value of the digit 3 is 0.3.

The digit 1 is in the hundredths place.
The value of the digit 1 is 0.01.

The digit 4 is in the thousandths place.
The value of the digit 4 is 0.004.

2.314 = 2 ones 3 tenths 1 hundredth 4 thousandths
= $(2 \times 1) + (3 \times 0.1) + (1 \times 0.01) + (4 \times 0.001)$
= 2 + 0.3 + 0.01 + 0.004

5 Thousandths can be represented on a number line.

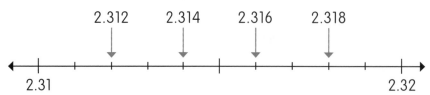

2.312 2.314 2.316 2.318

2.31 2.32

Hands-on Activity **Expressing thousandths as decimals**

1 Use 〔10〕〔1〕〔0.1〕〔0.01〕〔0.001〕 to show the following decimals and write them on the place-value chart.

Ones	Tenths	Hundredths	Thousandths

a 6.3
b 7.64
c 0.562
d 3.986

2 Find the value of the digit 6 in the decimals in **1**.

a _____ b _____ c _____ d _____

3 What do you notice about the values of each digit 6 in the decimals?

Write each decimal.

1  _____

2 _____

Express each of the following as a decimal.

3 627 thousandths = _____

4 $\frac{5}{1,000}$ = _____

5 $\frac{972}{1,000}$ = _____

6 $5\frac{718}{1,000}$ = _____

Find the decimal that each labeled point represents.

7

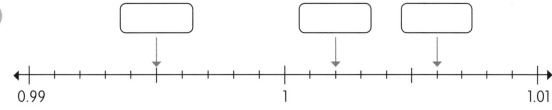

0.99   1   1.01

Fill in each blank.

8 In 2.315,

a the digit _____ is in the ones place.

b the digit _____ is in the tenths place.

c the digit _____ is in the hundredths place.

d the digit _____ is in the thousandths place.

9 In 4.072,

    a the value of the digit 4 is _____.

    b the value of the digit 0 is _____.

    c the value of the digit 7 is _____.

    d the value of the digit 2 is _____.

Fill in each blank.

10 $5 + 0.3 + 0.07 + 0.004 =$ _____

11 $6 + 0.4 + 0.08 +$ _____ $= 6.481$

12 $2.637 = 2 +$ _____ $+ 0.03 + 0.007$

13 $1.053 = 1 +$ _____ $+ 0.003$

Mathematical Habit 3 Construct viable arguments

Explain and show using a place-value chart or 10 1 0.1 0.01 0.001 why the following decimals are equal.

a   0.2   b   0.20   c   0.200

Ask your partner to show 0.08 in two different ways.

INDEPENDENT PRACTICE

Write each decimal.

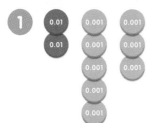

1 _____

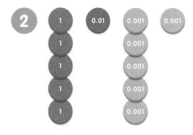

2 _____

Express each of the following as a decimal.

3 8 thousandths = _____

4 29 thousandths = _____

5 534 thousandths = _____

6 $\frac{706}{1,000}$ = _____

7 $4\frac{18}{1,000}$ = _____

8 $3\frac{891}{1,000}$ = _____

Find the decimal that each labeled point represents.

9

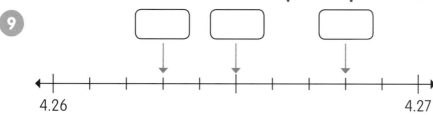

Fill in each blank.

10 In 5,349.106, the digit _____ is in the thousands place and

the digit _____ is in the thousandths place.

11 In 3.027, the digit 7 stands for _____.

12 In 2.814, the digit 1 stands for _____.

13 In 9.046, the value of the digit 9 is _____.

14 In 5.103, the value of the digit 3 is _____.

Fill in each blank.

15 $4 + 0.3 + 0.05 + 0.002 =$ _____

16 $7 + 0.6 +$ _____ $= 7.601$

17 $3.018 = 3 + 0.01 +$ _____

18 $5.246 = 5 +$ _____ $+ 0.04 + 0.006$

19 $6.901 = 6 + 0.9 +$ _____

Name: _____ Date: _____

 **Comparing, Ordering, and Rounding Decimals**

Learning Objectives:
• Compare and order decimals to 3 decimal places.
• Round decimals to the nearest hundredth.

THINK

Five decimals, 8.122, 8.126, 8.128, A, and B, can be ordered in various patterns. Find two possible sets of values of A and B.

ENGAGE

1 Using the digits 4, 1, and 7, make two decimals up to hundredths. One has to be the greatest and the other the least.

2 Find the least and greatest value of the digit A that makes the sentence true: 8.63 > A.59.

LEARN Compare and order decimals to 3 decimal places

1 Which is greater, 1.143 or 1.135?

▶ **Method 1**

Ones	Tenths	Hundredths	Thousandths
1	1	4	3
1	1	3	5

 STEP 1 The ones and tenths are equal.

STEP 2 Compare the hundredths.
4 hundredths are greater than **3** hundredths.

1.143 is greater than 1.135.
1.143 > 1.135

▶ Method 2

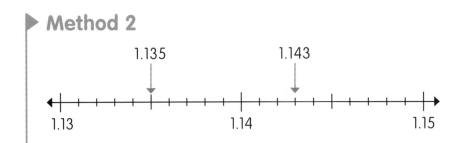

1.143 is greater than 1.135.
1.143 > 1.135

2 Order 0.72, 0.273, and 0.7 from least to greatest.

Ones	Tenths	Hundredths	Thousandths
0	7	2	0
0	2	7	3
0	7	0	0

STEP 1 Compare the ones.
They are the same.

STEP 2 Compare the tenths.
2 tenths are less
than **7** tenths.
So, 0.273 is the least.

STEP 3 Compare the hundredths
of the remaining numbers.
2 hundredths are greater
than **0** hundredths.
0.72 is greater than 0.7.
So, 0.72 is the greatest.

The order from least to greatest is 0.273, 0.7, 0.72.

Activity 1   Comparing decimals using ⑩ ① ⓪·¹ ⓪·⁰¹ ⓪·⁰⁰¹ **and number lines**

Work in pairs.

① Use ⑩ ① ⓪·¹ ⓪·⁰¹ ⓪·⁰⁰¹ to show 2.108 and 2.081. Then, use the number line to show the two decimals.

⟵├┼┼┼┼┼┼┼┼┼┼┼┼┼┼┼┼┼┼┼┼┼┼┼┼┼┼┼┼┼┼┤⟶

② Ask your partner to compare the decimals and explain which decimal is greater or less.

③ Trade places. Repeat ① and ② with each of the following.

   a   3.294 and 3.49

⟵├┼┼┼┼┼┼┼┼┼┼┼┼┼┼┼┼┼┼┼┼┼┼┼┼┤⟶

   b   1.079 and 1.077

⟵├┼┼┼┼┼┼┼┼┼┼┤⟶

Activity 2   Using 🔟 ① 🔘 🔘 🔘 to describe, compare, and order decimals

Work in pairs.

① Use 🔟 ① 🔘 🔘 🔘 to show each decimal.

    a 2.654   b 2.648   c 2.659

② Ask your partner to describe the decimals using **greater than**, **less than**, **greatest**, **least**, or **the same as**.

③ Order the decimals from greatest to least.

  _____   _____   _____

    greatest   least

④ Trade places. Repeat ① to ③ with the following.

    a 1.052,   1.2,   1.205

      _____   _____   _____

        greatest   least

    b 4.308,   4.31,   4.315

      _____   _____   _____

        greatest   least

TRY Practice comparing and ordering decimals

Compare each pair of decimals. Circle the greater decimal.

1 10.35   9.535

2 3.081   3.18

3 0.012   0.12

Compare each pair of decimals. Circle the lesser decimal.

4 6.423   6.427

5 2.16   2.611

6 0.303   0.33

Compare each pair of decimals. Write <, >, or =.

7 8.217 ◯ 8.235

8 4.24 ◯ 4.24

9 4.24 ◯ 4.218

Order the decimals from greatest to least.

10 0.7,   0.18,   0.315

_____   _____   _____
greatest   least

11 0.19,   0.2,   0.185

_____   _____   _____
greatest   least

12 1.43,   1.345,   1.453

_____   _____   _____
greatest   least

Order the decimals from least to greatest.

13 1.008,   0.08,   0.108

_____   _____   _____
least   greatest

14 0.505,   0.055,   0.5

_____   _____   _____
least   greatest

15 0.251,   0.25,   0.215

_____   _____   _____
least   greatest

ENGAGE

Draw a number line with 0.01 and 0.02 as the endpoints. How can you divide the number line into equal intervals to find 0.012? Explain your reasoning to your partner. Is 0.012 nearer to 0.01 or 0.02? Explain.
What decimals are nearer to 0.01 than to 0.02? Explain.

LEARN Rounding decimals to the nearest hundredth

1. A sheet of plastic is 0.014 centimeter thick. Round 0.014 centimeter to 2 decimal places.

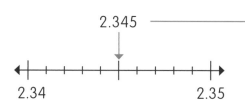

0.014 is between 0.01 and 0.02.
The digit in the thousandths place is 4.
So, it is nearer to 0.01 than to 0.02.

0.014 centimeter is 0.01 centimeter when rounded to 2 decimal places.

2. Round 2.345 to the nearest hundredth.

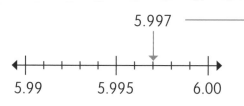

2.345 is exactly halfway between 2.34 and 2.35.

Rounding to the nearest hundredth is the same as rounding to 2 decimal places.

2.345 is 2.35 when rounded to the nearest hundredth.

3. Round 5.997 to 2 decimal places.

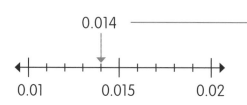

5.997 is between 5.99 and 6.00.
The digit in the thousandths place is 7.
So, it is nearer to 6.00 than to 5.99

5.997 is 6.00 when rounded to 2 decimal places.

6 is written as 6.00 to 2 decimal places.

TRY Practice rounding decimals to the nearest hundredth

Fill in each blank.

1 Round 99.826 to the nearest hundredth.

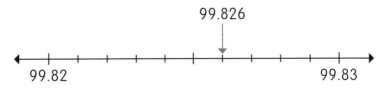

99.826 is between _____ and _____.

99.826 is nearer to _____ than to _____.

99.826 is _____ when rounded to the nearest hundredth.

Round each decimal to 2 decimal places.

2 6.457 _____

3 5.291 _____

4 9.035 _____

5 4.946 _____

6 2.198 _____

7 3.214 _____

INDEPENDENT PRACTICE

Compare each pair of decimals. Circle the greater decimal.

1 0.832   0.809

2 1.954   1.945

3 6.034   6.032

Compare each pair of decimals. Circle the lesser decimal.

4 0.052   0.205

5 8.763   8.736

6 13.574   13.475

Compare each pair of decimals. Write <, >, or =.

7 49.257 $\bigcirc$ 49.25

8 40.257 $\bigcirc$ 49.272

9 49.250 $\bigcirc$ 49.25

Order the decimals from least to greatest.

10 3.06,   3.6,   3.066,   3.006

_____   _____   _____   _____
　　least　　　　　　　　　　　　　　　　　　greatest

Order the decimals from greatest to least.

11 3.472,   2.472,   3.274,   2.427

_____   _____   _____   _____
　　greatest　　　　　　　　　　　　　　　　　least

Fill in each blank.

12 Rounding to the nearest hundredth is the same as rounding to _____ decimal places.

13 Round 1.038 to the nearest hundredth.

1.038 is between 1.03 and _____.

1.038 is nearer to _____ than to _____.

So, 1.038 rounds to _____.

Round each decimal to the nearest whole number, nearest tenth, and nearest hundredth.

	Decimal	Round to the nearest		
		Whole Number	Tenth	Hundredth
14	1.799			
15	31.999			

Name: _____ Date: _____

3 Decimals, Fractions, and Mixed Numbers

Learning Objective:
• Rewrite three-place decimals as fractions or mixed numbers in simplest form and vice versa.

 **THINK**

Jack ordered four decimals that are in thousandths. Two of the decimals are 0.003 and 0.005. What are the possible values of the other two decimals? Draw a number line to help you.

ENGAGE

a Write each decimal as a fraction: 0.002, 0.020, 0.200, 2.000.

b Write a list of decimals in thousandths that is nearer to 0.02 than 0.03.

LEARN Rewrite decimals, fractions, and mixed numbers

1 Rewrite 0.008 as a fraction in simplest form.

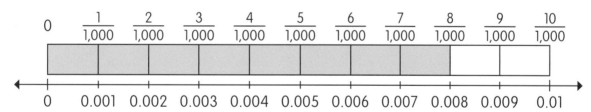

$0.008 = \dfrac{8}{1,000}$

$\quad\quad = \dfrac{1}{125}$

0.008 is $\dfrac{1}{125}$ in simplest form.

2 Rewrite 2.045 as a mixed number in simplest form.

$2.045 = 2\dfrac{45}{1,000}$

$\quad\quad = 2\dfrac{9}{200}$

2.045 is $2\dfrac{9}{200}$ in simplest form.

3 Rewrite $3\frac{5}{8}$ as a decimal.

$$3\frac{5}{8} = 3\frac{625}{1,000}$$
$$= 3.625$$

$3\frac{5}{8}$ is 3.625 as a decimal.

TRY Practice rewriting decimals, fractions, and mixed numbers

Rewrite each of the following as a fraction or mixed number in simplest form.

1 0.025

2 0.068

3 2.056

4 4.275

Rewrite each of the following as a decimal.

5 $1\frac{1}{125}$

6 $4\frac{7}{8}$

DECIMAL SNAP!

What you need:

Players: 4 to 5
Materials: Decimal cards, Fraction cards

What to do:

1. Put all the decimal cards face up on a table.

2. Shuffle the fraction cards and place the deck face down on the table. Then, turn over the top card.

3. Check to see if the fraction on the card is equivalent to any of the decimals on the cards on the table.

4. The fastest player to find a match will say, "Decimal snap!" and collects the two cards.

5. The other players check the answer. If the answer is wrong, the fraction card is put at the bottom of the card deck, and the decimal card is returned to the table.

6. Turn over the next fraction card and continue the game. Play until no more matches can be found.

Who is the winner?

The player who collects the most matching cards wins!

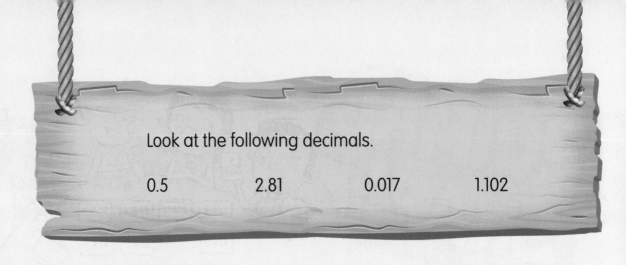

Look at the following decimals.

0.5   2.81   0.017   1.102

1. Fill in the decimals on a place-value chart. Write and insert a zero at any place in each decimal. Then, fill in the decimals formed on another place-value chart.

2. Compare the decimals formed with the given decimals.

3. Discuss with your classmates how inserting a zero in the different places of a decimal will change its value.

INDEPENDENT PRACTICE

Rewrite each of the following as a fraction or mixed number in simplest form.

1   0.064

2   0.175

3   1.035

4   2.179

5   5.552

Rewrite each of the following as a decimal.

6 $\frac{3}{8}$

7 $\frac{78}{125}$

8 $2\frac{9}{125}$

9 $5\frac{1}{8}$

10 $6\frac{9}{40}$

Mathematical Habit 3 Construct viable arguments

1 Van rewrote 1.024 as $1\frac{6}{25}$. Is he correct? Explain.

2 Ana rewrote 1.37 as $1\frac{3}{7}$. Is she correct? If not, what should the correct mixed number be?

Problem Solving with Heuristics

1 **Mathematical Habit 2** **Use mathematical reasoning**

The length of a car is measured in meters to 3 decimal places. The length of the car is 4.26 meters when rounded to the nearest hundredth. What are the least and greatest possible measurements of its actual length?

2 | **Mathematical Habit 2** Use mathematical reasoning

Read the example below.

> A number has 2 decimal places. It is 1.7 when rounded to 1 decimal place. What could the numbers be?
> Draw a number line to find the numbers.
>
>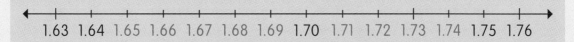
> 1.63 1.64 1.65 1.66 1.67 1.68 1.69 1.70 1.71 1.72 1.73 1.74 1.75 1.76
>
> The numbers in red are possible answers.

A number has 3 decimal places. It is 2.34 when rounded to 2 decimal places.

a What could the numbers be? List the possible numbers.

b Which of these numbers is the greatest?

c Which of these numbers is the least?

? What is the value of the second decimal place? What will be the value of the third decimal place?

Decimals

Understanding thousandths

Rounding to nearest hundredth

Comparing and ordering decimals

Rewriting decimals as fractions and mixed numbers

5.872 can be written in other ways.
- five and eight hundred seventy-two thousandths
- 5 ones 8 tenths 7 hundredths 2 thousandths
- $5.872 = 5 + 0.8 + 0.07 + 0.002$
- $5.872 = 5 + \frac{8}{10} + \frac{7}{100} + \frac{2}{1,000}$

3.02   3.152   3.052
- 3.152 is greater than 3.02. 3.152 is greater than 3.052. 3.152 is the greatest.
- 3.02 is less than 3.052. 3.02 is the least.
- The numbers arranged in order from least to greatest are 3.02, 3.052, 3.152.

- 1.493 rounds to 1.49.
- 2.349 rounds to 2.35.
- 0.685 rounds to 0.69.

- $0.8 = \frac{8}{10}$
  $= \frac{4}{5}$
- $1.42 = 1\frac{42}{100}$
  $= 1\frac{21}{50}$
- $2.016 = 2\frac{16}{1,000}$
  $= 2\frac{2}{125}$

Name: _____ Date: _____

Fill in each blank.

1　In 5.139, the digit _____ is in the thousandths place.

2　3 tenths 8 hundredths 6 thousandths written as a decimal is _____.

3　$17.208 = 17 + 0.2 +$ _____

$$= 17 \frac{208}{\boxed{}}$$

4　The decimal marked by ✗ on the number line is _____.

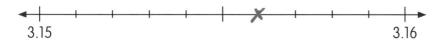

3.15　　　　　　　　　　　　　　　　3.16

5　8 hundredths = _____ thousandths

6　2 hundredths 5 thousandths = _____

Write each fraction as a decimal.

7　56 thousandths = _____

8　$\frac{14}{1,000} =$ _____

9　$\frac{516}{1,000} =$ _____

10　$3\frac{77}{1,000} =$ _____

Order the decimals from least to greatest.

11 6.018, 6.15, 3.978 _____

Round to the nearest hundredth.

12 0.675 _____

13 5.099 _____

14 35.214 _____

Rewrite each decimal as a fraction or mixed number in simplest form.

15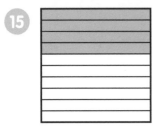

0.4 = _____

16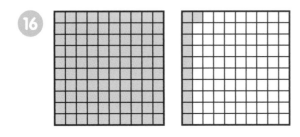

1.11 = _____

17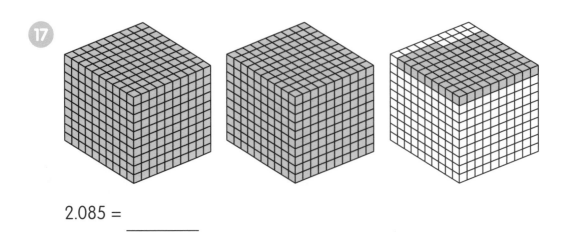

2.085 = _____

Rewrite each decimal as a fraction or mixed number in simplest form.

18 6.5 _____

19 9.06 _____

20 7.10 _____

21 3.005 _____

22 0.125 _____

23 5.258 _____

Rewrite each fraction or mixed number as a decimal.

24 $\frac{67}{200}$ = _____

25 $\frac{19}{40}$ = _____

26 $7\frac{133}{250}$ = _____

27 $11\frac{97}{500}$ = _____

Assessment Prep

Answer each question.

28 Which statement correctly expresses the decimal as a fraction?

Ⓐ $6.7 = \frac{67}{100}$

Ⓑ $6.07 = \frac{607}{1,000}$

Ⓒ $6.007 = 6\frac{7}{1,000}$

Ⓓ $6.077 = 6\frac{77}{100}$

29 Which is the value of the digit 3 in 4.093?

Ⓐ 0.003

Ⓑ 0.03

Ⓒ 0.3

Ⓓ 3

30 Which two statements about rounding decimals are correct?

Ⓐ 6.366 is 6.36 when rounded to the nearest hundredth.

Ⓑ 6.913 is 6.91 when rounded to the nearest hundredth.

Ⓒ 6.764 is 6.75 when rounded to the nearest hundredth.

Ⓓ 6.005 is 6.00 when rounded to the nearest hundredth.

Ⓔ 6.499 is 6.50 when rounded to the nearest hundredth.

Name: _____ Date: _____

Race Times

1 Six athletes from Greenville High School competed in the 200-meter race during a recent track and field meet. The individual times of five athletes for this race are listed in the table below.

Individual times for 200-meter race	
Athlete	**Times (in seconds)**
Justin	45.535
Ana	47.92
Luis	47.8
Tyler	48.042
Chloe	47.84

a Order the five athletes from fastest to slowest. Explain your answer.

b The sixth athlete, Zachary, finished with a time of 48.5 seconds. Did Zachary win the race? Justify your answer.

2 At the track and field meet, Greenville High School competed against Lee High School in the 400-meter relay race. Each member of the relay team had to run 100 meters. The individual times for each athlete are listed in the tables below.

Greenville High School		
Athlete	Time (in seconds)	Rounded time (in seconds)
Luis	19.549	
Ana	20.07	
Justin	19.4	
Tyler	19.482	

Lee High School		
Athlete	Time (in seconds)	Rounded time (in seconds)
Sara	19.6	
John	19.927	
Evelyn	20.093	
Mariah	19.45	

a The race officials decided to round each athlete's time to the nearest tenth of a second before determining which team won the race. Record each athlete's rounded time in the tables above.

© 2020 Marshall Cavendish Education Pte Ltd

b Round each time to the nearest whole number. Then, using these rounded times, find which high school team won the relay race. Justify your answer.

3 Liam competed in the long jump. The results of his three attempts are as follows:

4.5 meters

4.742 meters

4.67 meters

a Rewrite each decimal as a mixed number.

b Show the location of each decimal by drawing a ✗ on the number line below.

Rubric

Point(s)	Level	My Performance
7–8	4	• Most of my answers are correct. • I showed complete understanding of what I have learned. • I used the correct strategies to solve the problems. • I explained my answers and mathematical thinking clearly and completely.
5–6.5	3	• Some of my answers are correct. • I showed some understanding of what I have learned. • I used some correct strategies to solve the problems. • I explained my answers and mathematical thinking clearly.
3–4.5	2	• A few of my answers are correct. • I showed little understanding of what I have learned. • I used a few correct strategies to solve the problems. • I explained some of my answers and mathematical thinking clearly.
0–2.5	1	• A few of my answers are correct. • I showed little or no understanding of what I have learned. • I used a few strategies to solve the problems. • I did not explain my answers and mathematical thinking clearly.

Teacher's Comments

STEAM

Work for a Cause

Students across the country participate in different kinds of community service. Some organize events to raise money for charity.

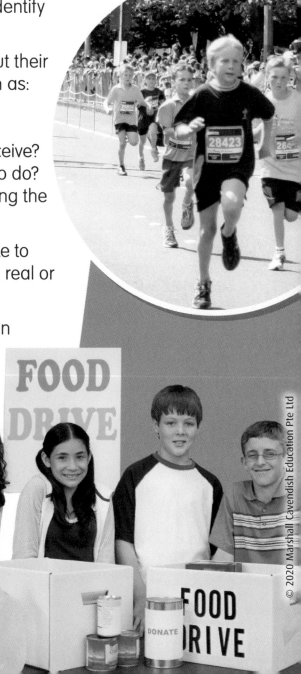

Task

Plan a Charity Event

Work as a class to plan an event to raise money for a charity.

1. Use the internet or local newspapers to identify charities in your community.

2. Research the charities to learn more about their work. Look for answers to questions, such as:
   - Who does the charity serve?
   - What is the charity's yearly budget?
   - How do they spend the money they receive? That is, what do they use their money to do? How much of each dollar goes to helping the people they serve?

3. Select one or more charities you would like to support. Work with your teacher to plan a real or imaginary fundraising event.

4. Record school announcements and design advertising posters you could use to encourage school participation.

5. If you carry out your plan, invite charity representatives to visit your class to receive the funds you collect. Then, to speak to your class about their work.

Four Operations of Decimals

Super Save Market

Item	Amount
Chicken 1 × $6.99	$6.99
Grapes	$4.45
Mangoes 2 × $2.25	$4.50
Total	**$15.94**
Cash payment	**$20.00**
Change	**$4.06**

Thank you for shopping with us!

Trevon, let's check if we paid the correct amount of money.

How can decimals be added, subtracted, multiplied, and divided?

Name: _____ Date: _____

Regrouping ones

a

10 ones = 1 ten

b   12 ones = 10 ones + 2 ones
            = 1 ten + 2 ones
            = 12

▶ Quick Check

Regroup. Fill in each blank.

1

_____ ones = _____ ones + _____ ones

= _____ ten + _____ ones

= _____

2

_____ ones = _____ ones + _____ ones

= _____ ten + _____ ones

= _____

© 2020 Marshall Cavendish Education Pte Ltd

Regrouping tenths

a

10 tenths = 1 one

b 13 tenths = 10 tenths + 3 tenths

           = 1 one + 3 tenths

           = 1.3

▶ Quick Check

Regroup. Fill in each blank.

③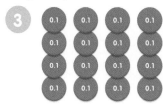

16 tenths = 10 tenths + _____ tenths

          = _____ one + _____ tenths

          = _____

④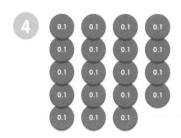

_____ tenths = _____ tenths + _____ tenths

            = _____ one + _____ tenths

            = _____

Regrouping hundredths

a  → 0.1

10 hundredths = 1 tenth

b 14 hundredths = 10 hundredths + 4 hundredths
= 1 tenth + 4 hundredths
= 0.14

▶ Quick Check

Regroup. Fill in each blank.

5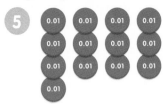

_____ hundredths = _____ hundredths + _____ hundredths

= _____ tenth + _____ hundredths

= _____

6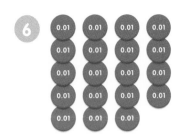

19 hundredths = 10 hundredths + _____ hundredths

= _____ tenth + _____ hundredths

= _____

Multiplying tens, hundreds, and thousands by a 1-digit number

a 3 × 2 = 3 ones × 2
        = 6 ones
        = 6

So, 3 × 2 = 6.

b 3**0** × 2 = 3 tens × 2
        = 6 tens
        = 6**0**

So, 3**0** × 2 = 6**0**.

c 3**00** × 2 = 3 hundreds × 2
        = 6 hundreds
        = 600

So, 3**00** × 2 = 6**00**.

d 3,**000** × 2 = 3 thousands × 2
        = 6 thousands
        = 6,**000**

So, 3,**000** × 2 = 6,**000**.

▶ **Quick Check**

Multiply.

7 20 × 3 = _____

   200 × 3 = _____

   2,000 × 3 = _____

8 4 × 10 = _____

   4 × 100 = _____

   4 × 1,000 = _____

9 8 × 10 = _____

   8 × 100 = _____

   8 × 1,000 = _____

10 12 × 10 = _____

    12 × 100 = _____

    12 × 1,000 = _____

Dividing by a 1-digit number with and without remainder

a

```
       3, 2 0 4
   2 ) 6, 4 0 8
       6          ⟵── 2 × 3 thousands
       ─
       4
         4        ⟵── 2 × 2 hundreds
         ─
         0
           0      ⟵── 2 × 0 tens
           ─
           8
             8    ⟵── 2 × 4 ones
             ─
             0
```

So, 6,408 ÷ 2 = 3204.

b

```
       8 4 6
   6 ) 5, 0 7 9
       4 8        ⟵── 6 × 8 hundreds
       ───
       2 7
         2 4      ⟵── 6 × 4 tens
         ───
         3 9
           3 6    ⟵── 6 × 6 ones
           ───
             3
```

So, 5,079 ÷ 6 = 846 R 3.

▶ **Quick Check**

Divide.

11 9,063 ÷ 3 = _____

12 4,215 ÷ 5 = _____

13 2,169 ÷ 4 = _____

14 3,692 ÷ 7 = _____

Rounding decimals

8.453 is 8 when rounded to the nearest whole number.
8.453 is 8.5 when rounded to 1 decimal place or to the nearest tenth.

▶ Quick Check

Fill in the table.

		Rounded to the nearest	
		Whole number	Tenth
15	14.78		
16	59.32		
17	79.99		
18	85.55		
19	39.46		
20	45.45		

Adding Decimals

Learning Objectives:
- Add decimals without regrouping.
- Add decimals with regrouping.

 **THINK**

What do the digits A, B, C, and D stand for?
Explain how you arrived at your answers.

$$\begin{array}{r} \boxed{A}\,4\,.\,8\,\boxed{B} \\ +\quad\boxed{C}\,.\,\boxed{D}\,5 \\ \hline 4\,1\,.\,1\,6 \end{array}$$

ENGAGE

Use to add each pair of decimals.
- **a** one and three tenths   seven hundredths
- **b** seven hundredths   one and three hundredths

LEARN Add decimals without regrouping

1. Grace drank 1.1 liters of orange juice. Her sister drank 0.2 liter of orange juice. How much juice did they drink in all?

   1.1 + 0.2 = ?

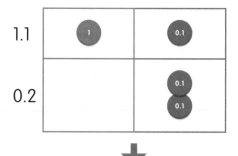

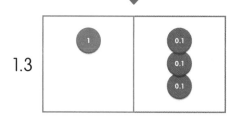

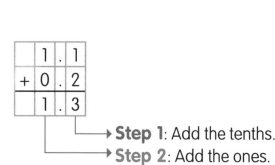

Step 1: Add the tenths.

Step 2: Add the ones.

1.1 + 0.2 = 1.3

They drank 1.3 liters of juice in all.

2 Find the sum of 2.63 and 7.12.

2.63 + 7.12 = ?

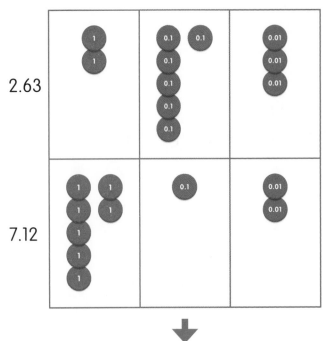

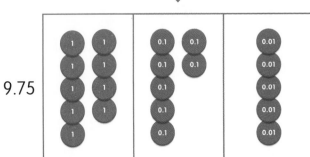

2.63 + 7.12 = 9.75

	2	.	6	3
+	7	.	1	2
	9	.	7	5

Step 1: Add the hundredth
Step 2: Add the tenths.
Step 3: Add the ones.

TRY Practice adding decimals without regrouping

Add.

1
```
    0 . 5
+ 2 . 4
```

2
```
    0 . 2 2
+ 0 . 3 6
```

3
```
    0 . 3
+ 1 . 0 7
```

Add.

④ 2.4 and 3.4

⑤ 3.84 and 11.15

⑥ 1.4 and 3.25

 Math Talk

Ana says you have to align the decimal points when adding decimals. Do you agree? Explain.

ENGAGE

① Add 2.45 and 3.76.

② Find the digits represented by A, B, and C.

$$
\begin{array}{r}
1\,.\,\boxed{A}\,8 \\
+\ 4\,.\,6\,\boxed{B} \\
\hline
\boxed{C}\,.\,0\ 5
\end{array}
$$

LEARN Add decimals with regrouping

① Add 3.65 and 9.75.

3.65 + 9.75 = ?

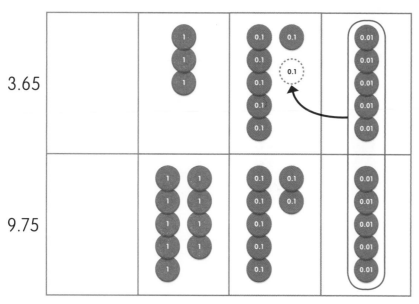

Step 1 Add the hundredths and regroup.

$$
\begin{array}{r}
{\scriptstyle 1}\quad\ \\
3\,.\,6\ 5 \\
+\ 9\,.\,7\ 5 \\
\hline
.\quad 0
\end{array}
$$

10 hundredths
= 1 tenth 0 hundredths

© 2020 Marshall Cavendish Education Pte Ltd

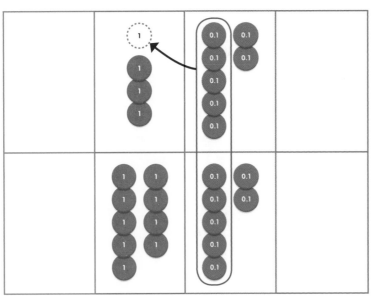

Step 2 Add the tenths and regroup.

		1		1	
		3	.	6	5
+		9	.	7	5
			.	4	0

14 tenths
= 1 one 4 tenths

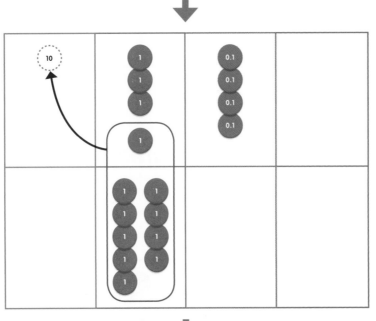

Step 3 Add the ones and regroup.

	1			1	
		3	.	6	5
+		9	.	7	5
	1	3	.	4	0

13 ones = 1 ten 3 ones

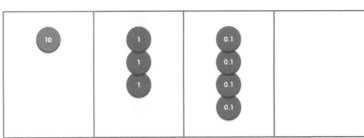

13.4

3.65 + 9.75 = 13.4

Work in pairs.

① Use 🔵100 🔵10 🔵1 🔵0.1 🔵0.01 🔵0.001 and a place-value chart to add the decimals and fill in the first column of the table. Then, add the whole numbers and fill in the second column of the table.

	Add each pair of decimals	Add each pair of whole numbers
a	3.1 + 2.85 = _____	310 + 285 = _____
b	0.16 + 0.2 = _____	16 + 20 = _____
c	1.81 + 0.17 = _____	181 + 17 = _____
d	0.9 + 0.6 = _____	90 + 60 = _____
e	12.97 + 79.43 = _____	1,297 + 7,943 = _____

② Compare the answers in the table in ①. What do you notice?

TRY Practice adding decimals with regrouping

Add.

1
```
  7 1 . 9
+ 3 9 . 2
─────────
```

2
```
  8 . 0 8
+ 4 . 9 9
─────────
```

3
```
1 1 . 6 5
+   4 . 3 5
─────────
```

Find the sum of each of the following.

4 0.8 and 0.5

5 7 and 6.35

6 36.08 and 3.99

Mathematical Habit 3 Construct viable arguments

1 Add 2.1 and 4.3.

> I added 2.1 and 4.3 mentally this way.
> 2.1 + 4.3 = ?
> 2 + 4 = 6
> 0.1 + 0.3 = 0.4
> So, 6 + 0.4 = 6.4.

2 Find the sum of 0.25 and 0.09.

> I found the sum of 0.25 and 0.09 mentally this way.
> 0.25 + 0.09 = 0.24 + 0.1
>   = 0.34

(0.24) (0.01)

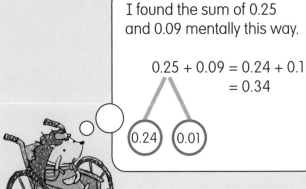

What other ways are there? Discuss with your classmates.

INDEPENDENT PRACTICE

Add.

1
```
   1 4 . 3
 +   3 . 2
 _____
```

2
```
   5 . 6 1
 + 2 . 2 5
 _____
```

3
```
   2 5 . 4 0
 +   3 . 1 9
 _____
```

4
```
   0 . 4 5
 + 3 . 3 3
 _____
```

5
```
   3 5 . 8
 +   7 . 4
 _____
```

6
```
   2 . 4 9
 + 1 . 8 6
 _____
```

7
```
   1 3 . 0 2
 +   6 . 9 9
 _____
```

8
```
   4 8 . 3 6
 +   5 . 6 5
 _____
```

Find each sum.

9 2.7 and 4.1

10 5.42 and 3.15

11 3.6 and 0.8

12 2.9 and 6.85

13 1.38 and 2.05

14 8 and 9.75

15 8.4 and 3.67

16 54.72 and 6.08

17 6.34 and 7.66

18 6.58 and 15.43

2 Subtracting Decimals

Learning Objectives:
- Subtract decimals without regrouping.
- Subtract decimals with regrouping.

THINK

What do the digits A, B, C, and D stand for?
Explain how you arrived at your answers.

$$
\begin{array}{r}
4\,\boxed{A}\ .\ 2\ 8 \\
-\quad 9\ .\ \boxed{B}\,4 \\
\hline
\boxed{C}\,4\ .\ 2\,\boxed{D}
\end{array}
$$

ENGAGE

1. Use to explain how you can subtract 1.35 from 4.87.

$$
\begin{array}{r}
7\ .\ \boxed{A}\,9 \\
-\ B\ .\ 2\,\boxed{C} \\
\hline
\boxed{4}\ .\ 3\ 3
\end{array}
$$

2. Find the digits represented by A, B, and C.

LEARN Subtract decimals without regrouping

1. A pumpkin weighs 1.3 kilograms. A watermelon weighs 0.2 kilogram less than the pumpkin. What is the mass of the watermelon?

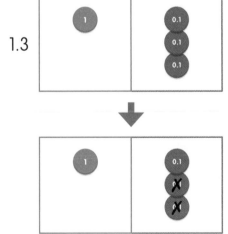

Step 1 Subtract the tenths.

$$
\begin{array}{r}
1\ .\ 3 \\
-\ 0\ .\ 2 \\
\hline
.\ 1
\end{array}
$$

Step 2 Subtract the ones.

$$
\begin{array}{r}
1\ .\ 3 \\
-\ 0\ .\ 2 \\
\hline
1\ .\ 1
\end{array}
$$

1.3 − 0.2 = 1.1

The mass of the watermelon is 1.1 kilograms.

2 Subtract 1.42 from 3.96.

3.96 − 1.42 = ?

3.96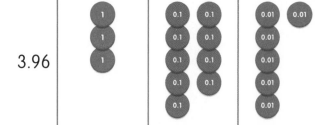

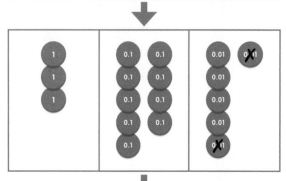

Step 1 Subtract the hundredths.

	3	.	9	6
−	1	.	4	2
		.		4

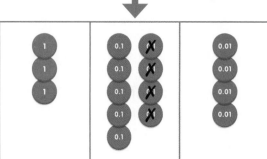

Step 2 Subtract the tenths.

	3	.	9	6
−	1	.	4	2
		.	5	4

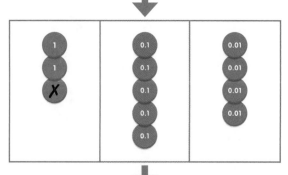

Step 3 Subtract the ones.

	3	.	9	6
−	1	.	4	2
	2	.	5	4

3.96 − 1.42 = 2.54

2.54

TRY Practice subtracting decimals without regrouping

Subtract.

1
```
  3 . 4 8
− 3 . 3 7
─────────
```

2
```
  5 . 4 9
− 3 . 1 6
─────────
```

Subtract.

3 $3.6 − 2.1 =$ _____

4 $18.56 − 7.14 =$ _____

ENGAGE

Anthony has $31.24. He spends $18.85 on groceries. How much does he have left? Use 💯 🔟 ① ⓪.₁ ⓪.₀₁ ⓪.₀₀₁ to show your thinking. What is another method to find the answer?

LEARN Subtract decimals with regrouping

1 Find the difference between 29.98 and 42.31.

$42.31 − 29.98 = ?$

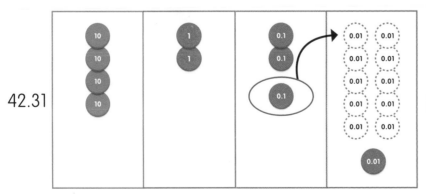

Step 1 Regroup.
3 tenths 1 hundredth
= 2 tenths 11 hundredths

```
        2  11
  4 2 . 3̶ 1̶
− 2 9 . 9 8
───────────
       .
```

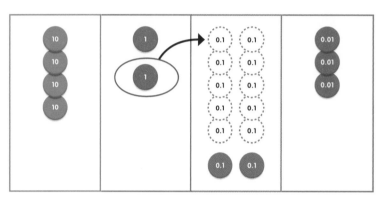

Step 2 Subtract the hundredths.

			2	11
4	2	.	~~3~~	~~1~~
− 2	9	.	9	8
		.		3

Step 3 Regroup.
2 ones 2 tenths
= 1 one 12 tenths

	1		12	11
4	~~2~~	.	~~3~~	~~1~~
− 2	9	.	9	8
		.		3

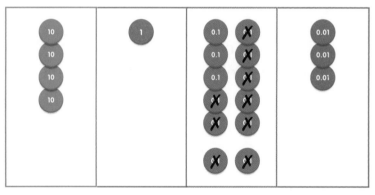

Step 4 Subtract the tenths.

	1		12	11
4	~~2~~	.	~~3~~	~~1~~
− 2	9	.	9	8
		.	3	3

Step 5 Regroup.
4 tens 1 one
= 3 tens 11 ones

3	11		12	11
~~4~~	~~2~~	.	~~3~~	~~1~~
− 2	9	.	9	8
		.	3	3

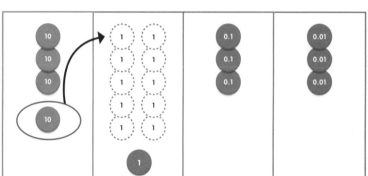

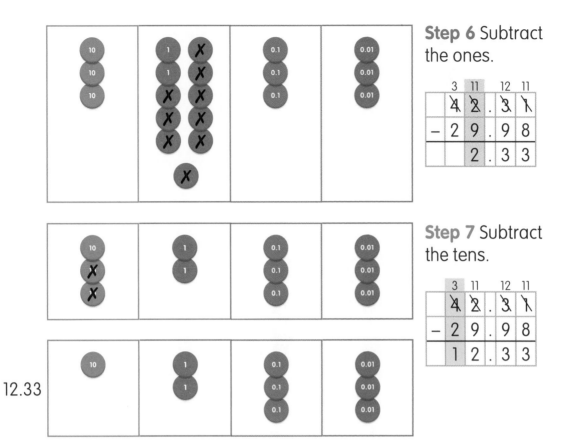

Step 6 Subtract the ones.

$$
\begin{array}{c}
{\overset{3}{\cancel{4}}}\ {\overset{11}{\cancel{2}}}\ .\ {\overset{12}{\cancel{3}}}\ {\overset{11}{\cancel{1}}} \\
-\ 2\ 9\ .\ 9\ 8 \\
\hline
 2\ .\ 3\ 3
\end{array}
$$

Step 7 Subtract the tens.

$$
\begin{array}{c}
{\overset{3}{\cancel{4}}}\ {\overset{11}{\cancel{2}}}\ .\ {\overset{12}{\cancel{3}}}\ {\overset{11}{\cancel{1}}} \\
-\ 2\ 9\ .\ 9\ 8 \\
\hline
1\ 2\ .\ 3\ 3
\end{array}
$$

42.31 – 29.98 = 12.33

The difference between 29.98 and 42.31 is 12.33.

2 Subtract 1.35 from 5.

5.00 – 1.35 = ?

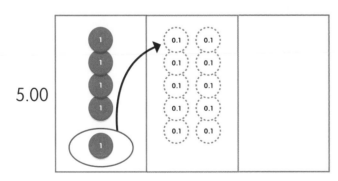

Step 1 Regroup.
5 ones = 4 ones 10 tenths

$$
\begin{array}{c}
{\overset{4}{\cancel{5}}}\ .\ {\overset{10}{\cancel{0}}}\ 0 \\
-\ 1\ .\ 3\ 5 \\
\hline
\ \ .\ \ \ \
\end{array}
$$

Step 2 Regroup.
10 tenths = 9 tenths 10 hundredths

$$
\begin{array}{r}
\overset{\;\;\;\;\overset{9}{}}{\overset{4}{}}\;\;\overset{10}{}\;\;10 \\
\cancel{5}\;.\;\cancel{0}\;\cancel{0} \\
-\;1\;.\;3\;\;5 \\
\hline
\;.\;\;
\end{array}
$$

Step 3 Subtract the hundredths.

$$
\begin{array}{r}
\overset{\;\;\;\;\overset{9}{}}{\overset{4}{}}\;\;\overset{10}{}\;\;10 \\
\cancel{5}\;.\;\cancel{0}\;\cancel{0} \\
-\;1\;.\;3\;\;5 \\
\hline
\;.\;\;\;5
\end{array}
$$

Step 4 Subtract the tenths.

$$
\begin{array}{r}
\overset{\;\;\;\;\overset{9}{}}{\overset{4}{}}\;\;\overset{10}{}\;\;10 \\
\cancel{5}\;.\;\cancel{0}\;\cancel{0} \\
-\;1\;.\;3\;\;5 \\
\hline
\;.\;6\;\;5
\end{array}
$$

Step 5 Subtract the ones.

$$
\begin{array}{r}
\overset{\;\;\;\;\overset{9}{}}{\overset{4}{}}\;\;\overset{10}{}\;\;10 \\
\cancel{5}\;.\;\cancel{0}\;\cancel{0} \\
-\;1\;.\;3\;\;5 \\
\hline
3\;.\;6\;\;5
\end{array}
$$

3.65

$5 - 1.35 = 3.65$

Work in pairs.

1 Use 100 10 1 0.1 0.01 0.001 and a place-value chart to subtract the decimals and fill in the first column of the table. Then, subtract the whole numbers and fill in the second column of the table.

	Subtract the decimals	Subtract the whole numbers
a	$0.97 - 0.25 = $ _____	$97 - 25 = $ _____
b	$0.9 - 0.4 = $ _____	$9 - 4 = $ _____
c	$1.48 - 1.23 = $ _____	$148 - 123 = $ _____
d	$3.2 - 0.54 = $ _____	$320 - 54 = $ _____
e	$50 - 37.42 = $ _____	$5,000 - 3,742 = $ _____

2 Compare the answers in the table in 1 . What do you notice?

TRY Practice subtracting decimals with regrouping

Subtract.

1
```
  1 8 . 3 2
-   4 . 3 6
_____
```

2
```
    4 . 0 0
-   2 . 8 7
_____
```

Find each difference.

3 0.8 − 0.09 = _____

4 8 − 2.5 = _____

5 7.1 − 2.06 = _____

6 6.12 − 3.58 = _____

7 27.43 − 5.65 = _____

8 16.78 − 5.9 = _____

Mathematical Habit 3 Construct viable arguments

1 Find the value of 2.8 − 1.5.

I found the value of 2.8 − 1.5 mentally this way.
2.8 − 1.5 = ?
2 − 1 = 1
0.8 − 0.5 = 0.3
1 + 0.3 = 1.3
So, 2.8 − 1.5 = 1.3.

2 Subtract 1.97 from 6.

I subtracted 1.97 from 6 mentally this way.
6 − 1.97 = ?   2
1.97 ≈ 2

1.97   0.03

STEP 1 6 − 2 = 4

STEP 2 4 + 0.03 = 4.03

So, 6 − 1.97 = 4.03.

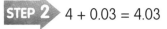

What other ways are there? Discuss with your classmates.

Name: _____ Date: _____

INDEPENDENT PRACTICE

Subtract.

1
```
  2 8 . 6
–   5 . 5
```

2
```
  9 . 7 3
– 1 . 4 1
```

3
```
  1 6 . 4 9
–   2 . 3 6
```

4
```
  4 2 . 5 9
– 4 1 . 3 6
```

5
```
  4 0 . 3
–   8 . 9
```

6
```
  5 . 3 5
– 2 . 7 8
```

7
```
  1 2 . 0 0
–   5 . 7 6
```

8
```
  2 0 . 0 1
–   1 . 2 3
```

Find each difference.

9 4.7 − 2.2 = _____

10 1.78 − 0.41 = _____

11 5.1 − 2.8 = _____

12 2.3 − 0.08 = _____

13 7.16 − 3.28 = _____

14 9 − 3.5 = _____

15 8.2 − 5.08 = _____

16 63.42 − 8.94 = _____

17 17.25 − 9.9 = _____

3 Multiplying Decimals

Learning Objective:
• Multiply decimals up to 2 decimal places by 1-digit whole numbers.

 **THINK**

Hiro estimated the product of 3.45 and 6 to be 18. Kayla estimated the same product to be 24, and Mika estimated it to be 30. Who is correct? Explain how each of them arrived at their estimates.

ENGAGE

Show 2 groups of 3  to find the product of 2 and 0.3. Explain how you would find the product mentally. Now, show 3 groups of 2 0.1. How do you show the product using a multiplication equation? What do you notice about your answers? Share your observation.

LEARN Multiply decimals by a whole number without regrouping

1 **a** What is 4 × 2?

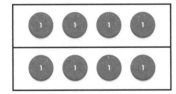

4 × 2 = 4 ones × 2
= 8 ones
= 8

b What is 0.4 × 2?

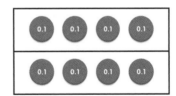

0.4 × 2 = 4 tenths × 2
= 8 tenths
= 0.8

c What is 0.04 × 2?

0.04 × 2 = 4 hundredths × 2
= 8 hundredths
= 0.08

What pattern do you notice?

2 Find the product of 3.1 and 2.

$3.1 \times 2 = ?$

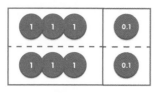

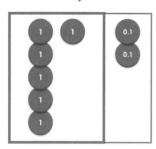

Step 1 Multiply the tenths by 2.
1 tenth × 2 = 2 tenths

	3	.	1
×			2
		.	**2**

Step 2 Multiply the ones by 2.
3 ones × 2 = 6 ones

	3	.	1
×			2
	6	.	2

$3.1 \times 2 = 6.2$

The product of 3.1 and 2 is 6.2.

TRY Practice multiplying decimals by a whole number without regrouping

Multiply.

1 $0.3 \times 2 =$ _____

2 $0.03 \times 2 =$ _____

3 $1.2 \times 3 =$ _____

4 $2.2 \times 4 =$ _____

A notebook cost $2.98. How much does it cost to buy 3 notebooks?
Use to show how you find 3 × $2.98. Explain how you can find the answer in two ways.

LEARN Multiply decimals by a whole number with regrouping

1 Multiply 13.34 by 3.

13.34 × 3 = ?

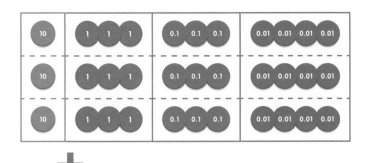

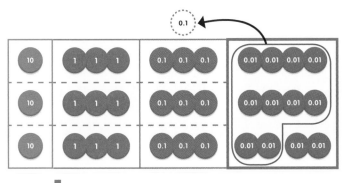

Step 1 Multiply the hundredths by 3.
4 hundredths × 3 = 12 hundredths

Regroup.
12 hundredths
= 1 tenth 2 hundredths

	1	3	.	3	4
					1
×					3
			.		**2**

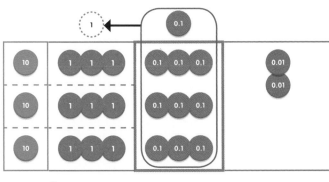

Step 2 Multiply the tenths by 3.
3 tenths × 3 = 9 tenths

Add the tenths.
9 tenths + 1 tenth
= 10 tenths

Regroup.
10 tenths = 1 one 0 tenths

	1	3	.	3	4
		1		1	
×					3
			.	**0**	2

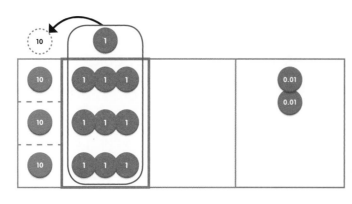

Step 3 Multiply the ones by 3.

3 ones × 3 = 9 ones

Add the ones.

9 ones + 1 one = 10 ones

Regroup.

10 ones
= 1 ten 0 ones

		1	1		1
		1	3	.	3	4
×						3
			0	.	0	2

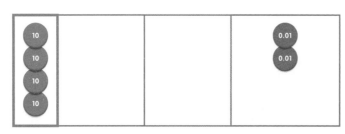

Step 4 Multiply the tens by 3.

1 ten × 3 = 3 tens

Add the tens.

3 tens + 1 ten
= 4 tens

		1	1		1
		1	3	.	3	4
×						3
	4	**0**	.	0	2

13.34 × 3 = 40.02

TRY Practice multiplying decimals by a whole number with regrouping

Multiply.

1
```
    2 . 3
×     7
───────
```

2
```
    1 . 0 7
×       9
─────────
```

3
```
   1 1 . 4 6
×         8
───────────
```

Find each product.

4 6.7 × 6 = _____

5 14.67 × 8 = _____

INDEPENDENT PRACTICE

Multiply.

1 2 × 3 = _____

2 0.2 × 3 = _____

3 0.02 × 3 = _____

Multiply.

4
```
  2 0 . 2 1
×       4
---------
```

5
```
  2 3 . 1 3
×       3
---------
```

6
```
  5 . 4
×   7
-------
```

7
```
  2 . 0 8
×     9
-------
```

8
```
  1 4 . 9
×     3
-------
```

9
```
  1 3 . 0 8
×       6
---------
```

10
```
  1 5 . 6 2
×       5
---------
```

11
```
  3 2 . 5 6
×       8
---------
```

Find each product.

12 8.3 × 3 = _____

13 2.6 × 4 = _____

14 5.8 × 7 = _____

15 77.5 × 2 = _____

16 8.23 × 5 = _____

17 6.07 × 9 = _____

18 11.82 × 3 = _____

19 27.13 × 6 = _____

20 70.59 × 4 = _____

21 63.58 × 9 = _____

Multiplying Decimals by Tens, Hundreds, Thousands, and Powers of Tens

Learning Objectives:
- Multiply decimals up to 3 decimal places by 10, 100, or 1,000, and their multiples.
- Multiply decimals up to 3 decimal places by powers of 10.

THINK

The mass of a dime is 2.274 grams. What is the mass of 200 such dimes? Share different ways to find the mass with your partner.

ENGAGE

1. What is $\frac{2}{10} \times 10$? What is 0.05×10?

   Use  to justify your answer.

2. Find each missing digit in the equation. $1.\bigcirc4 \times 10 = \bigcirc3.\bigcirc$

LEARN Multiply decimals by 10

Ones	Tenths	Hundredths	Thousandths
	1		
1			

$0.1 \times 10 = 1$

Ones	Tenths	Hundredths	Thousandths
		1	
	1		

$0.01 \times 10 = 0.1$

Ones		Tenths	Hundredths	Thousandths
	:			1
	:	1		

$$0.001 \times 10 = 0.01$$

2 What is $2.05 \times 10 =$?

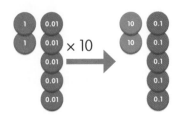

Tens	Ones	Tenths	Hundredths
	2	0	5
2	0	5	

$$2.05 \times 10 = 20.5$$

3 What is $0.345 \times 10 =$?

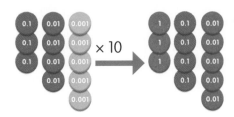

Ones		Tenths	Hundredths	Thousandths
	:	3	4	5
3	:	4	5	

$$0.345 \times 10 = 3.45$$

What pattern do you notice?

Work in pairs.

1. Use (100) (10) (1) (0.1) (0.01) (0.001) to show 0.4. Then, use (100) (10) (1) (0.1) (0.01) (0.001) to show the result of 0.4 × 10. Fill in the table. Draw arrows to show how each digit moves in the table.

	Tens	Ones	Tenths	Hundredths	Thousandths
0.4					
0.4 × 10					
0.13					
0.13 × 10					
0.751					
0.751 × 10					
2.34					
2.34 × 10					

2. **Mathematical Habit 8 Look for patterns**
   How is multiplying a decimal by 10 the same as multiplying a whole number by 10?

3. What is another way to multiply decimals by 10? Explain how you can tell whether you should shift the decimal point to the left or right.

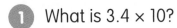
Multiply.

1 What is 3.4 × 10?

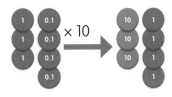

Tens	Ones	Tenths	Hundredths
	3	4	
_____	_____		

3.4 × 10 = _____

2 What is 0.23 × 10?

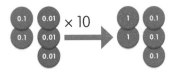

Ones	Tenths	Hundredths	Thousandths
	2	3	
_____	_____		

0.23 × 10 = _____

3 What is 0.102 × 10?

Ones	Tenths	Hundredths	Thousandths
	1	0	2
_____	_____	_____	

0.102 × 10 = _____

ENGAGE

Use 100 10 1 0.1 0.01 0.001 to show the products.
What is 0.2 × 2? What is 0.2 × 10? What do you think 0.2 × 20 equals?
Explain your thinking to your partner.

LEARN Multiply decimals by tens

1 What is 0.2 × 30?

▶ **Method 1**

0.2 × 10 = 2   2 × 3 = 6

0.2 × 30
= 0.2 × 10 × 3
= 2 × 3
= 6

▶ **Method 2**

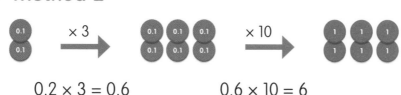

0.2 × 3 = 0.6   0.6 × 10 = 6

0.2 × 30
= 0.2 × 3 × 10
= 0.6 × 10
= 6

2 What is 0.02 × 30?

▶ **Method 1**

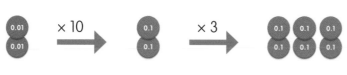

0.02 × 10 = 0.2   0.2 × 3 = 0.6

0.02 × 30
= 0.02 × 10 × 3
= 0.2 × 3
= 0.6

▶ **Method 2**

0.02 × 3 = 0.06   0.06 × 10 = 0.6

0.02 × 30
= 0.02 × 3 × 10
= 0.06 × 10
= 0.6

3 What is $0.002 \times 30 =$?

$0.002 \times 10 = 0.02$ $0.02 \times 3 = 0.06$

0.002×30
$= 0.002 \times 10 \times 3$
$= 0.02 \times 3$
$= 0.06$

TRY Practice multiplying decimals by tens

Fill in each blank.

1 $0.4 \times 30 = 0.4 \times \underline{\hspace{1.5cm}} \times 10$

$= \underline{\hspace{1.5cm}} \times 10$

$= \underline{\hspace{1.5cm}}$

2 $0.7 \times 20 = 0.7 \times \underline{\hspace{1.5cm}} \times 2$

$= \underline{\hspace{1.5cm}} \times 2$

$= \underline{\hspace{1.5cm}}$

3 $0.04 \times 30 = \underline{\hspace{1.5cm}}$

4 $0.07 \times 20 = \underline{\hspace{1.5cm}}$

5 $0.004 \times 30 = \underline{\hspace{1.5cm}}$

6 $0.007 \times 20 = \underline{\hspace{1.5cm}}$

Multiply.

7 $0.6 \times 40 = \underline{\hspace{1.5cm}}$

8 $50 \times 1.51 = \underline{\hspace{1.5cm}}$

9 $60 \times 0.312 = \underline{\hspace{1.5cm}}$

10 $2.03 \times 80 = \underline{\hspace{1.5cm}}$

1. Use 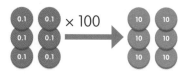 to find 0.2 × 100 and 0.2 × 1,000. Share an easier method to find the products with your partner.

2. What do you predict 0.02 × 100 and 0.02 × 1,000 equal? Explain your thinking to your partner.

3. Discuss how you find 0.02 × 120 in more than one way.

LEARN Multiply decimals by 100 and 1,000

1. a What is 0.6 × 100?

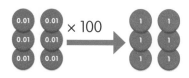

Tens	Ones	Tenths	Hundredths
		6	
6			

0.6 × 100 = 60

b What is 0.06 × 100?

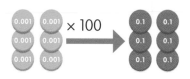

Ones	Tenths	Hundredths	Thousandths
		6	
6			

0.06 × 100 = 6

c What is 0.006 × 100?

Ones	Tenths	Hundredths	Thousandths
			6
	6		

0.006 × 100 = 0.6

What pattern do you notice?

2 **a** What is 4.1 × 100?

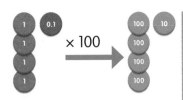

Hundreds	Tens	Ones	Tenths
		4	1
4	1		

4.1 × 100 = 410

b What is 0.012 × 100?

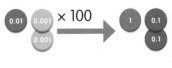

Ones	Tenths	Hundredths	Thousandths
		1	2
1	2		

0.012 × 100 = 1.2

3 **a** What is 0.6 × 1,000?

Hundreds	Tens	Ones	Tenths
			6
6			

0.6 × 1,000 = 600

b What is 0.06 × 1,000?

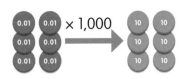

Tens	Ones	Tenths	Hundredths
			6
6			

0.06 × 1,000 = 60

c What is 0.006 × 1,000?

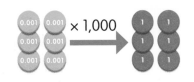

Ones	Tenths	Hundredths	Thousandths
			6
6			

0.006 × 1,000 = 6

4 **a** What is 0.036 × 1,000?

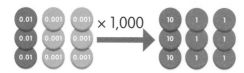

0.036 × 1,000 = 36

Tens	Ones	Tenths	Hundredths	Thousandths
			3	6
3	6			

b What is 0.81 × 1,000?

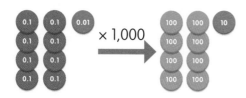

Hundreds	Tens	Ones	Tenths	Hundredths
			8	1
8	1			

0.81 × 1,000 = 810

TRY Practice multiplying decimals by 100 and 1,000

Multiply.

1. 2.9 × 100 = _____

2. 3.09 × 100 = _____

3. 1.259 × 100 = _____

4. 4.7 × 1,000 = _____

5. 4.75 × 1,000 = _____

6. 0.475 × 1,000 = _____

Fill in each blank.

7. 3.1 × _____ = 310

8. 5.029 × _____ = 502.9

9. 14.03 × _____ = 14,030

10. _____ × 0.045 = 45

Mathematical Habit 3 Construct viable arguments

Explain how multiplying a decimal by 100 or 1,000 is the same as multiplying a whole number by 100 or 1,000.

Is there another way to multiply decimals by 100 or 1,000?

ENGAGE

1. Use (100) (10) (1) (0.1) (0.01) (0.001) to find a pattern.

   What is 4×100? What is 4×200?

   What is 0.4×100? What is 0.4×200?

   What do you notice? Share your observation.

2. Find each missing digit in the equation and mark the decimal point at the correct place. $0.3 \times 3\bigcirc\bigcirc = \bigcirc026$

LEARN Multiply decimals by hundreds and thousands

1. a What is 0.2×300?

   ▶ **Method 1**

   $0.2 \times 100 = 20$ $20 \times 3 = 60$

   0.2×300
   $= 0.2 \times 100 \times 3$
   $= 20 \times 3$
   $= 60$

   ▶ **Method 2**

   $0.2 \times 3 = 0.6$ $0.6 \times 100 = 60$

   0.2×300
   $= 0.2 \times 3 \times 100$
   $= 0.6 \times 100$
   $= 60$

b What is 0.02×300?

> **Method 1**

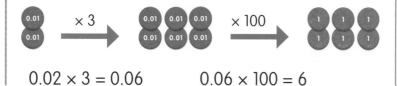

$0.02 \times 100 = 2$ $2 \times 3 = 6$

0.02×300
$= 0.02 \times 100 \times 3$
$= 2 \times 3$
$= 6$

> **Method 2**

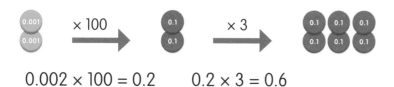

$0.02 \times 3 = 0.06$ $0.06 \times 100 = 6$

0.02×300
$= 0.02 \times 3 \times 100$
$= 0.06 \times 100$
$= 6$

c What is 0.002×300?

$0.002 \times 100 = 0.2$ $0.2 \times 3 = 0.6$

0.002×300
$= 0.002 \times 100 \times 3$
$= 0.2 \times 3$
$= 0.6$

2 **a** What is $0.2 \times 3,000$?

> **Method 1**

$0.2 \times 1,000 = 200$ $200 \times 3 = 600$

$0.2 \times 3,000$
$= 0.2 \times 1,000 \times 3$
$= 200 \times 3$
$= 600$

> **Method 2**

$0.2 \times 3 = 0.6$ $0.6 \times 1,000 = 600$

$0.2 \times 3,000$
$= 0.2 \times 3 \times 1,000$
$= 0.6 \times 1,000$
$= 600$

b What is 0.02 × 3,000?

▶ **Method 1**

0.02 × 1,000 = 20   20 × 3 = 60

> 0.02 × 3,000
> = 0.02 × 1,000 × 3
> = 20 × 3
> = 60

▶ **Method 2**

0.02 × 3 = 0.06   0.06 × 1,000 = 60

> 0.02 × 3,000
> = 0.02 × 3 × 1,000
> = 0.06 × 1,000
> = 60

c What is 0.002 × 3,000?

0.002 × 1,000 = 2   2 × 3 = 6

> 0.002 × 3,000
> = 0.002 × 1,000 × 3
> = 2 × 3
> = 6

TRY Practice multiplying decimals by hundreds and thousands

Fill in each blank.

1 0.8 × 200 = 0.8 × _____ × 100

= _____ × 100

= _____

2 0.7 × 400 = 0.7 × _____ × 4

= _____ × 4

= _____

3 0.08 × 200 = _____

4 0.07 × 400 = _____

5 0.008 × 200 = _____

6 0.007 × 400 = _____

7 $0.4 \times 3{,}000 = 0.4 \times \underline{\hspace{2cm}} \times 1{,}000$

$= \underline{\hspace{2cm}} \times 1{,}000$

$= \underline{\hspace{2cm}}$

8 $0.9 \times 5{,}000 = 0.9 \times \underline{\hspace{2cm}} \times 5$

$= \underline{\hspace{2cm}} \times 5$

$= \underline{\hspace{2cm}}$

9 $0.04 \times 3{,}000 = \underline{\hspace{2cm}}$

10 $0.09 \times 5{,}000 = \underline{\hspace{2cm}}$

11 $0.004 \times 3{,}000 = \underline{\hspace{2cm}}$

12 $0.009 \times 5{,}000 = \underline{\hspace{2cm}}$

Fill in each blank.

13 $200 \times 0.351 = \underline{\hspace{2cm}}$

14 $3{,}000 \times 1.6 = \underline{\hspace{2cm}}$

ENGAGE

1 What is 10^2? What do you think 0.2×10^2 equals? How does your answer compare to 0.2×100? Explain your thinking using a place-value chart.

2 Find each missing digit in the equation and mark the decimal point at the correct place. $0.23 \times 10^2 = \bigcirc\bigcirc\bigcirc$

LEARN Multiply decimals by powers of 10

1 **a** Find 0.125×10^2.

> Multiplying by 10 squared is the same as multiplying by 100. Multiplying by 10 cubed is the same as multiplying by 1,000.

	Thousands	Hundreds	Tens	Ones	Tenths	Hundredths	Thousandths
0.125				0	1	2	5
0.125×10^2		0	1	2	5		

$$0.125 \times 10^2 = 0.125 \times (10 \times 10)$$
$$= 0.125 \times 100$$
$$= 12.5$$

b Find 3.006×10^3.

	Thousands	Hundreds	Tens	Ones	Tenths	Hundredths	Thousandths
3.006				3	0	0	6
3.006×10^3	3	0	0	6			

$$3.006 \times 10^3 = 3.006 \times (10 \times 10 \times 10)$$
$$= 3.006 \times 1{,}000$$
$$= 3{,}006$$

When you multiply a decimal by 10^3 or 1,000, each digit of the decimal moves 3 places to the left in the place-value chart.

TRY Practice multiplying decimals by powers of 10

Multiply.

1 $0.6 \times 10^2 =$ _____

2 $3.09 \times 10^2 =$ _____

3 $5.3 \times 10^3 =$ _____

4 $0.421 \times 10^3 =$ _____

Fill in each blank with 10, 10^2, or 10^3.

5 $0.7 \times$ _____ $= 70$

6 $9.3 \times$ _____ $= 9{,}300$

7 $5.2 \times$ _____ $= 52$

8 $0.03 \times$ _____ $= 30$

INDEPENDENT PRACTICE

Fill in the table.

1

	0.136	3.54	2.079	24.5	42.015
× 10					
× 100					
× 1,000					

Multiply.

2 0.5 × 30 = _____

3 0.127 × 80 = _____

4 0.044 × 60 = _____

5 1.6 × 500 = _____

6 2.36 × 700 = _____

7 0.018 × 300 = _____

8 8.7 × 2,000 = _____

9 0.021 × 5,000 = _____

10 2.019 × 8,000 = _____

11 0.4 × 9,000 = _____

Fill in each blank.

12 6.75 × _____ = 67.5

13 0.498 × _____ = 4.98

14 2.01 × _____ = 201

15 0.055 × _____ = 5.5

16 0.47 × _____ = 470

17 _____ × 38.715 = 38,715

Multiply.

18 $3.09 × 10^3$ = _____

19 $0.421 × 10^2$ = _____

Fill in each blank with 10, 10^2, or 10^3.

20 3.5 × _____ = 350

21 0.008 × _____ = 8

Name: _____   Date: _____

Dividing Decimals

Learning Objectives:
- Divide decimals up to 2 decimal places by 1-digit whole numbers.
- Round quotients to the nearest tenth (1 decimal place) or hundredth (2 decimal places).

THINK

Jason is thinking of a decimal. When the decimal is multiplied by 7, the product is _____.52. Find the possible values of the missing digit. What is the decimal Jason is thinking of in each case?

ENGAGE

1 Use to model the problem.
Katelyn spent $0.60 to buy 3 small erasers. Show two different ways to find the cost of each eraser.

2 An eraser cost $0.46. Edward spent $1.84 on some erasers. How many erasers did he buy?

LEARN Divide decimals by a whole number without regrouping

1 a What is 4 ÷ 2?

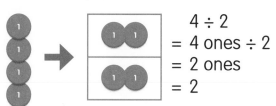

$$4 ÷ 2$$
$$= 4 \text{ ones} ÷ 2$$
$$= 2 \text{ ones}$$
$$= 2$$

b What is 0.4 ÷ 2?

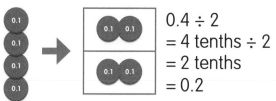

$$0.4 ÷ 2$$
$$= 4 \text{ tenths} ÷ 2$$
$$= 2 \text{ tenths}$$
$$= 0.2$$

c What is 0.04 ÷ 2?

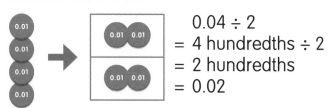

$$0.04 ÷ 2$$
$$= 4 \text{ hundredths} ÷ 2$$
$$= 2 \text{ hundredths}$$
$$= 0.02$$

© 2020 Marshall Cavendish Education Pte Ltd

2 Divide 8.4 by 2.

$8.4 \div 2 = ?$

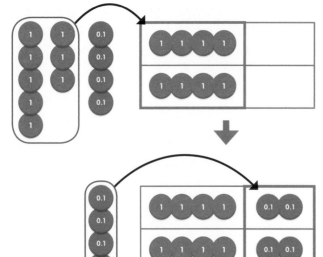

Step 1 Divide the ones by 2.

8 ones ÷ 2

= 4 ones in each group

Step 2 Divide the tenths by 2.

4 tenths ÷ 2

= 2 tenths in each group

$8.4 \div 2 = 4.2$

Let's recap!

Step 1	Step 2

TRY Practice dividing decimals by a whole number without regrouping

Divide.

1 $0.6 \div 3 =$ _____

2 $0.06 \div 3 =$ _____

3 $6.04 \div 2 =$ _____

4 $4.8 \div 4 =$ _____

1 Use to divide 5.25 by 3.

2 Leslie spent $28.50 to buy some shirts. The cost of each shirt is $4.75. Discuss to find out how many shirts he bought.

LEARN Divide decimals by a whole number with regrouping

1 Divide 6.12 by 3.

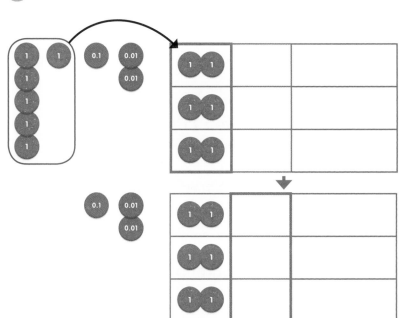

Step 1 Divide the ones by 3.

6 ones ÷ 3
= 2 ones in each group

Step 2 Divide the tenths by 3.

1 tenth ÷ 3
= 0 tenths in each group with a remainder of 1

Regroup.
1 tenth
= 10 hundredths
Add the hundredths.

10 hundredths
+ 2 hundredths
= 12 hundredths

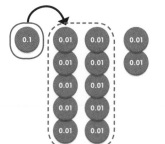

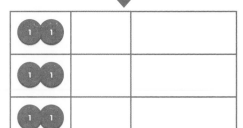

Step 3 Divide the hundredths by 3.

12 hundredths ÷ 3
= 4 hundredths in each group

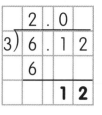

6.12 ÷ 3 = 2.04

Let's recap!

Step 1	Step 2	Step 3

Step 1:

```
    2 .
3) 6 . 1 2
   6
```

Step 2:

```
    2 . 0
3) 6 . 1 2
   6
          1
```

Step 3:

```
    2 . 0 4
3) 6 . 1 2
   6
         1 2
         1 2
             0
```

2 Divide 1 by 2.

$1 \div 2 = ?$

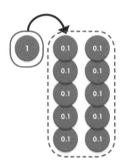

Step 1 Divide the ones by 2.

1 one ÷ 2 = 0 ones in each group with remainder of 1 one

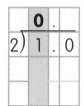

```
    0 .
2) 1 . 0
```

Regroup.

1 one = 10 tenths

```
    0 .
2) 1 . 0
```

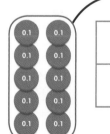 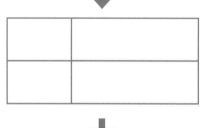

Step 2 Divide the tenths by 2.

10 tenths ÷ 2
= 5 tenths in each group

```
    0 . 5
2) 1 . 0
    1   0
        0
```

$1 \div 2 = 0.5$

Recall that $1 \div 2$ is the same as $\frac{1}{2}$.

So, $\frac{1}{2}$ is 0.5 when written as a decimal.

Let's recap!

Step 1	Step 2
``` 0. ```	``` 0 . 5 ```
``` 2)1.0 ```	``` 2)1.0 ```
	``` 1 0 ```
	``` 0 ```

③ Divide 2 by 3. Round your answer to the nearest tenth.
2 ÷ 3 = ?

Step 1	Step 2
``` 0. 6 ```	``` 0. 6 6 ```
``` 3)2.0 0 ```	``` 3)2.0 0 ```
``` 1 8 ```	``` 1 8 ```
``` 2 ```	``` 2 0 ```
	``` 1 8 ```
	``` 2 ```

To round a quotient to the nearest tenth or 1 decimal place, divide to 2 decimal places.

2 ÷ 3 = 0.7 (rounded to the nearest tenth)

④ Divide 0.72 by 6. Round your answer to the nearest tenth.
0.72 ÷ 6 = ?

Step 1	Step 2
``` 0. 1 ```	``` 0. 1 2 ```
``` 6)0.7 2 ```	``` 6)0.7 2 ```
``` 6 ```	``` 6 ```
``` 1 ```	``` 1 2 ```
	``` 1 2 ```
	``` 0 ```

0.72 ÷ 6 = 0.1 (rounded to the nearest tenth)

5 Divide 5.03 by 4. Give your answer correct to 1 decimal place.

$5.03 \div 4 = ?$

Step 1	Step 2	Step 3

Step 1:
```
      1 .
  4) 5 . 0 3
     4
     1
```

Step 2:
```
      1 . 2
  4) 5 . 0 3
     4
     1 0
       8
       2
```

Step 3:
```
      1 . 2 5
  4) 5 . 0 3
     4
     1 0
       8
       2 3
       2 0
         3
```

$5.03 \div 4 = 1.3$ (correct to 1 decimal place)

6 Divide 9 by 7. Give your answer correct to 2 decimal places.

$9 \div 7 = ?$

To round a quotient to 2 decimal places, divide to 3 decimal places.

Step 1	Step 2	Step 3	Step 4

Step 1:
```
      1 .
  7) 9 . 0 0
     7
     2
```

Step 2:
```
      1 . 2
  7) 9 . 0 0
     7
     2 0
     1 4
       6
```

Step 3:
```
      1 . 2 8
  7) 9 . 0 0
     7
     2 0
     1 4
       6 0
       5 6
         4
```

Step 4:
```
      1 . 2 8 5
  7) 9 . 0 0 0
     7
     2 0
     1 4
       6 0
       5 6
         4 0
         3 5
           5
```

$9 \div 7 = 1.29$ (correct to 2 decimal places)

Work in pairs.

① Use ⬤₁₀₀ ⬤₁₀ ⬤₁ ⬤₀.₁ ⬤₀.₀₁ ⬤₀.₀₀₁ and a place-value chart to divide the decimals and complete the first column of the table. Then, divide the whole numbers and complete the second column of the table.

	Divide decimals	Divide whole numbers
a	$4.6 \div 2 =$ _____	$46 \div 2 =$ _____
b	$0.84 \div 2 =$ _____	$84 \div 2 =$ _____
c	$0.93 \div 3 =$ _____	$93 \div 3 =$ _____
d	$3.2 \div 2 =$ _____	$32 \div 2 =$ _____
e	$6.25 \div 5 =$ _____	$625 \div 5 =$ _____

② Compare the answers in the table in ①. What do you notice?

TRY Practice dividing decimals by a whole number with regrouping

Divide.

① $3.5 \div 7 =$ _____

② $0.8 \div 5 =$ _____

③ $5 \div 4 =$ _____

④ $28.02 \div 6 =$ _____

Divide. Round each answer to the nearest tenth.

5 $8.7 \div 4 =$ _____

6 $7 \div 6 =$ _____

7 $1.7 \div 3 =$ _____

8 $5.12 \div 8 =$ _____

Divide. Give each answer correct to 2 decimal places.

9 $8 \div 3 =$ _____

10 $2.1 \div 4 =$ _____

11 $10.43 \div 5 =$ _____

12 $38.6 \div 9 =$ _____

MATH SHARING

Mathematical Habit 6 Use precise mathematical language

Fractions and decimals are closely related. How can you relate fractions and decimals using division? Use an example to explain your reasoning to your partner.

INDEPENDENT PRACTICE

Divide.

1 $0.8 \div 4 =$ _____

2 $0.08 \div 4 =$ _____

3 $4.08 \div 2 =$ _____

4 $0.9 \div 5 =$ _____

5 $9.87 \div 3 =$ _____

6 $63.72 \div 9 =$ _____

Divide. Round each answer to the nearest tenth.

7 $8 \div 7 =$ _____

8 $3.5 \div 3 =$ _____

9 $9.76 \div 4 =$ _____

10 $6.17 \div 2 =$ _____

11. $5.23 \div 9 =$ _____

12. $11.32 \div 5 =$ _____

Divide. Give each answer correct to 2 decimal places.

13. $9 \div 8 =$ _____

14. $0.37 \div 2 =$ _____

15. $5.6 \div 9 =$ _____

16. $7.55 \div 6 =$ _____

17. $19.03 \div 5 =$ _____

18. $41.8 \div 7 =$ _____

Dividing Decimals by Tens, Hundreds, and Thousands

Learning Objectives:
- Divide decimals up to 3 decimal places by 10, 100, or 1,000, and their multiples.
- Divide decimals up to 3 decimal places by powers of 10.

THINK

A roll of copper wire is 1,250 meters long. The roll of wire was cut equally into 200 pieces.

a How long is each piece?

b Juliet wants to buy some pieces of the wire. She has $230. If each piece of wire costs $7.20, how many pieces of wire can she buy?

ENGAGE

1 Use ⚫100 ⚫10 ⚫1 ⚫0.1 ⚫0.01 ⚫0.001 to show 0.2 and 0.25. Use ⚫100 ⚫10 ⚫1 ⚫0.1 ⚫0.01 ⚫0.001 to divide the decimals by 10.

2 Find each missing digit in the equation and mark the decimal point at the correct place. ◯.4◯ ÷ 10 = ◯3◯5

LEARN Divide decimals by 10

1 ⚫1 = [0.1][0.1][0.1][0.1][0.1][0.1][0.1][0.1][0.1][0.1] ÷ 10 → 0.1

Ones	Tenths	Hundredths	Thousandths
1			
	1		

$1 \div 10 = 0.1$

⚫0.1 = [0.01][0.01][0.01][0.01][0.01][0.01][0.01][0.01][0.01][0.01] ÷ 10 → 0.01

Ones	Tenths	Hundredths	Thousandths
	1		
		1	

$0.1 \div 10 = 0.01$

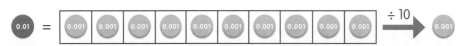

Ones	Tenths	Hundredths	Thousandths
		1	
			1

$0.01 \div 10 = 0.001$

2 **a** What is $50.1 \div 10$?

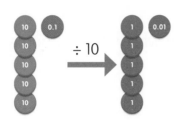

Ten	Ones	Tenths	Hundredths
5	0	1	
	5	0	1

$50.1 \div 10 = 5.01$

b What is $2.35 \div 10$?

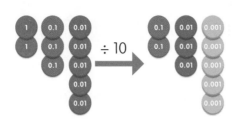

Ones	Tenths	Hundredths	Thousandths
2	3	5	
	2	3	5

$2.35 \div 10 = 0.235$

Hands-on Activity **Dividing decimals by 10**

Work in pairs.

1 Use 100 10 1 0.1 0.01 0.001 to show 12. Then, use 100 10 1 0.1 0.01 0.001 to show the result of $12 \div 10$. Fill in the table. Draw arrows to show how each digit moves in the table.

	Tens	Ones	Tenths	Hundredths	Thousandths
12					
$12 \div 10$					
0.13					
$0.13 \div 10$					

2 **Mathematical Habit 8 Look for patterns**

How is dividing a decimal by 10 the same as dividing a whole number by 10?

3 What is another way to divide decimals by 10? Explain how you can tell whether you should shift the decimal point to the left or right.

TRY Practice dividing decimals by 10

Fill in each blank.

1 What is 21 ÷ 10?

Tens	Ones		Tenths	Hundredths
2			1	
	___		___	

21 ÷ 10 = _____

2 What is 3.2 ÷ 10?

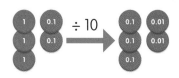

Ones		Tenths	Hundredths	Thousandths
3		2		
	___		___	

3.2 ÷ 10 = _____

© 2020 Marshall Cavendish Education Pte Ltd

3 What is 5.03 ÷ 10?

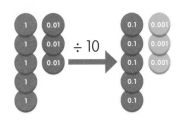

Ones		Tenths	Hundredths	Thousandths
5		0	3	
		_____	_____	_____

5.03 ÷ 10 = _____

Divide.

4 291 ÷ 10 = _____

5 49.1 ÷ 10 = _____

6 6.31 ÷ 10 = _____

7 4.07 ÷ 10 = _____

8 6.78 ÷ 10 = _____

9 89.02 ÷ 10 = _____

Fill in each blank.

10 45.6 ÷ _____ = 4.56

11 0.55 ÷ _____ = 0.055

12 _____ ÷ 10 = 39.14

13 _____ ÷ 10 = 1.008

14 _____ ÷ 10 = 40.05

15 _____ ÷ 10 = 0.006

ENGAGE

How can you use 8 ÷ 10 to find 8 ÷ 20? What is another way to find the answer? Explain your thinking to your partner.

LEARN Divide decimals by tens

1 **a** What is 6 ÷ 30?

▶ **Method 1**

6 ÷ 10 = 0.6   0.6 ÷ 3 = 0.2

$$6 \div 30$$
$$= (6 \div 10) \div 3$$
$$= 0.6 \div 3$$
$$= 0.2$$

▶ **Method 2**

6 ÷ 3 = 2   2 ÷ 10 = 0.2

$$6 \div 30$$
$$= (6 \div 3) \div 10$$
$$= 2 \div 10$$
$$= 0.2$$

b What is 0.6 ÷ 30?

▶ **Method 1**

0.6 ÷ 10 = 0.06   0.06 ÷ 3 = 0.02

$$0.6 \div 30$$
$$= (0.6 \div 10) \div 3$$
$$= 0.06 \div 3$$
$$= 0.02$$

▶ **Method 2**

0.6 ÷ 3 = 0.2   0.2 ÷ 10 = 0.02

$$0.6 \div 30$$
$$= (0.6 \div 3) \div 10$$
$$= 0.2 \div 10$$
$$= 0.02$$

c What is $0.06 \div 30$?

 ÷ 3 ➡ ÷ 10 ➡ 0.001 0.001

$0.06 \div 3 = 0.02 \qquad 0.02 \div 10 = 0.002$

$0.06 \div 30$
$= (0.06 \div 3) \div 10$
$= 0.02 \div 10$
$= 0.002$

TRY Practice dividing decimals by tens

Fill in each blank.

1 $8 \div 40 = 8 \div \underline{\hspace{1.5cm}} \div 10$

$= \underline{\hspace{1.5cm}} \div 10$

$= \underline{\hspace{1.5cm}}$

2 $6 \div 20 = (6 \div \underline{\hspace{1.5cm}}) \div 2$

$= \underline{\hspace{1.5cm}} \div 2$

$= \underline{\hspace{1.5cm}}$

3 $0.8 \div 40 = \underline{\hspace{1.5cm}}$

4 $0.6 \div 20 = \underline{\hspace{1.5cm}}$

5 $0.08 \div 40 = \underline{\hspace{1.5cm}}$

6 $0.06 \div 20 = \underline{\hspace{1.5cm}}$

Fill in each blank.

7 $15 \div 30 = \underline{\hspace{1.5cm}}$

8 $2.4 \div 40 = \underline{\hspace{1.5cm}}$

9 $0.21 \div 70 = \underline{\hspace{1.5cm}}$

10 $2.05 \div 50 = \underline{\hspace{1.5cm}}$

ENGAGE

Use 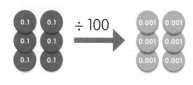 or a place-value chart to find each quotient.

a 200 ÷ 100   **b** 20 ÷ 100   **c** 2 ÷ 100   **d** 0.2 ÷ 100

What do you notice? Share your observations.

LEARN Divide decimals by 100 and 1,000

1   **a**   What is 60 ÷ 100?

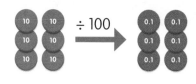

Tens	Ones	Tenths	Hundredths
6			
		6	

60 ÷ 100 = 0.6

b   What is 6 ÷ 100?

Ones	Tenths	Hundredths	Thousandths
6			
		6	

6 ÷ 100 = 0.06

c   What is 0.6 ÷ 100?

Ones	Tenths	Hundredths	Thousandths
	6		
			6

0.6 ÷ 100 = 0.006

What pattern do you notice?

2 **a** What is 24 ÷ 100?

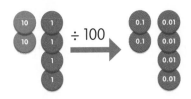

Tens	Ones	Tenths	Hundredths
2	4		
		2	4

24 ÷ 100 = 0.24

b What is 4.2 ÷ 100?

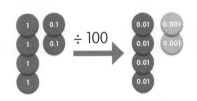

Ones	Tenths	Hundredths	Thousandths
4	2		
		4	2

4.2 ÷ 100 = 0.042

3 **a** What is 300 ÷ 1,000?

Hundreds	Tens	Ones	Tenths
3			
			3

300 ÷ 1,000 = 0.3

b What is 30 ÷ 1,000?

Tens	Ones	Tenths	Hundredths
3			
			3

30 ÷ 1,000 = 0.03

c What is 3 ÷ 1,000?

Ones	Tenths	Hundredths	Thousandths
3			
			3

3 ÷ 1,000 = 0.003

4 **a** What is 24 ÷ 1,000?

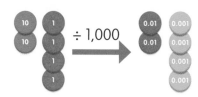

Tens	Ones		Tenths	Hundredths	Thousandths
2	4				
				2	4

24 ÷ 1,000 = 0.024

b What is 320 ÷ 1,000?

Hundreds	Tens	Ones		Tenths	Hundredths
3	2				
				3	2

320 ÷ 1,000 = 0.32

TRY Practice dividing decimals by 100 and 1,000

Divide.

1 308 ÷ 100 = _____

2 3.8 ÷ 100 = _____

3 30.8 ÷ 100 = _____

4 2,016 ÷ 1,000 = _____

5 201 ÷ 1,000 = _____

6 12 ÷ 1,000 = _____

Fill in each blank.

7 $420 \div \underline{\hspace{2cm}} = 4.2$

8 $70.5 \div \underline{\hspace{2cm}} = 0.705$

9 $1{,}061 \div \underline{\hspace{2cm}} = 1.061$

10 $890 \div \underline{\hspace{2cm}} = 0.89$

11 $\underline{\hspace{2cm}} \div 100 = 3.01$

12 $\underline{\hspace{2cm}} \div 1{,}000 = 67.25$

MATH SHARING

Mathematical Habit 3 Construct viable arguments

Explain how dividing a decimal by 100 or 1,000 is the same as dividing a whole number by 100 or 1,000.
Is there another way to divide decimals by 100 or 1,000?

ENGAGE

What is $20 \div 100$? Now, divide the result by 2.
What is $2 \div 100$? Now, divide the result by 2.
What is $0.2 \div 100$? Now, divide the result by 2.
What do you think $20 \div 200$, $2 \div 200$, and $0.2 \div 200$ are equal to? What is another way to find each quotient?

LEARN Divide decimals by hundreds and thousands

1 **a** What is $60 \div 300$?

▶ **Method 1**

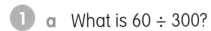

$60 \div 100 = 0.6$ $0.6 \div 3 = 0.2$

$60 \div 300$
$= (60 \div 100) \div 3$
$= 0.6 \div 3$
$= 0.2$

▶ **Method 2**

$60 \div 3 = 20$ $20 \div 100 = 0.2$

$60 \div 300$
$= (60 \div 3) \div 100$
$= 20 \div 100$
$= 0.2$

b What is 6 ÷ 300?

▶ **Method 1**

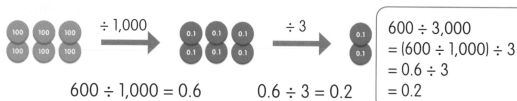

$$6 \div 100 = 0.06 \qquad 0.06 \div 3 = 0.02$$

$$6 \div 300$$
$$= (6 \div 100) \div 3$$
$$= 0.06 \div 3$$
$$= 0.02$$

▶ **Method 2**

$$6 \div 3 = 2 \qquad 2 \div 100 = 0.02$$

$$6 \div 300$$
$$= (6 \div 3) \div 100$$
$$= 2 \div 100$$
$$= 0.02$$

c What is 0.6 ÷ 300?

$$0.6 \div 3 = 0.2 \qquad 0.2 \div 100 = 0.002$$

$$0.6 \div 300$$
$$= (0.6 \div 3) \div 100$$
$$= 0.2 \div 100$$
$$= 0.002$$

2 **a** What is 600 ÷ 3,000?

▶ **Method 1**

$$600 \div 1,000 = 0.6 \qquad 0.6 \div 3 = 0.2$$

$$600 \div 3,000$$
$$= (600 \div 1,000) \div 3$$
$$= 0.6 \div 3$$
$$= 0.2$$

▶ **Method 2**

$$600 \div 3 = 200 \qquad 200 \div 1,000 = 0.2$$

$$600 \div 3,000$$
$$= (600 \div 3) \div 1,000$$
$$= 200 \div 1,000$$
$$= 0.2$$

b What is $60 \div 3{,}000$?

▶ **Method 1**

$60 \div 1{,}000 = 0.06$ $0.06 \div 3 = 0.02$

$60 \div 3{,}000$
$= (60 \div 1{,}000) \div 3$
$= 0.06 \div 3$
$= 0.02$

▶ **Method 2**

$60 \div 3 = 20$ $20 \div 1{,}000 = 0.02$

$60 \div 3{,}000$
$= (60 \div 3) \div 1{,}000$
$= 20 \div 1{,}000$
$= 0.02$

c What is $6 \div 3{,}000$?

$6 \div 3 = 2$ $2 \div 1{,}000 = 0.002$

$6 \div 3{,}000$
$= (6 \div 3) \div 1{,}000$
$= 2 \div 1{,}000$
$= 0.002$

TRY Practice dividing decimals by hundreds and thousands

Divide.

1 $280 \div 200 = (280 \div \underline{\hspace{1cm}}) \div 100$

$= \underline{\hspace{1.5cm}} \div 100$

$= \underline{\hspace{1.5cm}}$

2 $800 \div 4{,}000 = (800 \div \underline{\hspace{1cm}}) \div 1{,}000$

$= \underline{\hspace{1.5cm}} \div 1{,}000$

$= \underline{\hspace{1.5cm}}$

3 $28 \div 200 = \underline{\hspace{2cm}}$

4 $80 \div 4{,}000 = \underline{\hspace{2cm}}$

5 $2.8 \div 200 = \underline{\hspace{2cm}}$

6 $8 \div 4{,}000 = \underline{\hspace{2cm}}$

7 $45 \div 5{,}000 = \underline{\hspace{2cm}}$

8 $2164 \div 4{,}000 = \underline{\hspace{2cm}}$

INDEPENDENT PRACTICE

Fill in the tables.

1

	4,078	407	47.8	4.7	4.78
÷ 10					

	4,078	407.8	407	47.8	4.7
÷ 100					

	4,078	4,780	4,070	408	480
÷ 1,000					

Multiply.

2 $18 \div 30 =$ _____

3 $1.6 \div 40 =$ _____

4 $0.14 \div 70 =$ _____

5 $1.68 \div 80 =$ _____

6 $93 \div 300 =$ _____

7 $2.4 \div 400 =$ _____

8 $49.7 \div 700 =$ _____

9 $75 \div 5,000 =$ _____

10 $396 \div 6,000 =$ _____

11 $1,840 \div 8,000 =$ _____

Fill in each blank.

12 $23.5 \div$ _____ $= 2.35$

13 $0.79 \div$ _____ $= 0.079$

14 $260 \div$ _____ $= 2.6$

15 $80.3 \div$ _____ $= 0.803$

16 $1,928 \div$ _____ $= 1.928$

17 $354 \div$ _____ $= 0.354$

18 _____ $\div 10 = 89.51$

19 _____ $\div 100 = 7.26$

20 _____ $\div 1,000 = 41.65$

21 _____ $\div 1,000 = 1.001$

7 Estimating Decimals

Learning Objective:
- Estimate decimal sums, differences, products, and quotients.

**THINK**

Evelyn bought 4 story books at $11.75. Estimate the cost of each story book. She bought some pens for a sum of $26.95. If each pen cost about $4, how many pens did she buy? How can you check that your answer is correct?

ENGAGE

Heather bought a fruit for $6.75 and two bags of rice for $15.45.
Three students estimated the total cost of the items Heather bought.
Student A: $23   Student B: $21   Student C: $22
Explain how each student arrived at their answer. Whose estimate was closest to the correct answer?

LEARN Estimate sums by rounding to the nearest whole number

1 Just as you did with whole numbers, you can estimate the answers to problems involving decimals.

Estimate $6.75 + $15.45 by rounding to the nearest dollar.

To the nearest dollar, $6.75 rounds to $7.
To the nearest dollar, $15.45 rounds to $15.
$7 + $15 = $22
$6.75 + $15.45 is about $22.

2 Add 31.65 and 8.02. Then, estimate to check that your answer is reasonable.

Add:

```
  3 1 . 6 5
+   8 . 0 2
_____
  3 9 . 6 7
```

Estimate:
31.65 is about 32.
8.02 is about 8.
32 + 8 = 40

How close is your estimated answer to the actual answer?

39.67 is close to 40. The answer is reasonable.

TRY Practice estimating sums

Add. Then, estimate to check that each answer is reasonable.

1 $3.78 + 5.2 =$ _____

2 $12.9 + 3.26 =$ _____

3 $14.9 + 25.23 =$ _____

Estimate:
3.78 is about _____.

5.2 is about _____.

_____ + _____ = _____

_____ is close to _____.

The answer

is _____.

Estimate:
12.9 is about _____.

3.26 is about _____.

_____ + _____ = _____

_____ is close to _____.

The answer

is _____.

Estimate:
14.9 is about _____.

25.23 is about _____.

_____ + _____ = _____

_____ is close to _____.

The answer

is _____.

ENGAGE

Draw a number line to show 4.7 and 8.25. How does the number line help you estimate the difference between the two numbers? Explain your reasoning.

LEARN Estimate differences by rounding to the nearest whole number

1 Estimate the value of $7.13 - 5.7$ by rounding to the nearest whole number.

To the nearest whole number, 7.13 rounds to 7.
To the nearest whole number, 5.7 rounds to 6.
$7 - 6 = 1$
$7.13 - 5.7$ is about 1.

© 2020 Marshall Cavendish Education Pte Ltd

2 Subtract 1.86 from 11.09. Then, estimate to check that your answer is reasonable.

Subtract:

$$\begin{array}{r} \overset{0}{\cancel{1}}\overset{10}{\cancel{1}}.\overset{10}{\cancel{0}}9 \\ -\ 1\ .\ 8\ 6 \\ \hline 9\ .\ 2\ 3 \end{array}$$

Estimate:
11.09 is about 11.
1.86 is about 2.
11 − 2 = 9

How close is your estimated answer to the actual answer?

9.23 is close to 9. The answer is reasonable.

TRY Practice estimating differences

Subtract. Then, estimate to check that each answer is reasonable.

1 9.87 − 0.96 = _____ **2** 5.75 − 5.05 = _____ **3** 24.59 − 19.68 = _____

Estimate:
9.87 is about ____.

0.96 is about ____.

____ − ____ = ____

____ is close to ____.

The answer

is _____.

Estimate:
5.75 is about ____.

5.05 is about ____.

____ − ____ = ____

____ is close to ____.

The answer

is _____.

Estimate:
24.59 is about ____.

19.68 is about ____.

____ − ____ = ____

____ is close to ____.

The answer

is _____.

Melanie has $25. She wants to buy 2 novels that cost $12.35 each. She thinks that she has enough money. Is she reasonable? Explain your thinking.

LEARN Estimate the product of a decimal and a whole number by rounding the decimal

1 Estimate the value of 11.97 × 2 by rounding 11.97 to the nearest whole number.

To the nearest whole number, 11.97 rounds to 12.
12 × 2 = 24
11.97 × 2 is about 24.

2 Multiply 2.74 by 4. Then estimate to check that your answer is reasonable.

Multiply:

$$
\begin{array}{r}
\overset{2}{2}.\overset{1}{7}\,4 \\
\times \quad\;\; 4 \\
\hline
1\,0\,.\,9\,6
\end{array}
$$

Estimate:
2.74 is about 3.
3 × 4 = 12

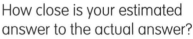
How close is your estimated answer to the actual answer?

10.96 is close to 12. The answer is reasonable.

TRY Practice estimating products

Multiply. Then, estimate to check that each answer is reasonable.

1 1.23 × 3 = _____

Estimate:

1.23 is about ____.

____ × ____ = ____

_____ is close to _____.

The answer is _____.

2 2.12 × 4 = _____

Estimate:

2.12 is about ____.

____ × ____ = ____

_____. is close to _____.

The answer is _____.

3 $0.98 \times 3 =$ _____

Estimate:

0.98 is about ____.

____ × ____ = ____

_____ is close to _____.

The answer is _____.

4 $3.15 \times 9 =$ _____

Estimate:

3.15 is about ____.

____ × ____ = ____

_____ is close to _____.

The answer is _____.

ENGAGE

Elijah has $26.52. He wants to find out if he has enough money to buy movie tickets for 3 persons. He thinks if each ticket costs less than $9, he can buy them. Is he reasonable? Explain your thinking.

LEARN Estimate the quotient of a decimal and a whole number

1 Estimate the value of $23.64 \div 3$.

Just as in division of whole numbers, to estimate the quotient, choose a number close to the dividend that can be evenly divided by the divisor.

Change 23.64 to the nearest whole number that can be evenly divided by 3.

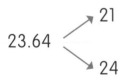

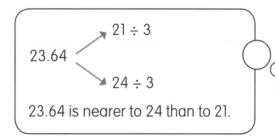

23.64 is nearer to 24 than to 21.

Then, divide.

$24 \div 3 = 8$

$23.64 \div 3$ is about 8.

2 Divide 40.4 by 5. Then, estimate to check that your answer is reasonable.

Divide:

```
      8 . 0 8
5) 4 0 . 4 0
   4 0
   ─────
        4
        0
      ─────
      4 0
      4 0
      ─────
         0
```

Estimate:
40.4 is about 40.
40 ÷ 5 = 8

How close is your estimated answer to the actual answer?

8.08 is close to 8. The answer is reasonable.

TRY Practice estimating quotients

Divide. Then, estimate to check that each answer is reasonable.

1 12.3 ÷ 3 = _____

2 17.73 ÷ 9 = _____

3 20.93 ÷ 7 = _____

Estimate:
12.3 is about ____.

____ ÷ ____ = ____

____ is close to ____.

The answer

is _____.

Estimate:
17.73 is about ____.

____ ÷ ____ = ____

____ is close to ____.

The answer

is _____.

Estimate:
20.93 is about ____.

____ ÷ ____ = ____

____ is close to ____.

The answer

is _____.

ENGAGE

What are two different ways to estimate each of the following?
a the sum of 4.5 and 6.35   **b** the product of 4.5 and 6.35
Explain which way gives you a better estimate for **a** and **b**.

LEARN Estimate by rounding to the nearest tenth

1 Estimate the value of 2.49 + 6.54 by rounding to the nearest tenth.

To the nearest tenth, 2.49 rounds to 2.5.
To the nearest tenth, 6.54 rounds to 6.5.
2.5 + 6.5 = 9
2.49 + 6.54 is about 9.

> You can estimate differences and products similarly by rounding to the nearest tenth.

TRY Practice estimating by rounding to the nearest tenth

Fill in each blank.

1 10.46 − 3.52

10.46 is 10.5 when rounded to the nearest tenth.
3.52 is 3.5 when rounded to the nearest tenth.

10.5 − 3.5 = _____

So, 10.46 − 3.52 is about _____.

> 5 tenths × 4 = 20 tenths
> = 2

2 0.47 × 4

0.47 is 0.5 when rounded to the nearest tenth.

0.5 × 4 = _____

So, 0.47 × 4 is about _____.

3 3.46 ÷ 4

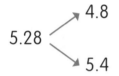

> Change 3.46 to the nearest tenth that can be evenly divided by 4.
> 36 tenths ÷ 4 = 9 tenths
> = 0.9

3.46 is nearer to 3.6 than to 3.2.

3.6 ÷ 4 = _____

So, 3.46 ÷ 4 is about _____.

4 5.28 ÷ 6

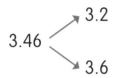

> 54 tenths ÷ 6 = 9 tenths
> = 0.9

5.28 is nearer to 5.4 than to 4.8.

5.4 ÷ 6 = _____

So, 5.28 ÷ 6 is about _____.

Calculate. Then, estimate to check that each answer is reasonable.

5 $12.42 + $12.64 = _____

6 $1.45 − $0.54 = _____

7 $1.79 × 3 = _____

8 $1.45 ÷ 5 = _____

INDEPENDENT PRACTICE

Add. Then, estimate to check that each answer is reasonable.

1 $6.3 + 3.52 =$ _____

2 $14.24 + 5.78 =$ _____

Subtract. Then, estimate to check that each answer is reasonable.

3 $2.45 - 0.54 =$ _____

4 $34.84 - 15.09 =$ _____

Multiply. Then, estimate to check that each answer is reasonable.

5 $6.47 \times 8 =$ _____

6 $14.97 \times 6 =$ _____

Divide. Then, estimate the quotient to check that each answer is reasonable.

7 $6.49 \div 5 =$ _____

8 $17.82 \div 3 =$ _____

Calculate. Then, estimate to check that each answer is reasonable.

9 25.09 + 4.92 = _____

10 9.49 + 23.86 = _____

11 7.51 − 3.48 = _____

12 76.84 − 24.18 = _____

13 3.21 × 3 = _____

14 7.28 × 9 = _____

15 11.68 ÷ 4 = _____

16 63.72 ÷ 6 = _____

8 Converting Metric Units

Learning Objectives:
- Convert from a larger metric unit to a smaller unit.
- Convert from a smaller metric unit to a larger unit.

THINK

1. The mass of 7,000 paper clips is 3.5 kilograms. How do you express the mass in grams?

2. A man drinks some glasses of water and twice as many cups of water each day. Each glass contains 150 milliliters of water and each cup is 100 milliliters. He drinks a total of 3.15 litres of water. How many cups of water does he drink?

ENGAGE

A gardener paves 6 tiles along the edge of a fence. Each tile measures 0.46 meter. Use 🔲 to model the length of the fence. How long is the fence in meters and centimeters?

LEARN Convert a measurement from a larger unit to a smaller unit

1. Express 0.8 meter in centimeters.

▶ **Method 1**

0 m	0.1 m	0.2 m	0.3 m	0.4 m	0.5 m	0.6 m	0.7 m	0.8 m	0.9 m	1 m
0 cm	10 cm	20 cm	30 cm	40 cm	50 cm	60 cm	70 cm	80 cm	90 cm	100 cm

0.8 m = 80 cm

▶ **Method 2**

1 m = 100 cm — 0.8

0.8 m = 0.8 × 100

= 80 cm

2 Express 0.5 kilogram in grams.

▶ **Method 1**

0 kg	0.1 kg	0.2 kg	0.3 kg	0.4 kg	0.5 kg	0.6 kg	0.7 kg	0.8 kg	0.9 kg	1 kg
0 g	100 g	200 g	300 g	400 g	500 g	600 g	700 g	800 g	900 g	1,000 g

0.5 kg = 500 g

▶ **Method 2**

1 kg = 1,000 g
0.5 kg = 0.5 × 1,000 ⟶ 0.5
      = 500 g

3 Express 3.28 kilometers in meters.

1 km = 1,000 m
3.28 km = 3.28 × 1,000
      = 3,280 m

4 Convert 1.205 liters to milliliters.

1 L = 1,000 mL
1.205 L = 1.205 × 1,000
      = 1,205 mL

> To convert from a larger unit to a smaller unit, you multiply.

5 Express 25.08 meters in meters and centimeters.

25.08 m = 25 m + 0.08 m
      = 25 m 8 cm

> 0.08 m = 0.08 × 100
>   = 8 cm

6 Express 16.55 kilometers in kilometers and meters.

16.55 km = 16 km + 0.55 km
      = 16 km 550 m

> 0.55 m = 0.55 × 1,000
>   = 550 m

7 Express 8.605 kilograms in kilograms and grams.

8.605 kg = 8 kg + 0.605 kg
= 8 kg 605 g

> 0.605 kg = 0.605 × 1,000
> = 605 g

8 Convert 8.028 liters to liters and milliliters.

8.028 L = 8 L + 0.028 L
= 8 L 28 mL

> 0.028 L = 0.028 × 1,000
> = 28 mL

TRY Practice converting a measurement from a larger unit to a smaller unit

Fill in each blank.

1 30.6 m = _____ × _____

= _____ cm

2 6.5 km = _____ × _____

= _____ m

3 10.72 kg = _____ × _____

= _____ g

4 15.924 L = _____ × _____

= _____ mL

5 4.35 m = _____ m + _____ m

= _____ m _____ cm

6 9.024 km = _____ km + _____ km

= _____ km _____ m

7 18.75 kg = _____ kg + _____ kg

= _____ kg _____ g

8 20.25 L = _____ L + _____ L

= _____ L _____ mL

ENGAGE

1 What is 1 centimeter in meters? What is 8 centimeters in meters? What are two ways to find the answer?

2 Some bricks are lined along the length of a rectangular patch that is 2 bricks wide. The perimeter of the patch is 1.6 meters. If each brick measures 8 centimeters by 8 centimeters, how many bricks are used in all?

LEARN Convert a measurement from a smaller unit to a larger unit

1 Express 30 centimeters in meters.

▶ **Method 1**

0 cm	10 cm	20 cm	30 cm	40 cm	50 cm	60 cm	70 cm	80 cm	90 cm	100 cm
0 m	0.1 m	0.2 m	0.3 m	0.4 m	0.5 m	0.6 m	0.7 m	0.8 m	0.9 m	1 m

30 cm = 0.3 m

▶ **Method 2**

100 cm = 1 m
30 cm = 30 ÷ 100 ——— 30
       = 0.3 m

2 Express 900 milliliters in liters.

▶ **Method 1**

0 mL	100 mL	200 mL	300 mL	400 mL	500 mL	600 mL	700 mL	800 mL	900 mL	1000 mL
0 L	0.1 L	0.2 L	0.3 L	0.4 L	0.5 L	0.6 L	0.7 L	0.8 L	0.9 L	1 L

900 mL = 0.9 L

▶ **Method 2**

1,000 mL = 1 L
900 mL = 900 ÷ 1,000 ——— 900
        = 0.9 L

3 Convert 2,500 grams to kilograms.

1,000 g = 1 kg
2,500 g = 2,500 ÷ 1,000
           = 2.5 kg

4 Convert 750 meters to kilometers.

1,000 m = 1 km
   750 m = 750 ÷ 1,000
            = 0.75 km

To convert from a smaller unit to a larger unit, you divide.

5 Express 33 meters 80 centimeters in meters.

33 m 80 cm = 33 m + 80 cm
              = 33 m + 0.8 m
              = 33.8 m

80 cm = 80 ÷ 100
         = 0.8 m

6 Express 3 kilometers 45 meters in kilometers.

3 km 45 m = 3 km + 45 m
             = 3 km + 0.045 km
             = 3.045 km

45 m = 45 ÷ 1,000
       = 0.045 km

7 Express 35 kilograms 600 grams in kilograms.

35 kg 600 g = 35 kg + 600 g
               = 35 kg + 0.6 kg
               = 35.6 kg

600 g = 600 ÷ 1,000
         = 0.6 kg

8 Express 2 liters 355 milliliters in liters.

$$2\ L\ 355\ mL = 2\ L + 355\ mL$$
$$= 2\ L + 0.355\ L$$
$$= 2.355\ L$$

| 355 mL = 355 ÷ 1,000 |
| = 0.355 L |

TRY Practice converting a measurement from a smaller unit to a larger unit

Fill in each blank.

1 123.5 cm = _____ ÷ _____

= _____ m

2 8,850 m = _____ ÷ _____

= _____ km

3 4,075 g = _____ ÷ _____

= _____ kg

4 48,060 mL = _____ ÷ _____

= _____ L

5 200 m 5 cm = _____ m + _____ m

= _____ m

6 75 L 800 mL = _____ L + _____ L

= _____ L

7 9 kg 5 g = _____ kg + _____ kg

= _____ kg

8 28 km 160 m = _____ km + _____ km

= _____ km

MATH SHARING

Mathematical Habit 3 Construct viable arguments

Find two examples of items that have measurements.
What are the uses of the different units of measurements?

INDEPENDENT PRACTICE

Fill in each blank.

1 16.02 m = _____ × _____

= _____ cm

2 4.95 km = _____ × _____

= _____ m

3 10.57 L = _____ × _____

= _____ mL

4 5.41 m = _____ m + _____ m

= _____ m _____ cm

5 2.068 kg = _____ kg + _____ kg

= _____ kg _____ g

6 37.19 L = _____ L + _____ L

= _____ L _____ mL

7 0.28 m = _____ cm

8 15.002 kg = _____ kg _____ g

Fill in each blank.

9 251.7 cm = _____ ÷ _____

  = _____ m

10 6,005 g = _____ ÷ _____

  = _____ kg

11 19,820 mL = _____ ÷ _____

  = _____ L

12 7 L 55 mL = _____ L + _____ L

  = _____ L

13 60 km 750 m = _____ km + _____ km

  = _____ km

14 135 kg 90 g = _____ kg + _____ kg

  = _____ kg

15 170 cm = _____ m

16 2,255 mL = _____ L

 **Real-World Problems: Decimals**

Learning Objective:
• Solve real-world problems involving decimals.

 **THINK**

The perimeter of a rectangle is 95.6 centimeters longer than that of a square with each side 16.7 centimeters long. The length of the rectangle is 50.5 centimeters. How do you find the breadth of the rectangle in different ways?

ENGAGE

Alex ordered a dessert that cost $5.90 and a meal that cost $3.05 more than the dessert. He also ordered a drink that cost $2.25 less than the dessert. Draw a bar model to show all the three costs. Discuss with your partner how you can use the model to find the total cost of food Alex ordered.

LEARN Solve one-step real-world problems

 A bucket contained 2.75 liters of water. A pail contained 1.26 liters more water than the bucket. How much water was there in the pail?

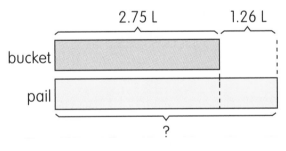

Estimate 2.75 + 1.26 to check that the answer is reasonable.

2.75 rounds to 3 and 1.26 rounds to 1.

3 + 1 = 4

4.01 is close to 4. The answer 4.01 is reasonable.

2.75 + 1.26 = 4.01

There were 4.01 liters of water in the pail.

2 Sara had $8.50. She spent $3.75 on a book. How much money did she have left?

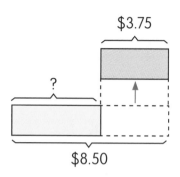

$8.50 − $3.75 = $4.75

She had $4.75 left.

3 Ms. Parker used 4.65 yards of cloth to make a dress. How much cloth did she use to make 4 identical dresses?

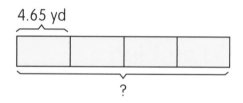

$4.65 \times 4 = 18.6$

She used 18.6 yards of cloth to make 4 identical dresses.

4 The length of a garden hose was 12.48 meters. David cut the hose equally into 6 pieces. What was the length of each piece?

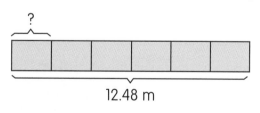

$12.48 \div 6 = 2.08$

The length of each piece was 2.08 meters.

Estimate $12.48 \div 6$ to check that the answer is reasonable.

12.48 rounds to 12.

$12 \div 6 = 2$

2.08 is close to 2. The answer 2.08 is reasonable.

TRY Practice solving one-step real-world problems

Solve. Use the bar model to help you.

1 Mr. Cooper used 3.9 pounds of flour and 5.45 pounds of sugar to make a loaf of bread. How much flour and sugar did he use altogether?

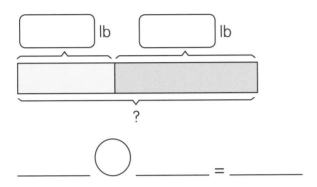

_____ ◯ _____ = _____

He used _____ pounds of flour and sugar altogether.

2 The height of an oak tree is 22.63 meters. It is 13.85 meters taller than a maple tree. What is the height of the maple tree?

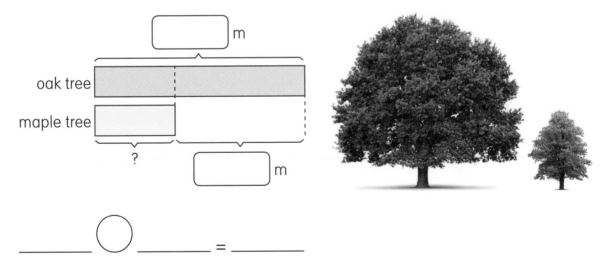

_____ ◯ _____ = _____

The height of the maple tree is _____ meters.

3 Brandon travels 6.17 kilometers from home to school. The distance from school to the park is twice the distance from home to school. How far is the park from the school?

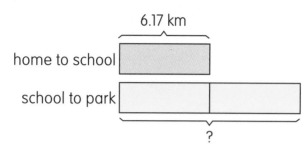

_____ ◯ _____ = _____

The park is _____ kilometers from the school.

4 8 similar packets of crackers cost $19.20. Find the cost of 1 packet of crackers.

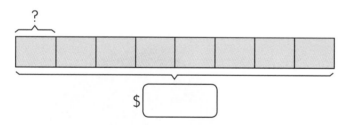

$_____ ◯ _____ = $_____

The cost of 1 packet of crackers is $_____.

ENGAGE

Luis had $12.45. Kyle had $3.50 more than Luis. How much money did both boys have in all? Draw a bar model to represent the problem. Share your bar model with your partner.

LEARN Solve two-step real-world problems

1. Jessica stacked 7 identical Mathematics textbooks.
    The height of the stack was 5.95 centimeters.
    a   What was the thickness of each textbook?
    b   What was the height of a stack of 9 such textbooks?

    STEP 1   Understand the problem.

    What do I need to find?

    STEP 2   Think of a plan.
    I can draw a bar model.

    STEP 3   Carry out the plan.

    a   ?
    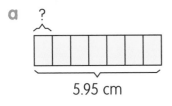
    5.95 cm

    $5.95 \div 7 = 0.85$

    The thickness of each textbook was 0.85 centimeter.

    b   0.85 cm
    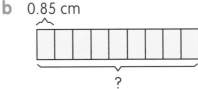
    ?

    $0.85 \times 9 = 7.65$

    The height of a stack of 9 textbooks was about 7.65 centimeters.

    STEP 4   Check the answer.
    I can work backwards to check if my answers are correct.

    Divide 7.65 by 9, I should get 0.85.
    Multiply 0.85 by 7, I should get 5.95.
    My answers are correct.

2 Sofia bought 5 storybooks at $4.75 each. She gave the cashier $30. How much change did she receive?

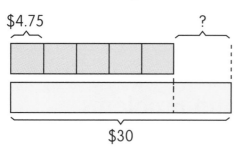

$4.75   ?

$30

Use the four-step problem-solving model to help you. Then, work backwards to check if your answer is correct.

5 × $4.75 = $23.75

The storybooks cost $23.75 altogether.

$30 − $23.75 = $6.25

She received $6.25 change.

3 The mass of a bag of peas was 1.2 kilograms. The mass of a bag of kidney beans was 0.85 kilogram. What was the total mass of 4 such bags of peas and 1 bag of kidney beans?

1.2 kg   0.85 kg

?

4 × 1.2 = 4.8

The mass of 4 such bags of peas was 4.8 kilograms.

4.8 + 0.85 = 5.65

The total mass of 4 such bags of peas and 1 bag of kidney beans was 5.65 kilograms.

Work in groups.

1 Use the information from the advertisement to write a two-step problem.

2 Exchange problems with your classmates and solve the problem in 1.

TRY Practice solving two-step real-world problems

Solve. Use the bar model to help you.

1 Jonathan made 18.4 liters of lemonade for a party. His guests drank 11.38 liters of lemonade. After the party, he poured the remaining lemonade equally into 3 containers.

a How much lemonade did he have left after the party?

b How much lemonade did each container contain?

a

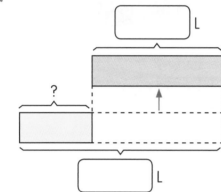

_____ ◯ _____ = _____

He had _____ liters of lemonade left after the party.

b

_____ ◯ _____ = _____

Each container contained _____ liters of lemonade.

2 7 similar packets of peanuts cost $27.30. Find the cost of 5 packets of peanuts.

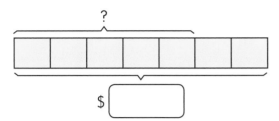

$_____ ◯ _____ = $_____

The cost of 1 packet of peanuts is $_____.

$_____ ◯ _____ = $_____

The cost of 5 packets of peanuts is $_____.

3 Hana saved $12.15. Mariah saved 3 times as much as Hana. Daniel saved $24.50 less than Mariah. How much did Daniel save?

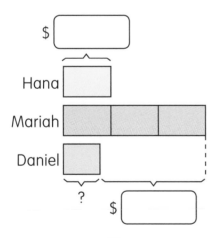

$_____ ◯ _____ = $_____

Maria saved $_____.

$_____ ◯ $_____ = $_____

Dan saved $_____.

4 Tristan jogged 0.93 miles on Monday. He jogged 0.56 miles more on Tuesday than on Monday. What was the total distance he jogged on both days?

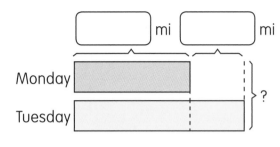

| Monday | |
| Tuesday | |

_____ ◯ _____ = _____

He jogged _____ miles on Tuesday.

_____ ◯ _____ = _____

He jogged _____ miles on both days.

5 A piece of wire 3.44 meters long is cut into two pieces. One piece is three times as long as the other. What is the length of the longer piece?

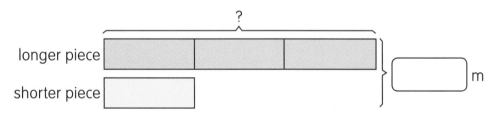

_____ units = 3.44 m

1 unit = _____ ◯ _____

= _____ m

_____ units = _____ ◯ _____

= _____ m

The length of the longer piece is _____ meters.

INDEPENDENT PRACTICE

Solve.

1 Kaden measures a table with a piece of stick and finds that it is 20 sticks long. The stick is 17.4 centimeters long. What is the length of the table?

2 Amanda poured 393 liters of paint equally into 15 containers. How much paint was there in each container?

3 Box A contained 1.67 kilograms of flour. Box B contained 8.6 kilograms of flour. Mr. Smith used all the flour from both boxes to bake some cakes. How much flour did he use in all?

Solve. Draw a bar model to help you.

4 Mr. Garcia had $15.50. He spent $9.65 on a doll. How much money did he have left?

5 Ms. Davis drove a total of 425.68 kilometers in June and July. She drove 72.6 kilometers less in June than in July. How many kilometers did she drive in June?

6 The sum of two numbers is 49.6. One of the numbers is 9 times the other. What are the two numbers?

Mathematical Habit 3 Construct viable arguments

1

I think 0.6 × 10 = 10.6.

You need to shift the decimal point one place to the right.

So, 0.6 × 10 = 6.

You write a zero at the end of the decimal.

So, 0.6 × 10 = 0.60.

You need to shift the decimal point one place to the left.

So, 0.6 × 10 = 0.06.

Who is right? Explain.

2 Are the following correct? If not, explain the error and show the correct answer.

a 3.8 + 5.6 = 9.4   b 69.8 − 2.01 = 49.7

Problem Solving with Heuristics

1 **Mathematical Habit 8** **Look for patterns**

A sheet of plastic is 0.12 centimeter thick. The sheet of plastic is folded so that the folded sheet is twice as thick after each fold.

a How thick will it be after 3 folds?

b What is the greatest number of folds you have to make before the folded plastic is thicker than 3.6 centimeters?

2 **Mathematical Habit 1** **Persevere in solving problems**

Ms. Lee packed 1.2 kilograms of rice crackers into 40-gram packets and 60-gram packets. There are 5 more 40-gram packets than 60-gram packets.

a How many 60-gram packets did she pack?

b How many 40-gram packets did she pack?

3 | **Mathematical Habit 3** Construct viable arguments

Sara bought a total of 20 sausage rolls and chicken pies. Each sausage roll cost $1.50 and each chicken pie cost $2.50. The chicken pies cost $18 more than the sausage rolls. How many of each item did she buy?

4 | **Mathematical Habit 2** Use mathematical reasoning

Find the missing digit.

$$
\begin{array}{r}
4\ \boxed{}\ .\ 8\ 2 \\
-\ 1\ 6\ .\ 3\ 5 \\
\hline
2\ 6\ .\ 4\ 7
\end{array}
$$

5 | **Mathematical Habit 8** Look for patterns

Find the sum.

1.5 + 2.7 + 4.6 + 0.4 + 2.3 + 3.5

CHAPTER WRAP-UP

Four Operations of Decimals

Addition and Subtraction

- Adding decimals

Without regrouping	With regrouping
2 . 4 + 1 . 3 ————— 3 . 7	2 .²⁸ + 3 . 1 4 ————— 5 . 4 2

- Subtracting decimals

Without regrouping	With regrouping
1 . 6 − 0 . 4 ————— 1 . 2	³4̶ .¹⁰0̶ ⁹¹⁰0̶ − 1 . 2 5 ————— 2 . 7 5

Multiplication

```
      2   1
    0 . 7 5
  ×       3
  —————————
    2 . 2 5
```

- To multiply by 10, move the decimal point 1 place to the right.

  $0.063 \times 10 = 0.63$

- To multiply by 100 or 10^2, move the decimal point 2 places to the right.

  $0.063 \times 100 = 6.3$

- To multiply by 1,000 or 10^3, move the decimal point 3 places to the right.

  $0.063 \times 1,000 = 63$

Division

```
        0 . 2 8
  3 ) 0 . 8 4
      0
      ———
        8
        6
        ———
        2 4
        2 4
        ———
          0
```

- To divide by 10, move the decimal point 1 place to the left.

  $1.9 \div 10 = 0.19$

- To divide by 100 or 10^2, move the decimal point 2 places to the left.

  $1.9 \div 100 = 0.019$

- To divide by 1,000 or 10^3, move the decimal point 3 places to the left.

  $19 \div 1,000 = 0.019$

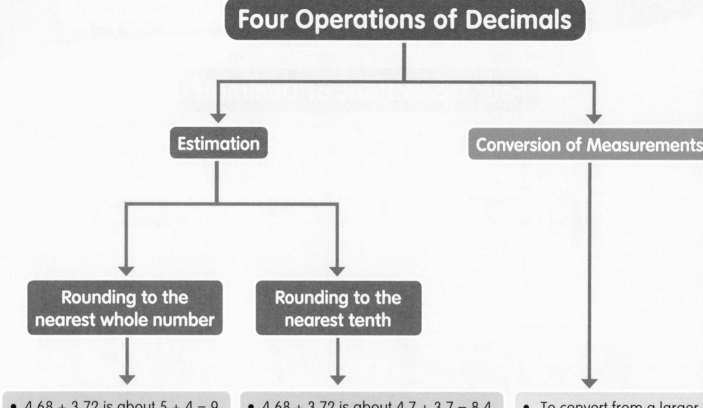

Four Operations of Decimals

Estimation

Rounding to the nearest whole number

- 4.68 + 3.72 is about 5 + 4 = 9.
- 6.25 − 2.41 is about 6 − 2 = 4.
- 7.19 × 3 is about 7 × 3 = 21.
- Change 21.57 to the nearest whole number divisible by 4: 21.57 ÷ 4 is about 20 ÷ 4 = 5.

Rounding to the nearest tenth

- 4.68 + 3.72 is about 4.7 + 3.7 = 8.4.
- 6.25 − 2.41 is about 6.3 − 2.4 = 3.9.
- 7.19 × 3 is about 7.2 × 3 = 21.6.
- Change 2.57 to the nearest tenth divisible by 5: 2.57 ÷ 5 is about 2.5 ÷ 5 = 0.5.

Conversion of Measurements

- To convert from a larger unit to a smaller unit, we multiply.

- 1 m = 100 cm
  1 km = 1,000 m
  1 kg = 1,000 g
  1 L = 1,000 mL

- To convert from a smaller unit to a larger unit, we divide.

Name: _____ Date: _____

Add.

1   3 . 4
    + 6 . 5
    ‾‾‾‾‾‾‾

2   3 . 6 2
    + 5 . 0 4
    ‾‾‾‾‾‾‾‾‾

3   9 . 8 1
    + 8 . 7 9
    ‾‾‾‾‾‾‾‾‾

Find each sum.

4 34.8 and 2.66

5 3.7 and 8.9

6 9.36 and 1.98

7 8.57 and 10.49

Add.

8 1.7 + 0.6 = _____

9 0.45 + 2.7 = _____

10 0.25 + 0.68 = _____

11 4.08 + 2.36 = _____

Subtract.

12
    5 . 3
− 2 . 1
─────

13
    3 0 . 3 8
− 1 2 . 6 2
─────────

14
    1 7 . 4 3
−   4 . 5 7
─────────

Find each difference.

15 0.6 and 0.28

16 9.02 and 8.77

17 7.62 and 3.99

18 20 and 4.78

Subtract.

19 4.5 − 2.6 = _____

20 8 − 2.98 = _____

21 0.7 − 0.32 = _____

22 32.4 − 10.84 = _____

Multiply.

23
```
    2 . 9
  ×     6
  ───────
```

24
```
    3 . 2 1
  ×       3
  ─────────
```

25
```
    6 . 0 7
  ×       4
  ─────────
```

Find each product.

26 $2.85 \times 2 =$ _____

27 $8 \times 5.96 =$ _____

28 $42.04 \times 2 =$ _____

29 $9 \times 0.34 =$ _____

30 $8.001 \times 10 =$ _____

31 $2.06 \times 400 =$ _____

32 $70.5 \times 30 =$ _____

33 $103.4 \times 70 =$ _____

Divide.

34 $2\overline{)8.2}$

35 $4\overline{)5.8}$

36 $3\overline{)4.11}$

Find each quotient.

37 $6.36 \div 3 =$ _____

38 $5.92 \div 8 =$ _____

39 $13.7 \div 2 =$ _____

40 $5 \div 4 =$ _____

41 $7.5 \div 100 =$ _____

42 $63.7 \div 70 =$ _____

43 825 ÷ 5,000 = _____

44 25.26 ÷ 30 = _____

Solve.

45 Divide 9.7 by 6. Correct your answer to the nearest whole number.

46 Divide 13 by 4. Correct your answer to the nearest tenth.

Fill in each blank.

47 3.07 kg = _____ kg _____ g

48 9.53 km = _____ m

49 25 cm = _____ m

50 6,004 mL = _____ L

Solve.

51 The area of a square is 49.2 square centimeters. The area of a rectangle is 19.8 square centimeters greater than the area of the square. The length of the rectangle is 12 centimeters. Find the breadth of the rectangle in centimeters, correct to the nearest tenth.

Solve.

52 The perimeter of a rectangle is 35.54 inches longer than the perimeter of a square with each side 6.75 inches long. Find the perimeter of the rectangle.

53 An apple and an orange cost $1.30. Kiara paid $13.40 for 12 apples and 8 oranges. Carla bought 9 oranges. How much did Carla pay for the oranges?

Solve. Draw a bar model to help you.

54 The sum of two numbers is 70.4. One number is 19 times the other. What are the two numbers?

55 The total mass of 8 identical chairs and 2 identical tables is 20 kilograms. The mass of one table is 4 times the mass of one chair. What is the difference between the mass of a table and a chair?

Assessment Prep

Answer each question.

56 Write your answer in the space below.

$19.46 + 38.54 =$ _____

57 Which **two** conversions are correct?

(A) 3 cm = 0.03 m

(B) 30 mm = 0.3 cm

(C) 300 m = 30 cm

(D) 3,000 m = 3 km

(E) 0.03 km = 3 m

58 Jacob wants to buy some apples for a class party. Shop A sells apples at $3.99 for 4. Shop B sells apples at $4.99 for 5. Jacob does some calculations and decided that the apples at Shop A are cheaper.
Explain if Jacob's reasoning is correct.
Write your explanation and answer in the space below.

Name: _____ Date: _____

Science Project

1 **a** Ms. Jones buys 8 boxes of clay for a science project. Each box contains 19 grams of clay. The clay is shared equally among the 20 students in the class. How many grams of clay will each student receive?

b Ms. Jones realizes that each student needs 8.8 grams of clay instead. How many more boxes of clay does Ms. Jones need to buy? Explain your work.

2 **a** In addition to the 8.8 grams of clay, the students will also need 8.8 grams each of sand, hummus, and topsoil. What will be the total mass of all the project materials that each student needs?

b Ms. Long decides to have her students conduct the same science project. She plans to buy all the necessary project materials for her class of 30 students that evening. What will be the total mass of all the project materials in kilograms? Given that Ms. Long can buy any amount of each material, explain whether she can reasonably carry the project materials home by taking a bus.

Rubric

Point(s)	Level	My Performance
7–8	4	• Most of my answers are correct. • I showed complete understanding of what I have learned. • I used the correct strategies to solve the problems. • I explained my answers and mathematical thinking clearly and completely.
5–6	3	• Some of my answers are correct. • I showed some understanding of what I have learned. • I used some correct strategies to solve the problems. • I explained my answers and mathematical thinking clearly.
3–4	2	• A few of my answers are correct. • I showed little understanding of what I have learned. • I used a few correct strategies to solve the problems. • I explained some of my answers and mathematical thinking clearly.
0–2	1	• A few of my answers are correct. • I showed little or no understanding of what I have learned. • I used a few strategies to solve the problems. • I did not explain my answers and mathematical thinking clearly.

Teacher's Comments

Glossary

B

- **base (of an exponent)**

  A number that is being multiplied the number of times indicated by the exponent.
  In 5^3, 5 is the base. The exponent indicates that 5 should be multiplied three times.

C

- **cube (of a number)**

  A number that is the product of three equal factors.
  27 is the cube of 3, because $3 \times 3 \times 3 = 27$.

D

- **division expression (in arithmetic)**

  An expression that contains only numbers and the division symbol.
  $2 \div 3$ is a division expression.

  $2 \div 3 = \frac{2}{3}$

E

- **exponent**

  A number that tells how many times the base is used as a factor.
  In 5^3, the exponent is 3. It means that this product is $5 \times 5 \times 5$.

P

- **power**

  Another word for exponent. See exponent.

R

- **reciprocal**

  $\frac{1}{3}$ is the reciprocal of $\frac{3}{1}$ or 3.

S

- **square (of a number)**

  A number that is the product of two equal factors.
  25 is the square of 5 because $5 \times 5 = 25$.

T

- **thousandth**

  One part out of a thousand is $\frac{1}{1,000}$ (one thousandth).

Index

Pages in **boldface** type show where a term is introduced.

fractions, *see* Fractions
mixed numbers, *see* Mixed numbers
reading and writing, 2

Order
    decimals, 301–302, 304–305, 320
        greatest to least, 304, 306, 310
        least to greatest, 306, 310, 320

Order of operations, 63–64, 66–67, 69, 94
    to simplify expressions, 186

Pictorial representations
    area models, *see* Area models
    bar models, *see* Bar models
    number lines, *see* Number lines
    place value charts, *see* Place value charts
    tables, *see* Tables

Place value-charts, *throughout, see for example,*
    298, 314, 343, 375, 395
    pictorial representations, *throughout, see for*
        example, 2, 12, 295–296, 376

Place-value chip–0.001, *throughout, see for example,*
    294–295, 297, 364, 366, 368

Place-value chip–0.01, *throughout, see for example,*
    290, 295, 297, 334, 340–341

Place-value chip–0.1, *throughout, see for example,*
    290, 295, 297, 333–334, 339–340

Place-value chip–1, *throughout, see for example,* 2,
    4–5, 33–34, 295, 379–382

Place-value chip–10, *throughout, see for example,* 2,
    12, 19–20, 390–391, 395–398

Place-value chip–100, *throughout, see for example,*
    2, 4–5, 12, 370–371, 396–397

Place-value chip–1,000, *throughout, see for example,*
    2, 4–5, 12, 23–24, 33–34

Place-value chip–10,000, *throughout, see for*
    example, 2, 12, 14, 20, 23–24

Place-value chip–100,000, *throughout, see for*
    example, 2, 12, 14, 24, 38

Place-value chip–1,000,000,
    11–12, 14, 20, 24–25, 45

Place-value chips, *throughout, see for example,*
    11–13, 19–20, 23, 25, 339

Place value strips, 23

Power, **29**

Powers of 10
    multiplying
        decimals by, 375–376
        whole numbers by, 29–30

Problem solving
    real-world problems, *see* Real-world
        problems

Proper fractions
    division
        by whole number, 245–246
    multiplying, 193, 273
        real-world problems, 201

Quotients, *throughout, see for example,* 50–52, 54,
    56, 75, 196
    of decimal and whole number, 407–408

Real-world problems, 75–76, 78–79
    division
        fractions and whole numbers, 261–262, 264
    fractional parts, 254, 256–257
        of remainder, 259–260
    with fractional remainder, 204, 206
    mixed numbers, 233
        multiplying, 233–234, 236–237
    multiplying fractions, 201–203
    one-step, 153–155, 421–423
    parts of a whole, 251–253
    two-step, 156, 159, 425–426, 428
    using models to solve, 9

Reciprocals, **242**, 247

Remainder, *throughout, see for example,* 6–7,
   50–52, 93, 204–207, 278
   fractional, 204, 206, 259–260

Rewrite, 320
   division expressions, 113–122
   decimals, fractions, and mixed numbers, 311–312,
      322–323, 328

Rounding
   decimals, 324, 338
      to nearest hundredth, 307–308, 310
      to nearest tenth, 292, 310
      to nearest whole number, 292, 310
   estimation, 440
      differences, to nearest whole number,
         404–405
      to nearest tenth, 409, 440
      product of decimal and whole number,
         406
      sums, to nearest whole number, 403–404

Simplest form, *throughout, see for example,* 109–110,
   119–121, 216–217, 311–312, 322–323

Square, **29**

Standard form, 2–3, 11–14, 94–95

Subtraction
   decimals, 347–350, 353, 439
   like fractions, 112
   with mixed numbers, 144–147, 166
   unlike fractions, 139–142, 166

Tables
   pictorial representations, *throughout, see for
      example,* 20, 42, 164, 325–326, 338

Thousandth, **293**–297, 299–302, 307, 320–321

Unit fraction
   division
      by whole number, 241–243, 247–248, 274

Unlike fractions, 108
   common denominator
      to add, 123–126, 166
      to subtract, 139–142, 166

Whole numbers
   division
      by 1-digit whole number, 114
      by 10,
         33–36
      by 100 and 1,000,
         37–40
      by hundreds and thousands, 40–41
      with proper fraction, 245–246
      real world problems, 261–262, 264
      by tens, 35–36
      with unit fraction, 241–243, 247–248
   estimate
      difference by rounding nearest, 404–405
      products, 406
      quotient, 407–408
      sums by rounding nearest, 403–404
   multiplying
      by 100 and 1,000,
         23–26
      decimals by, 357–360
      fraction by, 187–189, 273
      by hundreds and thousands, 27–28
      mixed number, 233–234, 274
      by powers of 10, 29–30
      by tens, 19–20, 22
   real-world problems, 75–76, 78–79
   division, 261–262, 264

Photo Credits

NOTES

NOTES

NOTES

NOTES

NOTES

NOTES

© 2020 Marshall Cavendish Education Pte Ltd

Published by Marshall Cavendish Education
Times Centre, 1 New Industrial Road, Singapore 536196
Customer Service Hotline: (65) 6213 9688
US Office Tel: (1-914) 332 8888 | Fax: (1-914) 332 8882
E-mail: cs@mceducation.com
Website: www.mceducation.com

Distributed by
Houghton Mifflin Harcourt
125 High Street
Boston, MA 02110
Tel: 617-351-5000
Website: www.hmhco.com/programs/math-in-focus

First published 2020

ISBN 978-0-358-10186-4

Printed in Singapore

3 4 5 6 7 8 9   1401   26 25 24 23 22 21
4500817280   B C D E F

The cover image shows a giant panda.
Giant pandas have thick, fluffy, black and white fur. They live in bamboo forests in China. Bamboo accounts for over 95% of their diet. Unlike other bears, pandas do not hibernate in the winter. They migrate to areas with warmer temperatures depending on the season. They used to be endangered in the past, but are now protected and their numbers are increasing once again.